SWITZERLAND'S
MOUNTAIN INNS

A WALKING VACATION IN A WORLD APART

SWITZERLAND'S
MOUNTAIN INNS

A WALKING VACATION IN A WORLD APART

MARCIA & PHILIP
LIEBERMAN

THE COUNTRYMAN PRESS
Woodstock, Vermont

Library of Congress Cataloging-in-Publication Data
Lieberman, Marcia
Switzerland's mountain inns : a walking vacation in a world apart
p.   cm.
ISBN 0-88150-406-8 (alk. paper)
1. Hiking—Switzerland—Alps, Swiss—Guidebooks. 2. Hotels—Switzerland—Alps, Swiss—
Guidebooks. 3. Switzerland—Alps, Swiss—Guidebooks. I. Lieberman, Philip. II. Title
GV199.44.S92A444 1998
914.94'70473—dc21   97-46866
                                                                        CIP

Cover and text design by Julie Duquet
Maps by Paul Woodward, copyright © 1998 The Countryman Press
Cover photograph of Berggasthaus Meglisalp, Appenzell, and all interior photographs by Philip
    Lieberman

Published by
The Countryman Press
PO Box 748
Woodstock, Vermont 05091

Distributed by
W. W. Norton & Company, Inc.
500 Fifth Avenue, New York, New York 10110

Printed in The United States of America
10 9 8 7 6 5 4 3 2 1

DEDICATION

For Eleanor Kirsopp Lieberman, whose birth we joyfully celebrated at the Rigi Kulm.

ACKNOWLEDGMENTS

Our thanks go to Rosemarie Bumann-Broger, Monika Breitenmoser, and Ruth Eberhard for their invaluable friendship and help. We'd also like to thank our editor, Helen Whybrow, and Kathleen Achor, Cristen Brooks, and everyone else at the Countryman Press who helped bring this book together.

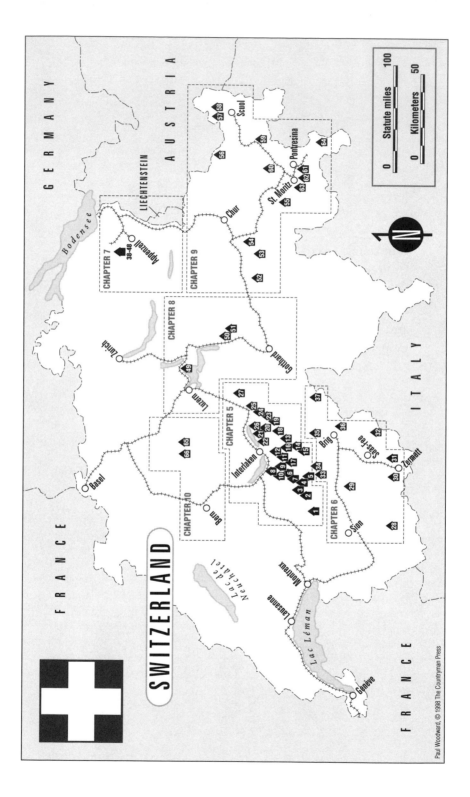

CONTENTS

INTRODUCTION: Simple Gifts • 13

PART I • WALKING IN THE SWISS ALPS • 17

CHAPTER 1. WHAT IS A BERGHAUS? • 19

CHAPTER 2. REACHING A BERGHAUS: *Getting There Is Half the Fun* • 33

CHAPTER 3. PACK LIGHTLY: *What You Need to Take for a Night at a Berghaus* • 37

CHAPTER 4. GENERAL INFORMATION ABOUT TRAVEL IN SWITZERLAND • 41

PART II • THE MOUNTAIN INNS BY REGION • 47

CHAPTER 5. THE BERNESE OBERLAND • 49

Inn 1. Berghaus Iffigenalp • 49

Inn 2. Hotel Waldhaus • 56

Inn 3. Hotel Steinbock • 61

Inn 4. Hotel Gasterntal • 61

Inn 5. Gasthaus zur Gletscher Heimritz • 62

Inn 6. Berghaus am Oeschinensee • 64

Inn 7. Berghotel Oeschinensee • 65

Inn 8. Hotel-Pension Waldrand at Pochtenalp • 68

Inn 9. Berggasthaus and Pension Golderli • 71

Inn 10. Berghaus Enzian, Bundalp • 73

Inn 11. Pension Suppenalp • 82

Inn 12. Restaurant-Pension Sonnenberg • 83

Inn 13. Berghaus Trachsellauenen • 88

Inn 14. Hotel Tschingelhorn • 88

Inn 15. Hotel Obersteinberg • 90

Inn 16. Restaurant-Pension Spielbodenalp • 93

Inn 17. Rotstockhutte • 95

Inn 18. Hotel des Alpes • 102

Inn 19. Bergrestaurant Stieregg • 103

CONTENTS

Inn 20. Bergrestaurant Waldspitz • *107*

Inn 21. Berghaus Faulhorn • *109*

Inn 22. Hotel-Restaurant Schynige Platte • *113*

Inn 23. Berghotel Grosse Scheidegg • *116*

Inn 24. Hotel-Chalet Schwarzwaldalp • *117*

Inn 25. Hotel Rosenlaui • *118*

Inn 26. Grand Hotel Giessbach • *122*

Inn 27. Berghaus Engstlenalp • *126*

CHAPTER 6. THE VALAIS • *131*

Inn 28. Hôtel de Mauvoisin • *138*

Inn 29. Hotel-Restaurant du Weisshorn • *143*

Inn 30. Hôtel du Trift • *148*

Inn 31. Hotel Fluhalp • *153*

Inn 32. Berghaus Almagelleralp • *158*

Inn 33. Berghaus Kummenalp • *160*

Inn 34. Berggasthaus Lauchernalp • *161*

Inn 35. Hotel Belalp • *163*

Inn 36. Hospice du Simplon • *166*

Inn 37. Hotel Ofenhorn • *171*

CHAPTER 7. APPENZELL • *175*

Inn 38. Berggasthaus Aescher • *178*

Inn 39. Gasthaus Schäfler • *180*

Inn 40. Berggasthaus Mesmer • *181*

Inn 41. Berggasthaus Forelle • *183*

Inn 42. Berggasthaus Seealp • *185*

Inn 43. Berggasthaus Meglisalp • *185*

Inn 44. Berggasthaus Rotstein • *187*

Inn 45. Berggasthaus Bollenwees • *189*

Inn 46. Fälenalp • *190*

Inn 47. Berggasthaus Plattenbödeli • *192*

Inn 48. Berggasthaus Staubern • *195*

CONTENTS

CHAPTER 8. CENTRAL SWITZERLAND • *197*
    Inn 49. Hotel Rigi Kulm • *199*
    Inn 50. Restaurant (Gasthaus) Golzernsee • *204*
    Inn 51. Hotel Maderanertal • *206*

CHAPTER 9. CANTON GRAUBUNDEN • *209*
    Inn 52. Ustaria Tgamanada • *211*
    Inn 53. Berggasthaus Turrahus • *215*
    Inn 54. Berggasthaus Beverin • *218*
    Inn 55. Berghaus Piz Plata • *222*
    Inn 56. Berghaus Vereina • *225*
LOWER ENGADINE
    Inn 57. Kurhaus Val Sinestra • *229*
    Inn 58. Berggasthaus Sinestra • *231*
    Inn 59. Parkhütte Varusch • *235*
UPPER ENGADINE
    Inn 60. Berggasthaus Suvretta • *238*
    Inn 61. Hotel Roseggletscher • *240*
    Inn 62. Berghaus Fuorcla Surlej • *242*
    Inn 63. Hotel Fex • *244*
VAL POSCHIAVO
    Inn 64. Ristorante Alpe Campo • *247*

CHAPTER 10. THE EMMENTAL • *251*
    Inn 65. Berghotel Napf • *253*
    Inn 66. Gasthof Riedbad • *255*

BIBLIOGRAPHY • *259*
INDEX • *261*

SIMPLE GIFTS

Engstlenalp is a place I dream of on winter afternoons at home. The old Berghaus there sits on a green terrace like a rich lawn, cradled between the two rocky walls of a U-shaped glacial valley. The ridge facing the inn is frosted with glaciers, icy bands gleaming above the meadows in the late afternoon sun. Just beyond the inn is a blue-green lake of such clarity that you can see the fish darting past and the precise reflection of the waterfalls and glaciers above. To the east rises the snowy head of the Titlis (3416 m); to the west, an impressive view of some of the giant peaks of the Bernese Oberland, most notably the Wetterhorn, which appears here, in John Tyndall's words, with "inexpressible nobleness."

Tyndall was a distinguished Victorian physicist and alpinist. President of the Royal Society of England, he did pioneering work in glaciology and atmospheric physics and also managed to achieve, during summers in Switzerland, some of the boldest first ascents of his time. Between climbs he tramped about the country, one of a whole class of Victorian scholars and clerics who discovered the Alps and invented the alpine walking tour. He first stayed at Engstlenalp in 1866 and in his memoirs called it "one of the most charming spots in the Alps. It had at that time," he noted, "a double charm for the handsome young widow who kept the inn supplemented by her kindness and attention within doors the pleasures extracted from the outer world."

My husband and I first came upon Engstlenalp while hiking across the Bernese Oberland. We knew nothing about Berghotels, the mountain inns of Switzerland. It was midafternoon and we were on our way to the next village, which we could easily have reached, but here was seductive loveliness. And what was this strangely tall (all of three stories, when farmhouses have only two) old house, overlooking the lake? Stepping inside, we discovered that it was a hotel, for we saw no sign in front.

"Let's see if we can stay," my husband suggested.

Suppenalp, Bernese Oberland

"But we planned to reach Engelberg tonight."

"Take another look. Are you sure you want to leave?"

I peered into a pine-paneled dining room, light and airy, with a high ceiling and tall windows facing the mountains. A mirror hung on one wall, in the kind of scalloped gilt frame one sees around 19th-century paintings. And indeed, we seemed to have stepped into an earlier time.

The answer to his question was self-evident. This was too good to pass up.

A pleasant white-haired lady behind the tall wooden counter summoned a young waitress who spoke English. Yes, a private room was available. She led us up to a room with two high, old-fashioned beds with plump down quilts between carved wooden head- and footboards. The walls and floors were light-colored pine, scrubbed spotless. In one corner stood an old-fashioned washstand with a pair of pitchers and basins; in another, a sturdy clothes cupboard. This wasn't a new room playing at being antique—it was the real thing. Best of all, it smelled clean, fresh, and sweet. Through the windows we saw the meadows shining in the sun. We dropped our packs and spent the rest of the afternoon lying on the shore of the lake and sauntering through the meadows. Behind the inn was a scattering of "alps," mountain farms to which cows are brought to graze in summer and where cheese is made; the mountains owe their name to these little summer farms. The farmhouses were built of dark brown, velvety wood with little shuttered windows. Below the eaves of one house hung a row of giant cowbells ranked by size, massive leather straps buckled around a wooden bar.

The pitchers on our washstand had been filled with fresh water, and we used them to wash before dinner. Little linen towels hung neatly on a wooden rack. Toilet and wash sink were down the hall; there are no private lavatories or baths at most Berghotels. Then down to dinner, which is à la carte at Engstlenalp; a barley soup thick with vegetables nearly filled me, but we had also ordered Schnitzel, Rösti (the Swiss potato specialty), and salad. As the sun set the Wetterhorn was flushed with rosy alpenglow and we wandered by the lake until it was nearly dark. We returned to hear the sounds of companionable laughter and found the dining room full of farmers and cowherds, in suspenders and work pants, sleeves still rolled up, chatting and drinking glasses of what we later learned is Kaffee-Zwetschge, black coffee with plum schnapps. But we didn't know then what they were drinking or why black coffee made them so jolly, and Phil and I ordered a small carafe of simple white wine.

I was awakened at dawn by cowbells. As each cow wears a bell of a different size and tone, the cows create random melodies. I looked out to see farmers and their children driving the cows out to graze, then drifted back to sleep for another hour. After a breakfast of bread and butter, jam and cheese, we shouldered our packs and returned to the trail.

Since then we have stopped at many Berghotels and enjoyed a variety of surprises: an interesting tablemate at dinner, an unusual menu, or a special occasion. When a Berghaus is near a cluster of alps, the farmers often drop in after dinner for a convivial evening, so the dining room functions something like a British neighborhood pub. One agreeable surprise awaited us on a return trip to Engstlenalp. The hostess was hesitant about giving us a

Engstlenalp, Bernese Oberland

room. "There will be an Alpfest, and you won't get much sleep," she apologized. The occasion was a midsummer festival called Nidlete, celebrating the first cream of the season. We happily replied that we certainly did want a room and were given one on the topmost floor. After dinner, a band arrived—four concertinas and a double bass, played with a bow. A corner of the dining room floor was cleared for dancing, and the music began: waltzes, polkas, country dance tunes.

The two young waitresses flew back and forth with trays of beer, wine, and of course Kaffee-Zwetschge. At 9:30 the Nidle was served, compliments of the house, to all present. The cream had been made with milk from the neighboring farms, whipped and unsweetened, with a slice of cake and sugar on the side. Even the waitresses, young and old, were dancing when Phil and I went to bed at 11. I woke up once, at 2 AM, and opened the window; I could hear the band still playing and an occasional merry whoop. Next morning, the waitresses told us that the band had played until 3:30 and then the staff had eaten a meal, but they were up and cheerful a few hours later to give us an early hiker's breakfast.

For the traveler who wishes to experience Switzerland off the beaten track, these mountain inns are the key. In themselves, they provide a sense of adventure. And they are a perfect way to meet other hikers. In the comfortable, informal atmosphere of a Berghaus, travelers often shed their reserve and share information and stories.

Every Berghaus is different. They are all individually owned, each one stamped by the history of the house and shaped by its owner's taste and personality. Yet their shared characteristics make them a type. This book will identify what makes a Berghaus and explain what to expect, how to reach them, and what to bring. It will then list a broad selection of many of Switzerland's most charming Berghotels, grouped according to region, with hiking routes used to reach each inn and walks that can be taken from them. A traveler who wants to sample the experience of a night at a Berghaus can pick one from the list or design a vacation based almost entirely at Berghotels. Whether it is one night or a dozen, the experience will be memorable.

PART I

WALKING IN THE
SWISS ALPS

CHAPTER ONE

WHAT IS A BERGHAUS?

The special type of mountain inn called a Berghaus, Berggasthaus, Berghotel, or *auberge de montagne* is a Swiss institution that arose in the 19th century to meet a largely British need. Existing only in Switzerland, it is uniquely Swiss; it has no real equivalent in the other alpine countries for reasons deriving from history and geography. Most are tucked away in quiet corners, undiscovered by foreign visitors, while the few non-Swiss who happen upon them are invariably charmed.

There are hundreds of mountain inns and mountain restaurants in Switzerland. This book cannot cover them all, but it attempts to provide a selection of the most charming or most historic inns, as well as some that merit a visit based on location alone. The book, moreover, includes a wide variety of mountain inns and hotels, from the simplest to a few that are more elaborate. There is no formal definition of the terms Berghotel and Berghaus, but the Swiss sometimes make an informal distinction between them: It's merely a matter of expectation. At the former they expect more amenities and comforts, such as better and maybe even private bathrooms and perhaps a sitting room or parlor. (In this book, the terms will be used almost without distinction.) This book also includes a few hotels that are more elegant than the usual mountain inn because of their historic character or associations, their scenic setting, or both. These few, at the upper end of the spectrum, remind us that in a bygone time when a summer vacation in the mountains was the fashion—before the discovery (or invention) of beach resorts—the rich and titled followed, to the extent possible, in the footsteps of the people who first drew attention to the mountains: artists, intellectuals, and many from the middle classes.

Although we are using the term *inn* to refer to these Swiss hostelries, there is no analogy between the Swiss mountain inn and what is now often termed an inn—a country inn—in North America. On the American continent, inns are reached by car and guests arrive with suitcases. You are pleased but not surprised to find a blazing fire in the hearth, plumply

Kummenalp, Lötschental; Overleaf: Fälenalp, Appenzell

stuffed chairs, silver and linen in the dining room, scented soap and thick bath towels in your private bathroom, maybe a chocolate on your pillow, and a freshly baked muffin beside your breakfast plate. As described in this chapter, the ambience of a Swiss mountain inn is very different.

People have not always flocked to the mountains for pleasure. Until quite recently, it was just the reverse. There is good reason to conjecture that early humans feared mountains, believing them to be sources of wild, dangerous power, home to supernatural beings and forces. Lightning strikes the highest point in any place; it flashes off high peaks, dances along mountain ridges. Zeus hurled thunder from atop Mount Olympus; Siva dwells on Mount Kailas. In a remote, rugged valley in the French Alpes Maritimes—the Vallée des Merveilles—prehistoric people carved symbols on the rocks. Archaeologists and historians believe that those people did not live in this high valley, but went up on special, ritual occasions; one petroglyph depicts a figure whose arms are lightning bolts, perhaps a shamanic leader who was believed able to take the power of the storm into his own body.

Besides their fearsome associations and physical dangers, mountains made life hard, obstructing the passage of humans and beasts. Flat land was fat land; rich farms were on land that was easy to plow and cultivate. The poorest people lived in the mountains, where the soil is thin, farming arduous, and herding cattle and sheep an aerobic exercise. Regarded as not just obstacles but actual physical blemishes, mountains would disappear on the Day of Judgment: "Every valley shall be lifted up, and every mountain and hill made low" (Isaiah 40:3).

Among the many sorts of revolutionary movements that sprang up in the 18th and early 19th centuries to shatter the ancient order of things was one, less obvious than others, that effected a change in the way leisured, educated people viewed landscape. The whole aesthetics of scenery was altered; one might say that the fashion in scenery changed. German philosophers began to extol "the sublime" as an aesthetic principle; Swiss artists began to climb into their own native mountains to paint. The perception of wildness shifted and wilderness, once shunned, began to be appreciated and admired. Rigid, formal garden design began to look artificial and went out of fashion, and the wilder, less deliberately artful garden was created. Wildness in nature began to be seen with different eyes.

The British Romantic poets (Shelley, Byron, Wordsworth) who ventured through the Alps found fascination instead of horror in the crags and mists that previous generations of wealthy travelers had avoided by taking the sea route to Italy. Soon their readers followed in their tracks.

Although the Alps extend from France to Slovenia, the mountains the British mostly flocked to were the Swiss Alps. And although so many were British, the Germans, French, Americans, and others came as well. The climbers came to Switzerland because many of the great challenges, of which the Matterhorn was only the most famous, were there. The hikers came because a constellation of advantageous features—topography, scale, and in the 19th century even its transportation network—made (and still make) Switzerland ideal for walking tours. The British had, moreover, the means and the leisure to do so, for the Industrial Revolution and her empire and overseas trading power had made Great Britain the richest country in the world. Not just the old landed aristocracy, but the newly prosperous upper middle classes could afford holiday travel. And just as the jet airplane, replacing the ocean liner, opened travel opportunities for millions in the later 20th century, so the replacement of the coach-and-four by the railway train facilitated travel for these British manufacturers and their families, and for the professional class. The British themselves came to call their standard, well-trodden tour route "the regular Swiss round" (the Reverend Harry Jones used the phrase as the title of his 1866 book about his adventures in Switzerland). In 1900, Sir William M. Conway sniffed at the term and at those who "with infinite docility . . . follow hour to hour the appointed path, ascending even in rain to points of view . . ." (Conway 1900, p. 119)

For centuries, alpine chamois hunters and smugglers had clambered about among the mountains to the extent necessary for their trade, not for sport. But some exceptions notwithstanding (the ascent of Mont Blanc in 1786 by two Frenchmen, Balmat and Paccard), the British virtually invented mountaineering as a sport; hiking and walking tours were the natural consequence. Poor men had always walked, while rich ones rode. Poor men got mud on their boots; rich ones wore silk stockings and clean pumps. Walking, as a leisure-time activity for people of means, was as much a revolution in social attitudes and practices as was the change in taste regarding mountains and wilderness.

The earliest climbers slept in farmhouses or shepherds' huts en route to a mountain, finding shelter wherever they could (dinner was often just a bowl of fresh milk and perhaps a hunk of cheese), and then at the mountain's base, sleeping out in the open, perhaps under the shelter of a rock wall. The first generation of alpinists were mainly from the British upper and middle classes, landed gentry, scholars, clergymen, and prosperous merchants. They were willing to rough it and did so, but they could pay for a bed to sleep in, and their wives and sisters could hike in with them if better lodging were available. As farmers began to take in guests, providing a room instead of space in the hayloft, more guests followed; the first mountain guesthouses were originally farmhouses that were later converted into simple lodges.

Most of these farms were alps. The word originally meant, and in Switzerland still means, a summer farm. As in other mountainous areas in the world where the soil is poor and people depend on their livestock, Swiss farmers send their herds and flocks up to high summer pastures to graze while raising grass as a crop in the lower farms. In a good summer the grass below, thus ungrazed, can be mowed up to three times, providing the winter's fodder. Up at the summer alp, farmers collect milk and make Bergkäse, alp cheese. At the end of summer the animals are brought back down from the various alps. Many scores of places with the word *alp* appended are small clusters of these summer farms.

Some of the old Berghotels served as climbing huts before the Alpine Club built its huts, and a few Berghotels (such as Fluhalp, above Zermatt) still serve as huts, providing climbers with the closest approach to a mountain. While huts and mountain inns are both simple and even have some common features, they are different from each other. Most huts were built from scratch by the Alpine Club, whereas Berghäuser (the German plural for Berghaus) may still look a little like the old farmhouses many once were. Huts are owned by the Alpine Club and run by hutkeepers or guardians on a concession basis (sometimes a whole family has been running a hut for many years), but Berghäuser are privately owned. (Occasionally, a community may own such an inn, as with Almagelleralp, and grant the concession to an individual.) Most are small, and many are open only in summer.

There are often slight inconsistencies between the names printed on the brochures or postcards and the way mountain inns are listed in telephone books, because the Swiss recognize any establishment labeled as a Berghaus, Berggasthaus, Berggasthof, Bergrestaurant, Berghotel, and so on as a mountain inn. In addition, some may be called simply Hotel, Restaurant, and sometimes even Hotel-Restaurant. (A Gasthaus or Gasthof is also an inn.) The word Pension may also be tacked on, as in Berggasthaus & Pension Golderli. But as long as the name is recognizable (e.g., Golderli), one need not be concerned about the "correct" designation: Any missive or reference using any of these descriptive titles—Berghaus, Bergrestaurant, and the name Golderli—will be understood. (When scanning in a Swiss telephone book for mountain inns, you have to look under several of the printed categories: try Berg, Hotel, and Restaurant. For one village, a near-by mountain inn may come under the label Berghaus; for another, it may appear under the label Hotel.)

In this book, following the hotel's telephone number is its postal address: a four-digit number and nearby town or village. The address for the inn at Golderli is CH-3723 Kiental. CH is the international postal abbreviation for Switzerland.

SWISS ALPINE CLUB (SAC) HUTS

Swiss Alpine Club (SAC is the German abbreviation, CAS the French) huts were built to facilitate climbs, so they are positioned as close as possible to the base of a mountain or the approach to a glacier, and the scenery is generally spectacular. But the distribution of huts conforms to the location of mountains that alpinists want to climb and they are not merely spaced along hiking routes, as is more often the case in Austria, a country to which the phrase "walking from hut to hut" is more appropriate. But mountain inns fill in the gaps. On a Swiss long-distance walking tour, you may walk from hut to Berghaus, and then perhaps from Berghaus to village hotel.

Alpine club huts are entirely functional, made for eating and sleeping; they consist of a dining room and dormitories (called Matratzenlager, Massenlager, Touristenlager, or just Lager in Swiss-German, *dortoirs* in French). There are no private rooms and no public sitting room apart from the dining room. There's no attempt to charm the visitor; the purpose is to provide a dry, sheltered place to sleep and a hot meal. Older huts may have an outdoor toilet, but newer ones have indoor toilets (many older huts are now converting their toilet facilities to an indoor space) and a cold-water wash sink—bring your own towel. A very few of the newest huts have solar-powered, coin-operated showers. The dorm space usually consists of sleeping shelves, wooden platforms on which pads are laid side by side. Pillows (uncovered) are provided for each space and a couple of woolen blankets, but no sheets. The dorms are shared by everyone, men and women, old and young. Boots must be parked at the front door, where there is a rack of clogs or scuffs to wear inside (many bring their own hut slippers).

At some alpine club huts, one meal is served to everyone; at others, guests can order from a menu. In either case, what's available is generally soup; meat, sausages, or eggs; spaghetti or potatoes; canned vegetables; and perhaps canned fruit or pudding; and always available are soft drinks, wine, and beer. A very few huts have no resident guardian and don't serve meals but have kitchens available.

Because climbers start early, often at 4 AM and sometimes even earlier, all guests are expected to turn in by 9 PM. Breakfast is laid out for those early risers, but others can have breakfast (bread, butter and jam, tea or coffee) at the usual hours.

BERGHOTELS

Berghotels are cozier and more homelike than huts; there may be wild-flowers on the tables and perhaps an old clock or an antique sideboard in the dining room, or a little parlor with comfortable chairs, books, and magazines. The food, whether one meal is served to all or guests order à la carte from a menu, is more varied; there may be fresh salad or homemade pastry. Although guests do not stay up late, lights don't have to be out at 9 PM.

At a Berghaus people are relaxed, at ease, and cheerful, and they are likely to linger over the meal and to chat with their neighbors at the table. A 19th-century British traveler noted that even the formality and constraint of his countrymen melted in this environment: "These table d'hôte dinners in the mountain inns are often very entertaining. The natural reserve of Englishmen gives way when you dine together in your shooting-jackets and slippers at some high and lonely spot." (Jones 1866, p. 226) Unlike the clientele at a hotel in town, who are there for different reasons, the Berghaus guests have a common interest: They like walking in the mountains. And as hiking is not a competitive sport, there's no tension about it. Guests don't try to impress or awe each other. Instead, there's a feeling of fellowship. An evening at a Berghaus is one of the best possible ways to meet a wide variety of Swiss people and get to know them.

After dinner on a fine evening one can stroll out to see the pink flush of the alpenglow on the mountains, or linger in the dining room for another glass of wine, or perhaps repair to a little Victorian parlor with a few old books and maps and some more or less recent magazines and paperbacks on its shelves. Television is almost always absent. The informal and relaxed atmosphere, the intimacy of a small inn, and the shared delight in hiking draw guests together. One meets other hikers (many of whom speak English), and part of the pleasure of a typical evening is when guests spread out their maps after dinner and discuss hiking routes with their tablemates or consult the host or hostess about neighborhood trails. Hosts and hostesses generally speak English and are friendly people, happy to share their knowledge of local hiking routes; they are often an invaluable source of information about walks off the beaten track.

While Berghäuser share certain characteristics, these guesthouses are individually owned. Each one is different, which adds to their charm. A Berghaus is almost invariably run by a family, and each has its own character, the stamp of their nature. Keeping such an inn is hard work, and it isn't done just for money. Alois Graber, who owns and runs Berghotel Waldrand with his wife, says there are easier ways to make a living, but for people like him it is almost a vocation. Many innkeepers were born at these old houses; they are attached to the house and the land—it's something in the blood.

What to Expect at a Berghaus

To a certain extent, alpine inns bring one back to the 19th or early 20th century. Cozy and charming as Berghotels are, they are also simple to a degree not generally seen in North America. They lack what many here consider basic amenities: Almost none has private bathrooms, some have no shower available, some have only cold running water. Many have no electricity or must generate their own. These inns would have been considered anachronisms elsewhere and would have been torn down or remodeled beyond recognition, but in Switzerland they have been lovingly preserved. These inns have a fresh, unstudied charm, rare today and immensely appealing. They are a national institution, beloved by the Swiss. They are "collected," their names passed on by word of mouth. Many Swiss people like to return with their families to a particular Berghaus they went to in childhood.

The first thing you need to know is that these places are popular, especially on weekends. Phone ahead. These simple inns almost never advertise; they don't have to. No matter how remote an inn may be, or how basic its facilities, it may be full on a Saturday night, especially if word gets out that it has some special charm or if it is known to enjoy a spectacular location. Switzerland is so small, and its transportation system so excellent, that many Swiss go to the mountains for only a weekend and spend Saturday night at a Berghaus. They are favorite spots for weddings. You should telephone in advance if you want a private room on a weekend, especially a Saturday night. Often it's sufficient to phone a few days in advance for a Saturday-night reservation, but some inns are in such demand that you should phone a week or two in advance. But it's always much easier to get a place in a Matratzenlager or dormitory than to get a private room, and if you're willing to sleep in the Lager, these strictures are much less applicable. Nevertheless, you should phone ahead for a weekend place even in a dormitory. If an inn is the only guesthouse on a popular hiking route, then even the dormitory can fill up on a Saturday night.

It's much easier to get a room for a weekday night, sometimes even on the same day, but you should still phone ahead.

Some inns are on a road and can be reached by bus or car, others only by foot. Unlike alpine club huts, inns usually won't have scuffs or clogs available for you, but many will ask that you not wear your hiking boots in the rooms or halls.

Arriving with just a rucksack for luggage, you'll be shown to a room that usually has scrubbed pine walls and floors, occasionally a carpet. The beds, possibly old-fashioned ones with wooden head- and footboards, will be piled high with a plump eiderdown comforter over a bottom sheet. There may or may not be top sheet and blanket; many Swiss use only a down quilt. There will often be a washstand, with a pitcher and basin filled with fresh water, which you can use for a sponge bath. As noted above, these are often converted 19th-century farmhouses (although in immaculate condition), and private bathrooms are almost never to be found. One might even say that one of the defining characteristics of the Berghaus is the shared bathroom.

The Matratzenlager or dormitory is often very much like those in alpine club huts. There may be wooden platforms with pads laid side by side; at each place there's an uncovered pillow and two folded woolen blankets. There may be a stack of additional blankets somewhere in the room, but two folded blankets are usually more than enough. Guests may be assigned to their places. Some few inns have bunk beds. Men and women share the dormitories. Guests lean their packs against the foot of their sleeping place. Bedtime is later than at alpine club huts, but many people turn in by 10 or certainly by 11. The rule is to be quiet in the dorm. You'll need a flashlight or headlamp if you get up during the night.

Berghaus toilets are usually found out in the hall. A few inns have sinks in the rooms (in which case the sink will have warm water), but most do not. The sink may be in the toilet or else is in a washroom for communal use. A type of sink often used both at these guesthouses and at alpine club huts is the metal trough sink, a long metal sink with three or four faucets so that several people can use it at once. Some have warm water, others only cold water. The major change occurring with respect to Berghaus facilities is that showers are now rapidly appearing, whereas until the early 1990s they were almost never found at these inns. They are still not universal but have become quite common. Some inns do not charge, but others charge a few francs for use of the shower. At some inns, especially those that do not charge for use of the shower, the shower is only for guests staying in private rooms, not in the Matratzenlager. The water may be heated by solar panels. The shower may also be controlled by a timer, giving you, say, 3 or 4 minutes for your coin or token. A few inns have separate sinks and washrooms for men and women, but often that is not the case. And a very few inns listed in this book have outdoor toilets or washing facilities. Towels are often provided, but these vary from very small hand towels to larger ones. When they are not provided, you can often get one by asking. (Towels are never provided at alpine club huts.)

Most inns are on an electric line or produce their own electricity and have electrically lighted rooms and toilets, but a few do not. You will need a headlamp or flashlight for those.

In case you stay at a Berghaus for several nights, you'll find that almost never will someone come in to "make up" your room.

It is the custom to ask guests to pay their bill in the evening after dinner, not on the morning of departure.

BERGHAUS FOOD

Some inns prepare one evening meal for all overnight guests, while at others guests order à la carte from a menu. A "half-pension" or "half-board" arrangement includes this fixed-price dinner.

Whether you take the half-pension or order from the menu, you'll find certain standard fare. This is not necessarily what Swiss people ordinarily eat at home, but rather what they look for when they go up to the mountains for a day's outing, a weekend, or a full holiday. Certain dishes can therefore be expected on almost every Berghaus menu, although there are variations, as will be noted here in the descriptions of individual inns.

Every menu offers soup, often several kinds. The Tagessuppe (soup of the day) can be any type of soup; there may also be Consommé or Bouillon. Two kinds of soup frequently seen on Berghaus menus are Gerstensuppe, a thick soup of barley and vegetables, and Gulaschsuppe, with vegetables and chunks of beef flavored with paprika. There will also be several kinds of salads. Grüner Salat is green lettuce salad and Gemischter Salat is mixed salad: This may be a plate with separate little servings of several vegetables, most of them raw (sliced tomato, cucumber, diced beets, corn, grated carrots, grated celery root, lettuce, or other vegetables). You can get a small or large mixed salad. A large salad, a Grosser Salatteller, with soup, is often enough for dinner. There is often also Thonsalat, a large mixed salad with tuna fish.

Soup and salad are served at restaurants in town, but certain dishes are considered particular to the mountains—foods associated with life in the alps, the high summer farms, and the fare of shepherds, cowherds, and dairy people. Platters containing slices of various kinds of smoked or air-dried meat (Trockenfleisch) and perhaps cheese (Käse) are particularly typical. These are often called *Teller* (a plate) with a prefix: Bauernteller (farmer's plate), Wanderteller (hiker's plate), Bergteller (mountain plate), or perhaps with the name of the inn prefixed, as in Waldhausteller.

Among the cheese dishes is Raclette, in which a wheel of special Raclette cheese is warmed, then the melted portion scraped onto a plate and served with boiled potatoes and pickled condiments. Another favorite is cheese fondue. Hobelkäse is a hard cheese cut into very thin slices or curls. Käseschnitte, a mixture of several cheeses, is melted and baked on bread.

Menus generally include several kinds of cooked meat, often pork. Schweinschnitzel is a pork cutlet, Schweinskotelett is a chop, and Schweinssteak is a steak. Rind means beef (menus list the country of origin for beef) and Lamm means Lamb. Kalbfleisch is veal. Chicken is called by its French name, *Poulet*—it is found occasionally on Berghaus menus although less often than the other meats—but turkey is called by its German name, Truthahn. There is usually a variety of sausages, such as Schüblig, Bauernwurst, Bratwurst, Wienerli, and others. Schinken is ham, Speck is bacon. A dish "mit Ei" means with egg; eggs are Eier. Fisch (fish) is very rare in the mountains, unless near a lake, where Forelle (trout) may be served.

Meat dishes are usually accompanied by potatoes or noodles, vegetables, or possibly salads. Rösti is practically the Swiss national potato dish: Potatoes are grated, then fried so that they form a slight crust, lightly browned (and very tasty). Rösti natur is the plain dish; other varieties of Rösti may be sprinkled with grated cheese or minced ham, or topped with a fried egg. French fries, listed on menus as *Pommes frites,* are also very common. Boiled potatoes, often served with fish, are known as Salzkartoffeln or *Pommes natur.* Mashed potatoes are Kartoffelpuree. Teigwaren refers to all sorts of pasta, macaroni, and noodles (Nudeln). Spätzli are unstuffed dumplings.

Vegetarians who don't eat cheese or eggs have several choices. They can order soup and a large salad plate or a portion of Rösti, Pommes frites, or Nudeln. A portion of Rösti with a salad makes a filling meal. Spaghetti is found on many menus: Spaghetti Bolognese is with meat sauce, but Spaghetti Napolitaine has no meat. Some restaurants offer a Gemüseteller or vegetable plate.

A vegetarian dish found at many mountain inns is Älpler Macaroni, spelled in various ways, such as Magronen, Maccaroni, Macaronen, Makkaronen. Macaroni is baked with grated cheese and slivers of onion and usually served with a side dish of Apfelmus, applesauce. Some restaurants pour cream (Rahm) into the casserole before baking it; ask for it "Ohne Rahm" if you don't want cream.

There is very little variety in à la carte desserts at mountain inns. Sometimes only ice cream is available, perhaps meringue (served with cream or ice cream), and sometimes pastry or cakes. But inns that offer a half-pension dinner may serve Fruchtsalat (fruit salad) or a pudding or custard.

A typical half-pension dinner consists of soup, then perhaps salad, a plate of meat with potatoes or noodles and vegetables, and often a dessert. Vegetarians can request the main course without the meat. "Ich bin Vegetarier" means "I am a vegetarian."

Breakfast is light. The standard, basic Berghaus fare is bread, butter, and jam with coffee or tea, or Pfefferminze Tee (peppermint tea) for a noncaffeine beverage. The butter and jam often come in individual wrapped portions. Anything beyond that is an additional nicety: There may be a slab of butter instead of a foil-wrapped cube, and there may be a bowl of jam instead of separate portions. There may be cheese, either in wrapped portions or else slices of fresh alp cheese. Some inns serve orange juice, and some offer cold cereal such as Muesli or cornflakes. Some offer a plate of sliced cold meat. Some few provide a roll as well as bread.

Wine and beer are available at every mountain inn (as at every alpine club hut), except at those few inns that list themselves as "alkoholfrei." Wine is generally sold by measurement, in fractions of a liter: A glass of wine may be listed as either 20 or 30 cl (centiliters) or 2 or 3 dcl (deciliters); a half-liter bottle is 5 dcl or its equivalent in centiliters, 50 cl. Offenweine (open wine) is served by the glass or in a carafe. Flaschenwein is a bottle of wine. Beer is available in smaller or larger bottles and sometimes vom Fass (from the tap). Some inns also serve brandy or cordials. A very popular drink is coffee with liqueur, Kaffee mit Schnapps, or sometimes with the name of the restaurant as a prefix, as in Stieregg-Kaffee. Pfefferminze Tee is available almost everywhere, a good alternative for those who want a hot drink without caffeine. Soft drinks and mineral water are always available; Apfelsaft (apple juice) is a popular drink, and sweet and hard apple ciders are great favorites in Appenzell.

PRICES

This book uses a code to indicate general price range. Prices at many mountain inns are very similar, with variations of a few francs. This code is based on a rate per person per day, for overnight in a private room, with breakfast and dinner, excluding drinks and lunch. Staying in a Matratzenlager (dormitory) reduces the price by approximately 10–20 Swiss francs (Sfr).

     less than 60 Sfr. Lower price.

     60–85 Sfr. Medium price.

85–120 Sfr. Higher price.

Some inns offer half-pension or half-board rates: This includes a fixed-price dinner from a set menu, plus breakfast. Some inns offer only half-pension, while at others half-pension is not available—meaning that dinner must be ordered à la carte—and some offer a choice between the two alternatives. Breakfast is normally included in all Swiss hotel overnight rates; if it is not, the description mentions that. Service is almost always included. Some inns are required by their community to charge a Kurtaxe, usually about 1 Sfr per person.

Some inns give a reduced rate if guests stay for a certain minimum number of nights, perhaps three. And at many inns there is a reduced rate for children, such as half price (and at some, very young children may stay free of charge), but there are various cutoff points as to age. These variations are not specified in this book; in dealing with individual inns, inquire as to the rate per child and give the age of the child or children.

At nearly all mountain inns you must pay with cash. Except for a very, very few of the fanciest hotels, these inns do not take credit cards. Some might take travelers' checks but in Swiss francs only.

General price range for drinks

A half liter of wine (they usually come in bottles but are called open or Offenweine) costs anywhere from 14 to 23 Sfr, depending on the type of wine, but most half liters average around 18. Inns generally list a choice of about four or five open wines on their menus. A small beer is usually about 3.50 Sfr, and a large one, 4–5 Sfr.

Average prices for dishes commonly found on Berghaus menus
Soup averages 5–6 Sfr; a small green salad is 6 Sfr on average, a small mixed salad 7–8, and a large salad 12–14. A plate of spaghetti is about 10.50. There are many varieties of sausage, which if ordered with Rösti cost about 14–15. They can be ordered with bread alone, for about 8–9. Various platters of cold cuts, air-dried meat, cheese, etc., cost about 15–20. A main course of meat or perhaps chicken, with potatoes and vegetables or with several kinds of salad (a dish of meat or chicken with salads is called a Fitness Teller, despite the meat), ranges from 17 to 26 (but could cost more or less). A portion of Rösti may cost 6.50–10. Älpler Macaroni runs about 10.50–15. A portion of cake may cost 2.50–6.

A Gaststube, sometimes called by its diminutive, Stübli, is a small, cozy, informal room in which food or drink may be ordered. If a large hotel has a room with such a name, it is generally meant to suggest a cozy, informal space smaller than the dining room, a bar or parlor where coffee, wine, or beer may be ordered after dinner.

CHAPTER TWO

REACHING A BERGHAUS: GETTING THERE IS HALF THE FUN

Some of the inns described in this book are on a road and can be reached by bus or car; others can be reached only by walking. The listing of each inn shows its elevation, whether you can get there on wheels or on foot, and if the latter, how long the walk will take. The code symbols in the margin beside the inn's name signify the following:

 for access by foot.

 for access by mechanized transportation—by car, bus, or train.

for access by cable car.

A few inns are also accessible by such unusual means as horse carriage and lake steamer.

THE SWISS TRANSPORTATION SYSTEM

The Swiss have one of the best public transportation systems in the world. Trains and buses are frequent. You do not need a car to get to any place listed in this book that's on a road: You can get there by public transportation unless it is accessible only by foot.

Information on how to get from one place to another is quickly and easily available. All travel schedules are computerized; at any rail station they will give you a printout, free of charge, with a schedule for your trip including all the connections, by rail and bus, for anywhere you want to go in Switzerland and for the time of day when you want to travel. The complete transportation schedule for the entire country is also published annually, called the Kursbuch or *Indicateur Officiel:* one book for train and another for bus travel. Hotels often have a copy. And little regional timetable cards and leaflets are available free of charge, placed on display for

Piz Plata, Canton Graubunden

travelers to pick them up.

A Swiss Pass will allow you to travel without buying a ticket anywhere in Switzerland by train, bus, lake steamer, or even city bus, and will give you a discounted rate on many cable cars, for a specified amount of time. A Swiss Card will give you a discount on such travel. (The Pass and Card are not valid on a very few private bus lines.) You can purchase these at travel agencies outside of Switzerland or at airports or rail stations within the country. Upon arrival, take your Pass or Card to the railroad desk at the airport terminal, where it will be stamped and the dates of validity entered. For details and current prices, contact one of the offices of Switzerland Tourism, the network of Swiss national tourist offices.

TRAINS

At rail stations, the large yellow posters give the time of departing trains (Abfahrt, *Départ*) and the white ones of arriving trains (Ankunft, *Arrivée*). Railroad cars are labeled first or second class, and smoking and nonsmoking sections are indicated by signs.

If you plan to hike for a few days and then wish to go to a city or town, you can send off a suitcase or bag with your city clothes from any rail station (except for a very few small ones) by the excellent Gepäck or *bagages direct* system. Leave it at the Aufgabe or *Dépots bagages* counter; pick it up at the Ausgabe or *Retrait bagages* one. You must have a ticket or travel pass to do this and will pay a small fee. Your bag will arrive anywhere in the country within a day or two. Bags are also transported to places where there are bus but no train stations.

BUSES

When an inn is described in this book as reachable by bus, it means by a PTT bus. A bus network that covers virtually the entire country is run by the Swiss post office, known as the PTT or Post-Telephone Telegraph. Known in German as Postautos, in French as *Autobus* or *cars postales,* these PTT buses are immediately recognizable by sight and sound: They are painted bright yellow with red writing, and their horns produce a three-note sound. Upon hearing this sound, car drivers are supposed to yield, as the buses deliver the mail and have right of way. Bus schedules are posted at the bus stops and at PTT offices.

Passes that reduce travel costs (see above) are valid on all buses except for the handful of private lines.

A few inns are on roads that are private. Cars are allowed on some (and are charged a toll), but are restricted from others. This book indicates when those conditions apply.

Large bags or large rucksacks are stowed in a compartment under the bus (or sometimes in a little cart attached to the bus). If there are few passengers, the bus driver may let you take a big pack onto the bus.

WALKING ROUTES

Most inns, however, are on hiking trails, and in many ways these are the most fun. There is not only the exercise of the walk itself and the often glorious scenery along the way, but walking to your evening's resting place enables you most fully to enter into the Berghotel experience. You arrive on foot, with nothing but the rucksack on your back and a keener interest in dinner. Because these inns enable one to escape the slickness of the contemporary world, they complement perfectly the experience of hiking in the Alps. After a day's walking through meadows and past little farms, with glorious snow peaks above—a landscape both peaceful and utterly unspoiled—it enhances the delight to stay at an inn that does not break the spell. The comfortable but old-fashioned simplicity of a Swiss mountain inn is balm to the soul.

Trail conditions may change from year to year. A portion of trail can be washed out after heavy rain or covered with a rock slide after a winter storm. Moreover, a trail that can be easily and safely hiked on a dry, clear day may be dangerous in rain, snow, or mist.

REACHING INNS BY FOOT

For each inn described here that's accessible by foot, this book explains how to walk there and what that will entail. For round-trip walks (walks that return you to your starting point), the time given will be for both ways—that is, the entire walk. One-way times are given for walks that can be used to link inns or to descend into another valley. In general, descent time is 30–50 percent less than ascent time. Walking times are approximate and generally include a lunch break of a half hour. A walk may take some people a little more or a little less than the time given here.

Trail Signs and Markers

Trails are generally very well marked, blazed, and signposted. A blaze is a dash of paint on a stone or tree. The most usual blaze mark is white/red/white, the colors of the Swiss flag, but sometimes you may see another color. Any paint mark indicates that you are on a trail. A bent blaze, like an inverted V, indicates that the trail takes a turn.

Throughout the country you'll find yellow metal signs on posts indicating trail destinations and the time it should take to get there (supposedly calculated for an ascent rate of 300 meters an hour, but in places the posted signs are a little fast). Distances are never posted, as what counts most to calculate hiking time is how much ascent the trail requires. An easier, gentler trail is called a Wanderweg or *chemin pédestre,* indicated by signs that are all yellow. Trails that require more ascent or that are rougher or more difficult have a white/red/white tip and are called Bergweg, mountain trails.

Note: The abbreviation "m" is given in this book for meters and "km" for kilometers.

CHAPTER THREE

Pack Lightly: What You Need to Take for a Night at a Berghaus

Even when inns are on a road and can be reached by bus or car, no one arrives at a Berghaus with a suitcase or duffel bag. Hiking in Switzerland is a kind of backpacking, although not in the sense of camping out, because hikers sleep and eat indoors. Hikers carry only what they want or absolutely need. If you see someone toiling up a trail beneath a towering pack, he or she is most likely a climber, headed for an alpine club hut with a pack stuffed full of gear. Hikers carry a pack as small and as light as possible.

As explained in chapter 1, you don't need to bring a sleeping bag or pad to a mountain inn. Even if you stay in a dormitory, ample blankets will be provided along with a pad or mattress. Neither do guests bring bathrobes, nor even pajamas. People sleep in a T-shirt and underpants or whatever they choose, even in the unisex dorms, and head to the communal bathroom in the same or in a parka. Sheet sacks (called, oddly, *sacs à viande* in French) can take the place of sheets for dormitories, but most Swiss hikers don't use them.

Berghaus Necessities

Necessities are few. Most inns request that you remove your hiking boots. You can pad around in your socks, but many hikers pack some lightweight slippers or scuffs. Camping supply stores and mail-order houses now provide very lightweight scuffs. You should also carry a small supply of hand soap—you can cut a small piece off a larger bar and carry it in a self-sealing plastic bag—and for a trip of several days, perhaps another bag with a few spoonfuls of detergent powder for washing undergarments. Most inns now supply a towel, sometimes large, sometimes quite small, or will provide a towel on request. If there is a sink near the inn's restaurant, there will sometimes be a supply of paper towels there and a liquid soap dispenser. If you decide to bring your own towel, pack a very small one, as lightweight as possible; investigate the viscose towels sold by camping supply houses or sometimes pet supply stores. We are all used to large, luxurious bath towels at home, but you will be surprised at how well you can manage with a small one. You can buy very small tubes of toothpaste almost anywhere these days, including Switzerland, or put some toothpaste into a plastic film can. A dollop of face or shaving cream can also go into a film can. It's a good idea to carry a small, lightweight headlamp or flashlight as well.

That is all you will *need* for a night at a Berghaus; the rest is up to you.

WHAT TO PACK FOR A HIKING TRIP IN SWITZERLAND
These are the things you should bring for hiking in Switzerland, whether you will stay in a mountain inn or a hotel in a village or in town.

* a two-piece rain suit of laminated "breathable" cloth
* a warm garment, such as a fleece or pile jacket or pullover, or a woolen sweater
* long pants, comfortable and loose-fitting (synthetic fabrics are best as they dry quickly; jeans are heavy and also slow to dry)
* shorts for hot weather
* a long-sleeved shirt, synthetic or cotton, with sleeves you can roll up
* a T-shirt (again, synthetic fabrics wick your sweat and dry much faster after you wash them)
* a sun hat, preferably with a brim that will shade your face
* gaiters to keep snow and mud out of your boots, particularly if you think you will be on snow
* sunglasses
* sunblock, and protective sunstick for lips
* trekking poles (these cannot be described as essential, only as invaluable! They protect knees on a downhill slope, give you purchase on an uphill one, help you stabilize yourself on a narrow passage, and keep you steady on a slippery surface. Collapsible, made in three sections, they can fit into packs or be strapped beside them)
* a water bottle
* a pair of wool gloves and a wool cap, which are very comforting if the weather turns cold or windy

A few words about boots: If your boots are new, you should break them in at home before your trip by wearing them as much as possible. For greatest comfort wear two pairs of socks—a thin liner sock and a heavier outer wool or synthetic fiber sock—and use an insole pad for cushioning. If you need to buy new boots, try them on over this sock arrangement and with an insole pad in the boot. Look for boots with Vibram soles. Despite the advertisements, lightweight boots are less comfortable in the end than sturdy, mediumweight ones as they give your feet less protection from rocks underfoot and provide less ankle support. We prefer leather boots, which we treat with a sealant, to boots with panels of laminated cloth, which may fail to keep your feet dry in very wet conditions.

Your pack: Like your boots and clothes, your pack should fit you well. You need to try on a new pack just as you would try on a new pair of boots, as they are sized to different body lengths. Look for a lightweight pack with an internal frame that conforms to the shape of your back, and a load-bearing waistbelt. Packs can be found with shoulder straps set closer together, which are more comfortable for smaller persons. No pack is completely waterproof: Line your pack with a plastic trash bag or waterproof inner bag to keep clothes dry, or obtain a rain cover that fits over the pack.

CHAPTER FOUR

GENERAL INFORMATION ABOUT TRAVEL IN SWITZERLAND

BUSINESS HOURS

These are generally 8.00 to 12.00 and 13.30 or 14.00 to 18.30, based on a 24-hour clock. In large cities, department stores often stay open during the lunch break. Stores may also close at 16.00 on Saturday afternoons, although not in busy resorts. In some large cities, stores may be closed on Monday mornings as well, and some shops remain closed throughout the day. Most shops are closed on Sunday, although some bakeries may remain open.

CURRENCY

Banks accept travelers' checks; you can also exchange currency at railway stations. Most hotels, restaurants, and stores in cities and towns accept major US credit cards. Mountain inns with very few exceptions and alpine club huts, however, do not accept credit cards and usually do not accept travelers' checks.

FOOD AND DRINK

See chapter 1 for the type of meals you can expect at mountain inns. In towns and cities you'll find a wider variety of food on restaurant menus. Note that most Swiss restaurants also double as bars or pubs. People go not only to cafés but also to restaurants for a beer or a glass of wine after dinner.

While all mountain inns serve lunch and refreshments, hikers often carry picnic supplies for lunch, especially on a route where no inn will be available at midday. Upon request, many inns can make you a picnic lunch to take on the trail. Hikers buy picnic supplies when they pass through a village. The large supermarket chains, such as Migros and Coop, offer lower prices than smaller shops. Photographic film at competitive prices is always available in supermarkets.

Monika Breitenmoser on the route to the Rotsteinpass, Appenzell

The classic alpine picnic lunch consists of bread and cheese or sausage or sliced cold meat, but there are other possibilities as well, such as canned tuna or sardines. Mustard is available in tubes, both large and small, useful for picnics. Vegetarians can make an excellent sandwich of sliced tomato, cucumber, green pepper, and onion. "Reform" means a health food store or section in a supermarket, and you may find tofu-, soy-, or wheat-based luncheon meat substitutes. You can buy packaged trail mix or make your own, much cheaper, from bags of peanuts, raisins, and various sorts of sliced dried fruit. Fruit is excellent. And it is hard to pass up the goodies at the bakery counter. But the bread itself is as good as cake: It is superb, among the best in Europe, and the variety of breads is astonishing. (Bread connoisseurs, look for your loaf at a bakery, not a supermarket.) Many of the breads are made of whole grain (Vollkorn) and breads with names such as Funfkorn and Siebenkorn (five-grain, seven-grain) contain a mixture of grains. There are many others as well. Halbweiss, the most common bread, is a little like Jewish rye but without the seeds. Bread is sold by the loaf or by weight. If a loaf of Halbweiss is too large for you, they'll sometimes give you a half (ein Halb), or you can buy a roll or two (Brötli).

It's safest to fill your water bottle at your inn or hotel in the morning. No guarantee can be made about mountain stream water.

LANGUAGES

There are four official ones: German, French, Italian, and Romansch. Swiss children must learn High German in school but the native Germanic language is actually Schwyzer Dütsch, which sounds and looks and is different from High German in many respects. But if you know any German, everyone will understand you. Many people speak English: railway conductors, for example, and others who work in any way with travelers, as well as large numbers of ordinary Swiss.

MAPS

Swiss maps are excellent, and you should buy a topographic map for any region where you are planning to walk. Maps labeled Wanderkarte have hiking trails marked on them, often in red (ski trails may be marked as well, in blue), and are easy to follow. Get the map with the smallest scale—1:25,000 rather than 1:50,000—for the best details. The place to find maps is in the region that they cover. They're sold at a variety of places: bookstores, food shops, railway stations, shops or kiosks that sell newspapers and magazines, and tourist offices.

On the Vereinapass route

One point is important to note: You may reach a place that has a name on a map (or a trail sign) but find nothing there. This occurs often in Switzerland. It doesn't mean that you are lost or that the map is wrong; rather, it may be the name of a meadow or pasture or perhaps was the name of a farm that no longer exists. Such names are useful markers. Also, names may have slightly different spellings on maps and signposts.

SAFETY

A few basic rules and tips that apply to hiking in any mountains, anywhere: Don't start out on a long hike if the weather looks threatening, and turn around in time if a storm approaches. Lightning strikes high points and ridges, so get down to a lower place if a thunderstorm is brewing. Always carry your rain suit and a warm jacket or sweater to avoid getting wet and chilled, conditions that lead to hypothermia. Carry some snack food for energy.

Don't hike alone, unless you're on a short trail with lots of other hikers.

Be watchful when you pass below a steep slope. Animals or hikers above may knock over stones. Don't take a lunch break under a cliff or slope covered with loose rock.

Stay off glaciers unless you're with a licensed guide and properly equipped. And take special care if you must cross a snow-covered slope. Wet grass is also slippery, and when steep grassy slopes are wet, they are as dangerous as snow slopes.

Rabies exists across Europe. Beware of animals that appear ill or unnaturally friendly. Poisonous snakes also exist in Switzerland but are very rare. Before you sit down on a rock, poke it with your trekking pole to make sure nothing is beneath it.

A few points specific to hiking in Switzerland: Many farmers use electrified fencing around pastures. When this is the case, you'll see little plastic spools around the wire, and you may hear a low clicking sound. These fences are meant to keep the animals in, not to keep hikers out (and not to harm the farmers), and so there are always safe-passage gates. Grasp the plastic handgrip, unhook the wire, then replace it.

Do not touch any metal tube or shiny object you may see lying in the ground. The Swiss army practices maneuvers in the mountains and very rarely may overlook a piece of ordnance when the soldiers clean up (as they assiduously do). Report any such object when you get to your inn or to the next village.

Telephones and Telephone Numbers

Important: When calling within Switzerland, use the initial 0 of Swiss area codes; if calling from outside the country, do not use the initial 0. There are telephones at coin boxes and at PTT offices. You can buy a calling card (Taxkarte, Taxcard) at PTT offices and rail stations, for 10 or 20 Sfr, to use instead of coins. Telephones that take these are labeled Taxphone.

The word Natel in a telephone book means the number of a cellular phone. The letters "w.k.a." (wenn keine Antwort) mean that if there is no answer for the first number given, try this number.

Walking Tips

If you have not hiked in the mountains before, here is some general advice.

Give yourself a little time to acclimatize to higher altitudes. Reactions vary, but usually people acclimatize after a few days at moderate altitudes. Almost all mountain inns are at what would generally be called moderate altitude. Although there are no altitudes in Switzerland to compare with the Himalayas or Andes, most people will feel light-headed if they take a cable car or cog railway that lofts them quickly up to 3000 meters.

Don't start off on your first day with a long, challenging hike. Start with something less demanding until your muscles are warmed up for extended uphill/downhill walking.

Foot pain may result from lacing your boots too tightly across the instep. But keep boots laced firmly enough around your ankles (but not too tightly) so that your foot doesn't slide forward when you walk downhill; your toes should not strike the front of the boot.

Most important of all: When climbing uphill, go slowly. The proper pace makes the difference between arriving at your destination exhausted and out of breath or feeling good. Take a slow, rhythmic pace that lets you breathe easily; if you start to huff and puff, slow down. It is both conditioning and also proper pacing that enables so many Swiss people in their 70s and 80s to hike in the Alps.

Weather

Summer in Switzerland is variable: There may be a spell of cool, rainy weather followed by very hot, dry weather. Be prepared for either. On a sunny day in the mountains, it rarely gets above 80 or perhaps 85 degrees Fahrenheit. Evenings are always cool, depending on your altitude, and you will certainly need a sweater or pile jacket or pullover. Although the country is small, the weather varies because of the mountain barriers. The Bernese Oberland generally gets more rainfall, the Valais less, and it can be raining or showery in the former while sunny and dry in the latter.

If the spring was late, snow may linger in high places and on north-facing slopes into early July. Some people think that the weather is more stable and more likely to remain warm in August (although this is not guaranteed by statistics); on the other hand, the alpine flowers show best in July.

Weather forecasts are excellent. You can dial 162 anywhere in the country and get the forecast in the language of the region, if you can understand it.

THE MOUNTAIN INNS
BY REGION

CHAPTER 5

THE BERNESE OBERLAND

The high country above the Swiss capital city of Bern is known by this name, sometimes called simply the Oberland. It is one of the most magnificently scenic regions in the Swiss Alps. The mountains in the Valais are higher, but the Oberland receives more rainfall (its only drawback) and so is more lushly, lavishly green. But the sun does shine on the Bernese Oberland, and on a fine day, with its rich meadows profusely full of brilliant wildflowers, dazzling against the backdrop of snowy peaks, the heart leaps.

The great Oberland mountains form a long chain, running east to west, and there is considerable variety along the chain. The highest peaks are toward its center.

IFFIGENALP

Almost at the western end of the Bernese Oberland, the Rawilpass connects the Oberland with the Rhône Valley and the Valais. At one end of the pass route is the small ski resort of Lenk, at the other, the Valaisian capital, Sion. French-speaking Sion is home to several attractions: a handsome old castle, the world's oldest playable organ (there's a summer music festival), and some good restaurants with French cuisine.

Iffigenalp, a cluster of a few farms and a little inn, is the last settlement on the Oberland side of the pass. It is often an overnight stop for hikers crossing the pass or taking other routes, or for people who want the pleasure and the respite of a little Berghaus in the mountains. It's a well-loved place, its charm deriving from its simplicity and the warmth and friendliness of the family that runs it.

1 • BERGHAUS IFFIGENALP • 1600 M

The inn is a little chalet only two stories high, its weathered wood a deep, rich brown. An enclosed porch with glass windows has been added to the front, extending the small dining room, and a few tables have been placed outside—the extra space proves very useful on fine Saturday and Sunday

Bernese Oberland between the Rotstockhütte and Mürren; Overleaf: The Matterhorn from the route to Mettelhorn, the Valais

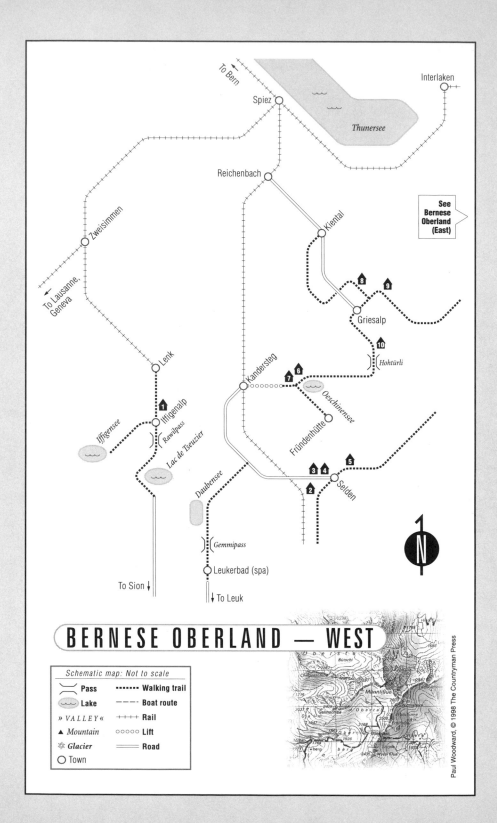

To Bern

Interlaken

Spiez

Thunersee

Reichenbach

See
Bernese
Oberland
(East)

Kiental

Zweisimmen

8 **9**

To Lausanne,
Geneva

Griesalp

Lenk

10

Hohtürli

1

Iffigenalp

Kandersteg

7 **6**

Rawilpass

Iffigsee

Lac de Tseuzier

Oeschinensee

Fründenhütte

Daubensee

3 **4** **5**

2 Selden

Gemmipass

N

To Sion

Leukerbad (spa)

To Leuk

BERNESE OBERLAND — WEST

Schematic map: Not to scale

	Pass	▪▪▪▪▪	Walking trail
	Lake	– – –	Boat route
» *VALLEY* «		++++	Rail
▲	*Mountain*	○○○○○	Lift
☀	*Glacier*	═══	Road
○	Town		

Paul Woodward, © 1998 The Countryman Press

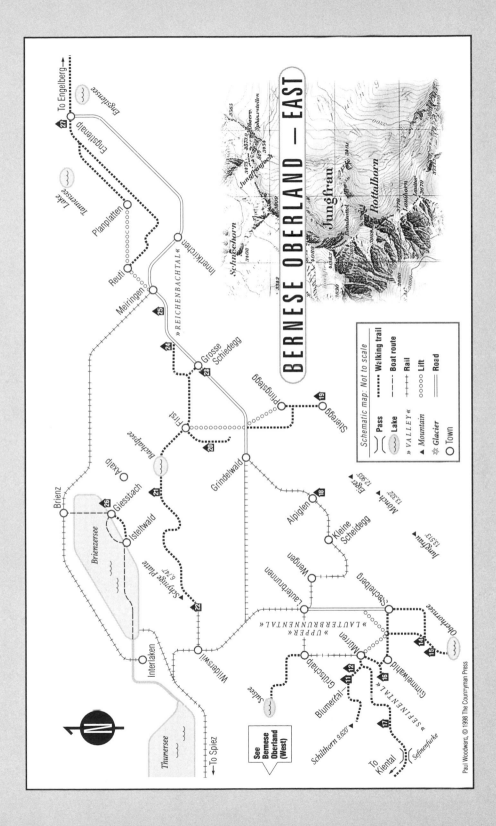

BERNESE OBERLAND — EAST

Schematic map: Not to scale

Pass ······· **Walking trail**
          --- **Boat route**
Lake ++++ **Rail**
»VALLEY« ooooo **Lift**
▲ **Mountain** ──── **Road**
☀ **Glacier**
○ **Town**

To Engelberg →

Engstlenalp

Lake Tannensee

Planplatten

Reuti

Meiringen

Innertkirchen

»REICHENBACHTAL«

Grosse Schiedegg

Pfingstegg

Stieregg

Grindelwald

First

Bachalpsee

Axalp

Brienz

Giessbach

Isteltwald

Brienzersee

Schynige platte 6,747

Alpiglen

Kleine Scheidegg

Eiger 12,903

Mönch 13,322

Jungfrau 13,513

Wengen

Lauterbrunnen

Stechelberg

Oberhornsee

»UPPER «LAUTERBRUNNENTAL«

Mürren

Gimmelwald

»SEFINENTAL«

Grütschalp

Blumertal

Sulsee

Schilthorn 9,620

Sefinenfurke

To Kiental →

Wilderswil

Interlaken

Thunersee

To Spiez →

See Bernese Oberland (West)

Jungfrau

Rottalhorn

Schneehorn

Jungfraujoch

Paul Woodward, © 1998 The Countryman Press

afternoons, when many hikers coming from various directions congregate here for refreshments. The dining room itself has been divided into two sections in order to create a feature most unusual in a mountain inn: a space for nonsmokers. This is typical of the thoughtfulness of the family that runs the inn.

Overnight guests who take private rooms stay in the Dépendance, another old house just beside the inn. This annex, a rather curious structure, is also an old wooden house, 100 years old—older, in fact, than the inn itself, which was rebuilt in 1929 after a fire. One side of the older building consists of open galleries, alongside which are some of the rooms, so that

Rawilpass

when you leave your room to go to the toilet or shower, you pass along a corridor that is covered by a roof but open on one side to the air. The rooms are basic—with down quilts, blankets, washstand, and little table—but very plain: The wooden floors are not as bright or lustrous as at some other inns. The Matratzenlager are also in a separate building, a rustic old barn, where they are divided into several rooms upstairs off the hayloft area. Two more simple rooms are below, beside the barn (but the cows, we were informed, are not inside the barn at night), next to a sort of common room with a rough table and benches and a tile stove. For dormitory guests the toilet is in a little wooden cubicle outside, and for washing there's an open-air trough.

Dinner is à la carte, from a menu with no surprises. Along with the customary farmers' platters of dried and smoked meat and cheese, sausages, Schnitzel and cutlets, and of course Rösti, is Älpler Macaroni with apple-sauce, as well as spaghetti, cheese fondue, soups, and salads.

We stayed here one unseasonably cold night and were given hot water bottles to warm our beds—a gesture typical of the very warm-hearted Tschanz-Schönmann family who have been running the inn since 1980. They are friendly, helpful folk, and for those who can't speak any German or French, Frau Tschanz can summon up a little English.

There are 14 private rooms and 50 Matratzenlager places. It's open from mid-May to mid-October. Tel. 033/733 13 33; 3775 Lenk.

Getting there: Most people approach Iffigenalp from Lenk, the small, low-key ski resort at the upper end of the Simmental. From the Lenk rail station, you can take a van that makes several runs a day up to Iffigenalp (a distance of 8 kilometers) and back again. For the schedule or to reserve places, phone Taxi Gobeli, 033/733 14 12 (on fine weekend afternoons, they may send up a bus instead of the van to accommodate all the hikers coming down). You can hike up from Lenk in about 2½ hours; on the way you'll pass a superb waterfall, the Iffigfall.

Walks: You can hike in several directions from the inn. A very popular route goes to the Iffigensee, a little blue lake at 2065 meters, reachable in 2 hours. Another hour would bring you up to the Wildhorn alpine club hut below the peak with the same name. From the lake you can also hike westward to the Lauenensee and from there continue on to Gstaad. From Lenk you can take the Betelberg lift, then hike in a loop around the Stigel-berg Ridge to come down to Iffigenalp. The Simmenfälle is another spectacular waterfall, also reachable by hiking trail.

WALK 1 • Rawilpass Route from Iffigenalp: 10 kilometers; 830 meters up/655 meters down; 6 hours.

The hike over the Rawilpass (also spelled Rawyl; Col du Rawil in French) begins or ends at Iffigenalp. This pass should not be hiked in foggy, misty weather or too early in the season, when there may be snow on the pass. The main difficulty of the Rawil is that, unlike other passes, it has a long passage (essentially level, with ups and downs) across the top connecting the two slopes, and although the trail is well blazed, the paint marks are on rather low rocks, and one could lose the track under snow or in mist.

If you look up from Iffigenalp at the great cliffs that seem to bar the way to the pass, it looks as if there's no possible way up. But there is a very good trail to the top; it simply cannot be seen from below.

From Iffigenalp, follow the signposted trail across the meadows. It reaches the base of the cliffs and begins a steep ascent on switchbacks. You'll pass a small lake of a beautiful deep turquoise color and then reach the top of the pass (2429 meters). Follow the blazes and the track (easy to see in good weather and without snow) across the top to another lake of less vivid color, then descend less steeply on the Valaisian side, with an excellent view of the grand spread of the long snowy wall of the Valaisian Alps. You'll descend to the Lac de Tseuzier, where you can get a bus down to Sion, an hour's ride.

Note that if you approach the pass from Sion and start from the Lac de Tseuzier, you'll have less to climb but more to descend. Starting from Sion, pick up the bus for the Lac de Tseuzier at the big outdoor bus plaza just outside the Sion rail station: The sign on the bus may say BARRAGE DE RAWIL instead of LAC DE TSEUZIER. Also, this bus route may be listed under Barrage de Rawil in the Kursbuch or Indicateur Officiel, which lists all bus schedules. Starting from Sion, you may also have to change to another bus at Botyre or Ayent; simply name your destination to the bus driver—you don't really need to speak French to do that—and he'll tell where or when to change. There's a morning bus that in 1997 left at 9:20, but the schedule may change from year to year and should be checked. If you start from Iffigenalp, in 1997 the last bus down to Sion left at 5 PM but check the current schedule.

KANDERSTEG

Kandersteg is one of the most appealing little towns in the Swiss Alps. Very small, quiet, and unspoiled, it is set on a broad meadow—surprisingly level and richly green in summer—at the foot of a fan-shaped wall of mountains and glaciers: a stunning backdrop. The little Reformed

Church on Kandersteg's main street, dating from 1510, is a jewel, with tiny stars, a moon, and a sun painted on the ceiling, and a beautiful pulpit of inlaid wood.

Kandersteg is the departure point for the Gasterntal, a lovely, quiet, and undeveloped high valley, and for a beautiful lake, the Oescheninsee.

THE GASTERNTAL

The unspoiled character of the Gasterntal, empty except for a few farms and four Berghotels, will be preserved because there is strict control on new building. Two of the guesthouses are located very near each other at Selden, which—although it has a place-name—is neither a village nor even a hamlet. There is no electricity in the valley except for that generated by individual microhydroelectric turbines.

Getting there: The easiest way is to take one of the little red-and-white Kanderreisen vans from the Kandersteg station; it's a good idea to reserve places. You can do that at the tourist office, on the main street, just 5 minutes from the rail station: From the station, walk up the street toward the mountains and turn left at the big intersection; the tourist office is on the right, a little past the small food market. You can also phone for reservations: 033/671 11 71. A round-trip fare is Sfr 17, one way is 10. The dramatic, spectacular road climbs through a steep, narrow gorge in galleries cut through sheer walls of rock—the road being only just wide enough for the van.

Mark Twain traveled through the Gasterntal in 1878 and described its torrent as "lashing and thrashing its way over and among monster boulders, and hurling chance roots and logs about like straws. The path by the side of the torrent was so narrow that one had to look sharp when he heard a cow-bell, and hunt for a place that was wide enough to accommodate a cow and a Christian side by side, and such places were not always to be had at an instant's notice. The cows wear church-bells, and that is a good idea in the cows, for where that torrent is you couldn't hear an ordinary cow-bell any further than you could hear the ticking of a watch." (Twain 1996, p. 363)

The road twists through a series of curves that snake through walls of rock. It then emerges onto the initially comparatively level, high shelf of the Gasterntal, beside the Kander stream. There is a special stop for Hotel Waldhaus soon after you reach the shelf. From the van stop, cross the bridge and bear left on a gravel road; you'll reach the Waldhaus in 5 minutes. The van continues as far as the two inns at Selden, then turns around.

2 • HOTEL WALDHAUS • 1358 M

The Waldhaus (literally, "forest house") is immensely charming—all the more so for being unself-conscious about it. In the style and spirit of the Berghaus tradition, it is devoid of quaintness or cuteness. Simple as it is, relaxed, informal, and not in the least hokey, it is considered one of the most special and romantic old hotels in the region because, having no electricity and using no generator, guests dine and get about by candlelight. Besides being a Berghotel, it is a working farm, with two barns full of cows at milking time, and pigs as well. Its facade is hung with cowbells, a decoration often seen on Swiss farms but not on Berghotels.

Its front porch faces a splendid view across the meadow that includes the snow-streaked wall that closes off the valley and grand rock walls on both sides, striped with glistening waterfalls. With so pleasing a scene and a long summer evening, we chose to eat dinner on the porch, a simple space with weathered wooden chairs and tables. During dinner we watched farmers mowing the fields, lofting the hay into the barns, and driving the cows out to graze for the evening.

After dinner we visited the barns, which were being swept and mucked out. Milking stools hung on pegs in the little dairy room, and milk cans were cooling in a basin of cold water. The herd consists of 15 cows and 15 calves, producing all the milk and some of the cheese used here. The cows come up in June from Kandergrund and go back down in September, but they return for one more month in late autumn to eat the hay harvested in the summer.

Toward dusk, we repaired to the dining room for a carafe of wine. The house is about 100 years old. Along with a floor of rough, broad boards that betray its farmhouse origin and an unusual corner chimney and fireplace, the room has the traditional wood-paneled ceiling and red-and-white-checked tablecloths and curtains. It is fairly small, with only six tables and an adjoining alcove for groups. As evening approached, some local farmers came in for a treat—sunburned men in their work clothes, sleeves still rolled up from the day's toil. Nine of them sat together at one table, ordered food and drink, and were quietly jolly.

The Waldhaus is famous for its Raclette, which is made in the old way: The huge cheese is laid upon a large brick and heated before a wood fire in the dining room's open chimney; the melted end is then scraped onto a plate with a knife. Few mountain inns serve Raclette, and no other that we ever saw makes it over a wood fire. But other dishes are available as well, and

Hotel Waldhaus, Gasterntal

guests order from the menu, as we did. For dessert we managed to nab—and perforce had to share—the very last slice of a delectable, fresh, homemade strawberry pie. At breakfast slices of very good alp cheese were served and thickly cut fresh bread, along with the customary butter and jam.

We slept in a private room furnished with two old-fashioned bedsteads with high, dark wooden head- and footboards. On the marble-topped washstand were basins and pitchers, filled with water, and a tiny sink out in the hall had cold running water. Besides the candles that lit the dining room after sunset, lighted candles were also placed in the toilets, and we had a candlestick on our night table.

The inn is run by Marianne Ryter and her husband, Albert Aellig, but everyone in the family, from grandma to the children, helps out. Frau Ryter explained that although they use a generator to power the milking machines, they don't want to use one to provide electricity for the house; people like it old-fashioned, she said.

Hotel Waldhaus has four double rooms and 30 dormitory places; it's open from May to October. Tel. 033/675 12 73 or 671 36 34; 3718 Kandersteg.

Getting there: Take the van from Kandersteg and get off at the stop for the Waldhaus.

Walks: From the Waldhaus you can hike up to the Daubensee, or you can catch the morning van from Kandersteg up to Selden and then hike to the Kanderfirn (see Walk 1 under Selden).

WALK 1 • Waldhaus to the Daubensee: round-trip 14 kilometers; 900 meters up; 6½–8 hours. (The Gemmipass, leading down to Leukerbad, is about 40 minutes beyond the lake.)

About a minute from the hotel at a signposted junction, turn right for the locations on the Gemmipass route: Gurnigel, Stock, and the Gemmipass itself.

The path leads through woods, then climbs steeply beside a waterfall for about 40 minutes and passes through a gorge. Here the trail is a little exposed and there are some fixed cables to hold onto. About 1 hour after starting, the trail emerges beside a lovely stream, becoming more gradual. You'll reach a signposted junction at Stierenbergli; turn left for Spittelmatte, Schwarenbach, and the Gemmipass. (A trail to the right leads to Stock, from which a lift descends to the lower valley; the cable car station below is connected by a shuttle bus with Kandersteg, running every 30 minutes.)

Beyond Stierenbergli, a nearly level gravel road leads through a broad valley. You'll reach a signposted junction at Spittelmatte. (From this point, another trail to the right also leads to the upper cable car station at Stock.) Continue straight ahead and soon reach another signposted junction, where you could turn right for the Arvensee, a very clear, shallow, little green lake—a nice lunch spot.

The trail to the Gemmipass continues through a narrow valley; a plaque commemorates the disaster of 1895, when a section of the Altels Glacier fell onto an alp below, killing six men and many cows. There is a Berg-hotel at Schwarenbach (a historic building, which still has a portion of its 13th-century roof; we found it a rather cold, impersonal place—quite unusually so among the many inns we have visited), above another small lake. In another 40 minutes reach the Daubensee, a gray lake between slabbed rock walls; in contrast to the Arvensee, it is a rather bleak spot. This lake has no visible outlet and is drained by an underground channel. Another 40 minutes brings you to the Gemmipass, from which the trail makes a dizzying, precipitous plunge to the very well-appointed spa at Leukerbad, to which you can also descend by cable car. In former times many travelers rode down by mule or horse, until 1861, when the Count-ess d'Herlincourt, a young bride, fell out of her saddle and plunged down the cliff to her death. Subsequently, travelers were not allowed to descend this pass on horseback.

SELDEN 1537 M

Formerly also called Gastern, Selden is not a village but a couple of sweetly simple farmhouses, clearly much changed in the last century. The *Baedeker Guide* of 1893 describes it as "a group of hovels, the first a small cabaret." It is the site of two pleasant inns, the Steinbock and the Gasterntal. At Heim-ritz, another 10 or 15 minutes up the gravel path from Selden, is a third and simpler inn, Gasthaus zur Gletscher Heimritz (which is also an alp). The elder Herr Künzi of Hotel Steinbock says that the Gasterntal, now so very sparsely populated, was inhabited even before Kandersteg, indeed, even inhabited year-round, which is no longer the case. Traffic through the val-ley can be dated to at least the early 14th century and perhaps even earli-er, when the valley served as a route for the transport of salt and pepper from the south. The name Gastern has nothing to do with things gastric, such as gastroenterology, but instead is said to derive from the Latin word

Christian Künzi and the 1696 Bible, Gasterntal

castrum, encampment; apparently the Romans also used this pass. The valley provides access to the Lötschenpass (see p. 160), which connects with the Valais, and before the construction of the Lötschberg railway tunnel in 1906–1912, it served as an important link with the south. The Lötschenpass was considered a safer passage than the only other access route to the Valais, the Gemmipass, before the construction of a bridle path on the latter. Another small and simple inn, **Berghaus Gfällalp,** is found at 1850 meters, partway up the rise to the pass, below a high shelf. It is open June to October. Tel. 033/675 11 61.

Getting there: Take the van from Kandersteg; it stops at both the Steinbock and Gasterntal inns, then turns back.

3 • HOTEL STEINBOCK • 1537 M

This inn, now partially renovated, was built around 1920 and served as a way station for hikers crossing the Lötschenpass. Christian Künzi, a mountain guide, and his Scottish-born wife, Ann, provide a warm, friendly atmosphere. The Künzi family has the keeping of a great leather- and brass-bound Bible, dated 1696, given at that time by the government in Bern to the people of the Gasterntal because they were so isolated and poor and to thank them for helping to build the trail over the Lötschenpass. The Bernese Protestants had fought several battles with the Valaisian Catholics at or near that pass, and the men of the Gasterntal had helped build a paved mule track on the Bernese side of the pass.

Tasty meals are served in the cheerful small public room that serves as dining room and bar or outdoors at a few tables on the front porch. As at the Waldhaus, dinner is à la carte. The Künzi family generates its own electricity with a small hydro.

The hotel has six double rooms and two single ones, and 30 Matratzenlager places. A shower and sink are available in the hall. Hotel Steinbock is open from mid-May or June to mid-October. Tel. 033/675 11 62 or 675 14 72; 3718 Kandersteg.

4 • HOTEL GASTERNTAL • 1538 M

About 2 minutes farther up the road from Hotel Steinbock, in a house said to be about 100 years old, Hotel Gasterntal looks older, smaller, and simpler than the neighboring inn. It was the first Bergrestaurant in the Gasterntal Valley when the others were only tearooms. The small dining room is plain and old-fashioned, and its deep brown pine walls and ceiling give a rather dark effect. There is a small terrace in front and benches facing a lawn to one side. There are six double rooms, an additional two single rooms that could also hold two people, and four single rooms. A large new bathroom has warm-water sinks and showers; towels are provided upon request. There are 40 Matratzenlager places in three rooms above an old barn; dormitory guests cross the lawn to the main house to use the toilet and sinks off the dining room. The hotel is run by the Holzer family. Meals may be à la carte or half-pension. Our dinner was undistinguished, but it was cooked by old Herr Alfred Holzer, who is retiring; his son, Adrian, usually does the cooking, and starting in 1998, Adrian will run the hotel.

Hotel Gasterntal is open from mid-May or June to mid-October. Tel. 033/675 11 63; 3718 Kandersteg.

5 • GASTHAUS (BERGGASTHAUS) ZUR GLETSCHER HEIMRITZ
• 1635 M

A real alp, with a barn and six cows, this pleasant, quiet house is the smallest, simplest establishment in the Gasterntal, with three private rooms and 24 places in the Matratzenlager. The sink and washing place are outside.

Heimritz, run by the Rauber family, is open from the beginning of June to the beginning of October. Hikers can also stop here for drinks and refreshments. Tel. 033/675 14 34 or 671 22 35.

WALK 1 • The Kanderfirn, from Selden: round-trip 8 kilometers; 850 meters up; 6½ hours.

The Kanderfirn (2415 meters) is the glacier that closes off the upper end of the valley. The trail to its edge provides a scenic view across the glacier as well as down the valley. From Heimritz, cross the river on a bridge, or continue on the right bank through a small area of larch and spruce and cross another bridge higher up. The path continues through meadows, then ascends up along a knife-edge moraine, crosses a few boulder areas, and climbs the steep slope to the right of the glacier. The approach is scenic all the way, with a grand view of the impressive rock wall and its waterfall that blocks the end of the valley, and of the tongue of the Kanderfirn hanging over the rock. You can climb to a sort of belvedere and look down onto the glacier, which is open, with crevasses glinting azure blue. The scene extends across the expanse of glacier to a distant mountain with a hanging glacier above. The valley is enclosed by big rock walls.

THE OESCHINENSEE 1578 M

This stunning mountain lake, on a shelf just above Kandersteg, is one of the most startlingly beautiful places in the Alps. Its turquoise water is set like a gem below vertical walls of sheer rock, glistening with waterfalls, that wrap partway around the lake; shining above the cliffs are the mountains and glaciers of the superb Blümlisalp group. This cluster of mountains includes the Blümlisalphorn (3663 meters), the Weisse Frau (3650 meters) and Wilde Frau (3260 meters)—the "white wife" and the "wild wife"—the Morgenhorn (3627 meters; "morning peak"), and still more, all shining with ice and snow. The Blümlisalphorn was first climbed in 1860 by Leslie Stephen (see p. 98). He wrote of "the exquisite Oeschinen lake—a lake, so far as I know, of a beauty unrivalled in any of the High Alpine districts." (Lunn 1973, 55)

It is possible to walk partway around the Oeschinensee, although the path is interrupted by the rock walls on the eastern side of the lake. You can also rent a rowboat to go out on the water. Energetic hikers can go much farther. Beyond the lake, the trail rises past splendid mountains and glaciers to the Hohtürli Pass, which connects Kandersteg and the Upper Kiental (see Inns 8, 9, and 10).

Getting there: Most people take the Sesselbahn (chairlift) from the edge of Kandersteg; it runs daily from 7:30 AM to 6:30 PM. From the Tourist Office on the main road, continue up the street away from the center of town, cross a bridge, and turn right; signs will direct you to the Sesselbahn. From the upper chairlift station (at Lager), a broad path leads down to the lake in about 20–25 minutes. If you are returning from the lake to catch the last chairlift down to Kandersteg, remember that you'll have a slight uphill walk to reach the station at 1682 meters; give yourself close to 30 minutes to get there. You can also reach the lake by walking from Kandersteg: 3.5 kilometers; 417 meters up; 1½ hours.

The small meadow leading to the lake was formerly the site of a couple of little alps, whose farmers brought cows up for summer grazing. As visitors—mainly Victorian British climbers and walkers—began finding their way up here, the farmers started selling their milk and cheese and were soon offering their haylofts as well. Long before the chairlift was installed, these farms became a useful as well as a beautiful stop on the way to the big mountains above, the Blümlisalp group.

There are now two inns right next to each other on the western shore of the lake and another inn somewhat farther away. Evenings at these guesthouses are very quiet. Their restaurants close fairly early because most people come up to the lake only for the day and descend to Kandersteg before evening. But the handful who stay overnight have the silence and beauty of the lake nearly to themselves; then it becomes almost a magical place.

6 • BERGHAUS AM OESCHINENSEE • 1593 M

Of the two inns on the lakeshore, this is by far the smaller, quieter, simpler, and more intimate one. Sleeping accommodations are in one little house and the kitchen and dining room are in the other. There are only three private rooms and Matratzenlager space for 27, and a bathroom with shower is available. The dining room in the older house (which dates from 1880) is small, neat, and snug, with traditional wood paneling and a low ceiling. In fine weather you can eat outdoors on its little balcony overlooking the lake, and there is a terrace below for drinks, snacks, and lunch. Most visitors leave by late afternoon to catch the last chairlift down, and

Hohtürli—the high point between Kanderstag and the Kiental

the kitchen staff, quite worn out, are eager to get some rest. Therefore dinner is served early—not later than 6 PM. For the few overnight guests, this offers the advantage of time after dinner to wander around the lake and admire the alpenglow as it turns the glaciers first rosy pink, then yellow. Dinner is à la carte: We enjoyed a plate of Rösti with sliced mushrooms and vegetables. Breakfast, which is not included in the overnight rate, is notably good: orange juice, a warm croissant and homemade bread, and very good jam.

This Berghaus, owned by Herr Hirschi, is open from the end of May to mid-October. Tel. and Fax 033/675 11 66; 3718 Kandersteg.

7 • BERGHOTEL (HOTEL RESTAURANT) OESCHINENSEE • 1600 M

This is the largest and most elaborate of the three inns on or near the lake. There is a large dining room with a few gourmet dishes on the menu along with the traditional and customary Schnitzels and Röstis. The restaurant serves until 6:30 or maybe 7 PM. A terrace in front is used for lunch and snacks. There is a sitting room and television (a most uncommon item in any Berghotel). The private rooms have an "old" look because of their pine-paneled walls and pine floors, but are quite modernized, with the unusual luxury of warm-water sinks. The Matratzenlager are also new and attractive, with cold-water sinks. Showers are available.

Both private rooms and Matratzenlager places cost more on weekends, and breakfast is included. Although both this Berghotel and the smaller, plainer Berghaus next door are both within the moderate-price category, the rates here are higher. There are 12 private rooms and 35 dormitory places.

The Berghotel Oeschinensee is run by the David Wandfluh family. It is open from mid-May to mid-October. Tel. 033/675 11 19; Fax: 675 16 66 or 675 16 76; 3718 Kandersteg.

The **Hotel zur Sennhütte** (1650 meters) is another inn near the lake. A quite new structure, built only a little more than 20 years ago, it makes no pretense of looking old. Its dining room is contemporary and tasteful, with windows on three sides. There are private bedrooms and no Matratzenlager. Although it overlooks the lake, it is set quite far back from it, about 70 meters above the shore. In the medium-price range, it is open from May to October. Tel. 033/675 16 42.

Walks:

WALK 1 • round-trip 11 kilometers; 1200 meters up; 7 hours.

The main walk from the lake is to or over the Hohtürli Pass (see pp. 77–78). This is a steep, long hike, quite challenging if you cross over the pass. The scenery along the ascent, however, is magnificent, and it's worth going partway to the pass and then turning back.

WALK 2 • round-trip 7 kilometers; 990 meters up; 5 hours.

From the southwest corner of the lake, a path leads steeply up to the Fründenhütte (2562 meters), which overlooks the lake from the southeast.

THE KIENTAL

In the heart of the Bernese Oberland, this fairly unknown valley is packed with surprises. It is one of the approaches to the Oberland's two grandest, highest passes, Hohtürli and the Sefinenfurke. The charm of the Kiental is that although it leads to these great passes, it contains nothing resembling a resort, but only a few unassuming hamlets and a cluster of Berghotels, including two of the most pleasant mountain inns in Switzerland. There are no cable cars up here, no means of getting anywhere but by your own legs, and nothing to do but climb and hike or read a book in a peaceful meadow.

At one of these charming Berghotels, we once shared a table at dinner with a Dutchman who was staying there for a week. He told us he needed a very quiet place for a restorative spell of perfect tranquility and physical exercise, and, he said happily, he had found it.

Getting there: From Kandersteg or the Lauterbrunnental, you can hike over the great passes and reach the Upper Kiental on foot, or you can travel by rail to Spiez, on lovely Lake Thun, and change there for the train to Reichenbach. (This is not the site of the celebrated Reichenbach Falls, where Sherlock Holmes wrestled Dr. Moriarty to his death—they are above the town of Meiringen.) At Reichenbach, take a PTT bus to Griesalp. The road meanders along through several sleepy little hamlets (one of which is also named Kiental) set in gentle, placid farmland, then suddenly bolts upward through a steep gorge, climbing through a corkscrew of hairpin turns blasted out of walls of sheer rock; the road is

The Oeschinensee

often only an inch or so wider than the PTT bus. (The latter part of the road, beyond the hamlet of Kiental, is privately owned; cars are allowed up as far as Griesalp, but must pay a toll.) Bus passengers with a Swiss Pass must pay a fare of 3.5 Sfr beyond Kiental.

At Griesalp (1407 meters), the last bus stop, there is a parking area, a Berghaus, a public telephone, and a tiny shop that sells refreshments. Although the road extends for a short distance beyond Griesalp, only Kiental inhabitants are allowed to drive farther. There is no electricity beyond the hamlet of Kiental, and the Berghotels use generators to make their own.

Three of the Berghotels are quite near each other, in the vicinity of Griesalp, and a fourth is some distance higher up the slope. The cluster of three are the inns at Griesalp and at Golderli and the Hotel Waldrand at Pochtenalp. The latter two are among the most engaging of all mountain inns. Berghotel Griesalp, however, is a rather cold and impersonal place; it has also been modernized to the extent that it has lost any vestige of charm. It is difficult to select between Golderli and the Waldrand, as each has its own distinctive character and both are stamped with the personality of their owners. Moreover, both Herr Jost at Golderli and Herr Graber at the Waldrand are well acquainted with the hiking trails in the area and are happy to discuss these and advise their guests about trail conditions of the moment. (You cannot look for any such personal attention at Griesalp.) Should there be no room at any of these inns, the **Hotel Bären** in the hamlet of Kiental, partway down the valley, is an agreeable, old-fashioned hotel.

8 • HOTEL-PENSION WALDRAND AT POCHTENALP • 1364 M

Hotel Waldrand (the name means "forest rest") is a lovely, old-fashioned country hotel, set back from the road in a meadow from which you can hear the Gamchibach mountain torrent. The house, formerly an alp, was built between 1910 and 1913, and the family still keeps a flock of sheep. A film version of Thomas Mann's *The Magic Mountain,* with Rod Steiger and Charles Aznavour, was filmed here in 1981.

There's a little terrace outside the hotel, where you can have a drink or watch the sunset. The pleasant dining room, with many windows and light pine walls, is bright and airy. White linen tablecloths provide a touch of crisp but simple elegance not seen in most other Berghotels, while a large, old-fashioned wooden sideboard and shelves with plants bespeak a country home rather than the stiffness of a formal restaurant. There's also a rather plain, informal room with small tables that serves as a Gaststube.

One evening menu is served to all guests, and substitutions are cheerfully made to accommodate vegetarians. On a recent visit the evening meal was cream of cauliflower soup, a large platter of meat and vegetables, and cut-up fresh fruit. At breakfast there were bowls of jam.

We once spent August 1, the Swiss national holiday, at the Waldrand. The celebration was sweet and simple: We were served the little rolls with tiny paper Swiss flags in them that are customary for this holiday, soup, roast chicken, homemade potato chips, vegetables, and ice cream cake.

Dining room of the Hotel-Pension Waldrand

After dinner, the bonfire traditional for this holiday was lit in a meadow beside the hotel.

Our bedroom had an old-fashioned high double bed that looked even higher under its thick down quilt (it also had sheets and a blanket), and the customary washstand with pitchers and basins. A cold-water sink was down the hall, as well as a bathroom with a warm-water shower, available for guests.

Since 1989, when a turbine was installed, the Waldrand has had electricity.

They cook mainly with wood but also use some electricity.

The Waldrand is owned by the Graber-Kohli family. Alois Graber's father bought the Waldrand in 1939, and Alois now runs it with his wife, Maya Kohli. They are warm and genial hosts. Alois's philosophy is to keep the hotel old-fashioned and quiet, and in the family. They love the place, he says—not because it's a good business (a look in his eye says there are easier ways to support a family), but for Alois, the Waldrand is home. "I was born here," he says emphatically, in fluent English; "I've been here for the last 50 years." He says he tries to think how he would like a holiday place to be. "I would not like to be pushed around, told that you have to go here or there, but to feel at home. It's not a 'business,'" he adds, trying to define more closely something that may be indefinable, a practice of innkeeping that survives today perhaps only in remote mountain valleys like this one and has as much to do with love and choice as with money.

The Waldrand has nine double and nine single rooms, and no Matratzenlager. It is open weekends in May, and then every day from mid-June to the end of September. No groups are allowed, because they can be noisy. Tel. 033/676 12 08 or 676 30 08; 3723 Kiental.

View from the Abendberg, Kiental

Getting there: This is the lowest of the group of Berghotels, although by less than 100 meters. If you come up by bus, ask the driver to stop at Pochtenalp, which is just below Griesalp. If you are walking down from the high passes or from Golderli, the Waldrand is about a 10-minute walk down by path; from Griesalp, a little less. In descent from the Sefinenfurke, Golderli will be on your left; about 1 minute later, just before the bridge, turn onto a path (signpost) that leads to Waldrand in about 10 minutes. In descent from Hohtürli, a fork in the route permits descent to either Golderli (via Steinenberg) or Griesalp; take the trail to the right toward Golderli, then take the signed path to the left.

9 • BERGGASTHAUS AND PENSION GOLDERLI • 1440 M

The area around the inn, consisting of a few scattered summer farms and houses, is named Golderli on maps and is sometimes also called Gorneren. Many years ago (no one remembers precisely when), the Friends of Nature, a Swiss organization devoted to the outdoors (more about this below), had opened a sort of hostel here and asked the baker in the hamlet of Kiental to open a small shop for their guests. This shop was then expanded into a little restaurant, and later a few beds were added. This became the Pension Golderli, to which people came for three- or four-week holidays in the 1930s and '40s. For many years the inn was run by two old ladies. The present owners, Georges and Beatrice Jost, bought it in 1989. Beatrice was formerly the hutkeeper at the Gspaltenhorn alpine club hut, where Georges met her on a climbing trip. Deciding they wanted to work together, Georges left his job as a word processor with IBM for a new life as an innkeeper. Together they managed a youth hostel in Pontresina, saved their francs, and looked for a Berghaus to purchase. Golderli is the culmination of their dreams, and they have poured as much loving care into the old hotel as if they had been born to it. Georges Jost, moreover, is dedicated to the very concept of the Berghaus and to its survival. He has posted notices at Golderli about other mountain inns to bring them to the attention of hikers, and he wishes to create a sort of mutual supporting network of such inns.

Golderli is a thoroughly charming, inviting sort of place, one of the finest of Swiss mountain inns today. With excellent taste, intelligence, and sensitivity, the Josts have successfully managed a delicate undertaking: They have slightly modernized the inn, making it a little more comfortable, while retaining its appearance and essential character as a Berghaus.

For example, Georges Jost replaced upstairs floors that squeaked so loudly underfoot that guests below could hear every step. The floors, now silent to the tread, are pine, in the Berghaus style. There's a cold-water sink on the second floor, but Georges installed a warm-water sink on the third, toilets on each floor, and a shower (solar-powered) in the basement; there's a charge of 3 Sfr for the shower. Everything is immaculate: The light-colored pine walls, ceilings, and floors shine as if they had been scrubbed down yesterday. The private rooms are spare and simple—beds with down quilts, washstand with pitchers and basins, a small table—however, instead of looking coldly austere, the simplicity of these light, fresh rooms is soothing. Such a room seems to invite you to unclutter your thoughts, to lay aside all petty and mundane distractions, all the things that keep you from seeing clearly—after all, isn't this part of the reason you came to the mountains?

A herd of cows often graze behind the hotel. One evening I fell asleep to the gentle music of their bells.

The rooms downstairs are in a different spirit. The spacious, pretty dining room is lined on one side with windows facing the high mountains that close off the valley. It's attractively decorated with a grandfather clock and chests painted in folk-art style. On every table is a tiny vase of fresh flowers. There's a cozy little Gaststube for coffee or drinks before or after dinner and an even cozier little parlor with an old stove, an antique clock, and shelves full of books and games. Outdoors, there's a terrace facing the view.

Beatrice cooks some of the best meals served at any Berghotel. There is a menu of the evening, although guests may also order à la carte. One evening we had an unusual, delicious bread soup (her own recipe—all the soups are homemade), Älpler Macaroni with fresh applesauce, and blueberry pudding. The salads are excellent and fresh. And breakfast is unusually good, starting with a bowl of Birchermuesli with yogurt and fresh berries and fruit, and then cheese, cold cuts, and homemade jam with your bread. One unusual dish on the menu is Gorner Nudle, a dish of green noodles with tomatoes, mushrooms, and basil cream sauce.

There are seven double rooms, two rooms with four beds each, and 20 Matratzenlager places. Berggasthaus Golderli is open from May or June to October. Tel. 033/676 21 92; 3723 Kiental.

Getting there: From Griesalp, turn left and follow the road (only farmers are allowed to drive beyond Griesalp) toward Steinenberg and the Sefinenfurke; reach Golderli in 10 minutes. In descent from the Sefinenfurke, Golderli will be on your left, just before you reach Griesalp; in descent from Hohtürli, bear right at a signposted fork where you can choose whether to descend via Steinenberg to Golderli or else to Griesalp.

NATURFREUNDEHAUS GORNEREN • 1470 M

One more establishment at Golderli should be mentioned here. Across the road from Hotel Golderli is the oldest house belonging to this organization (the Swiss Friends of Nature), which has a number of similar hostels around Switzerland. The one at Golderli has a tiny shop, where hikers on the Oberland Pass route can stock up on supplies: Bread is available (although you may need to reserve a loaf the day before) and a small selection of fruit, chocolate, cookies, and some canned goods. Nonmembers may stay in the house. Wool blankets are provided, but not sheets. (You can rent linen for 4 Sfr per piece.) There are cold-water sinks. The house does not generate electricity, so overnight guests need a flashlight or headlamp; gas and solar panels light the rooms downstairs. Many guests cook their own meals in the large kitchen, but this house also offers restaurant meals; prices are low to moderate.

The house is open from June 1 to the end of October. There are 16 rooms that can take up to eight people, and a total of 60 places. Tel. 033/676 11 40; NHF Gorneren, 3723 Kiental. For information on this organization, write to Natur Freunde Schweiz, Zentralsekretariat, Pavillonweg 3, Postfach 3001, Bern.

10 • BERGHAUS (BERGGASTHOF) ENZIAN, BUNDALP • 1860 M

This inn, at Ober Bundalp, is considerably higher than the Golderli-Griesalp-Pochtenalp cluster. It is partway up the slope on the route to the Hohtürli Pass. As such, it is convenient for Hohtürli hikers but less so for those on the Sefinenfurke route.

Berghaus Enzian is a working alp, with a herd of 20 cows. They make their own Bergkäse (alp cheese) and butter and use milk from the herd. Besides the barn there is a large old house, 300 years old and very plain, and a somewhat newer, smaller house, with a small porch and a row of cowbells for decoration. Enzian offers simple private rooms and very basic Matratzenlager accommodations in the large house, with a cold-water sink and toilet down the hall. Guests need a flashlight or headlamp. The dining room, in a somewhat newer, smaller house, is modestly cheerful. Electricity is provided by a generator for the kitchen (where they cook with wood) and dining room.

Owned by the Lengacher-Egli family, Berghaus Enzian is open from May to October. There are four double rooms, two rooms for three people, one single room, and two rooms for four people. Tel. 033/676 11 92; 3723 Kiental.

Getting there: To reach Berghaus Enzian from Griesalp, follow the trail sign to Bundalp and Hohtürli. You can walk up on the farm road that switchbacks up the slope or take the path that ascends more directly, cutting across the loops of the road. Signposts will point to Ober Bundalp. Although the time posted on the trail sign reads 1.15, the ascent can take about 1½ hours or a little longer. In descent from Hohtürli, on the network of trails halfway down the slope, the inn will be on your left.

Walks: Besides the approaches to the two passes (the Sefinenfurke and Hohtürli), several other walks can be taken here.

WALK 1 • Descent from Griesalp to Kiental hamlet: 6 kilometers; 460 meters down; 2 hours, 20 minutes.

Instead of walking down the road, you can take this trail along the river, the Gornernbach, which flows down from the Upper Kiental to join the Kiene River below the hamlet of Kiental. Follow the trail signs marked WILDWASSERWEG TO POCHTENSCHLUCHT This will take you past two impressive waterfalls that plunge through the gorge: the Hexenfall (or "witches' fall")—a thunderous explosion of water that bursts forth with tremendous force and volume—and the Dündenfall. Descend to Tschingel and its placid lake, and continue almost on the level on a path beside the stream, partly in the woods. From the hamlet of Kiental you can take the bus back up to Griesalp or down to Reichenbach and the rail station.

WALK 2 • The Abendberg: from Golderli or Pochtenalp: 2.75 kilometers; 524 meters; 2 hours. For a loop hike, another 3.5 kilometers; 1016 meters; 3 hours to descend via Spiggegrund to the Kiental bus stop.

This promontory above the east slope of the Kiental is a viewing point, a sort of peaklet. Its name means "evening peak." Ascend the Abendberg and return the way you came, or make this a loop trip by descending to the next valley, reaching the hamlet of Kiental, and returning to the Upper Kiental by bus.

From Golderli, walk up past the Naturfreunde house (from Pochtenalp, take the path up to Golderli to reach the Naturfreunde house) and in 10 minutes bear left, heading northwest. You'll pass through a metal cattle gate and turn left at a red/white blaze onto a gravel road. Above will be a band of cliffs, overlooking sloping meadows. After about 25 minutes, turn left onto a blazed, narrow dirt path that branches to the left from the gravel road. This steep dirt path rejoins the gravel road, passing several isolated alps. A signpost at 1670 meters indicates that you should continue straight ahead for the Abendberg. After this you'll soon reach an alp, where the gravel road ends. Follow a steep trail here to the left; occasionally the track is broken but the way is always clear. Climb through some woods, then up a steep grassy slope with some blazed rocks, and reach the ridge; this is Kanzel (1890 meters). Turn left, follow the track down a little, passing an alp, then up again to a tiny, conical peak—the Abendberg, with views into the Kiental and the valley to the north, the Spiggegrund.

Either retrace your steps or descend into the Spiggegrund. To do the latter, walk back to Kanzel and follow the path down northward to Schwand. Upon reaching the valley floor, turn left (northwest), with the stream on your right. Although the road before you is signposted for the hamlet of Kiental, cross a wooden bridge, turn left, and resume your descent on the right bank of the stream, which is also signposted for Kiental; this is the more direct way to the hamlet. Follow the narrow dirt path through the woods or the gravel jeep road, and about 50 minutes beyond the bridge reach the paved road. Turn right for Kiental and the bus stop. At the next fork, go either left or right: Both ways will take you onto the main road through the center of the hamlet of Kiental.

WALK 3 • The Dündengrat: round-trip 11 kilometers; 807 meters up; probably 6 hours.

This hike is said to be a fine one. However, at the time we planned to take it, Herr Graber at Hotel Waldrand advised us not to go because of a great deal of snow that had lingered that year on the ridge late into the season. A loop trip, it climbs south of Griesalp to Kistihubel, then over the Dündengrat to Ober Dünden, and returns to Griesalp through Mittelberg.

WALK 4 • Gspaltenhornhütte (2458 meters): round-trip 14 kilometers; 1100 meters up; 7 hours.

This alpine club hut is perched in a dramatic location overlooking the Gamchigletscher, just below the rugged cirque between the Gspaltenhorn (3437 meters) and the Morgenhorn (3612 meters). You can make a day hike of this excursion. Note that although a trail connecting this hut and the Sefinenfurke is marked on some maps, it is a very tricky and difficult route and cannot be recommended to any but highly experienced hikers.

From Golderli, start up the road toward the Sefinenfurke, southwest. At the farm at Bürgli, the road becomes a trail and bifurcates; continue to the right (still southwest). The trail hugs the base of a very steep slope, almost a cliff, and there's a gorge below to your right; its sheer walls drop to a turbulent stream that charges through the chasm. Then you'll come out into open meadows beside which the Gamchibach flows demurely as a braided stream. The little alp at Gamchi sells drinks. There you'll begin a steeper ascent. The trail is cut below a cliff, and you'll pass under a few waterfalls. A few spots have a cable you can hold onto to steady yourself on a rocky ledge, but although you must pay attention, the trail is not dangerous or tricky. It switchbacks upward to cross a scree slope and then reaches the rocky promontory on which the hut is sited. The trail sign at Golderli says 3.15 hours for this hike, but that is surely too little.

WALK 5 • Sefinenfurke from Golderli over the pass east to Mürren: 15 kilometers; 1270 meters up/1000 meters down; 7½ hours.

This is a spectacular but long hike, and the final section of ascent over the pass is very steep. It should not be attempted in snow or bad weather. Although scenic on both sides of the pass, the grandest views are on the descent to Mürren. This hike can be broken up by stopping overnight at the Rotstockhütte or Spielbodenalp, and very simple accommodations are available at Ober Dürrenberg.

A signpost facing Hotel Golderli points southwest up the road toward this pass. As you reach the farm at Bürgli, the road becomes a trail; bear left at the fork there. There are scenic views to your right of the snowy Blümlisalp group. As the valley narrows and the trail begins a steeper ascent, you'll pass the little alp of Ober Dürrenberg, where they sell goat cheese and drinks and offer Nachtlager—very simple overnight accommodations. The trail, up an eroded scree slope, becomes extremely steep as you approach the pass. Log steps have been set into the slope and there's a cable to hold onto, but there is no exposure. This final passage on scree is about 200 meters.

From the pass (2612 meters), a network of little paths descends the scree, very steeply at first and then more gradually. As the grade eases and you can look about you, you'll see that the scenery on this side is magnificent and remains so all the way to Mürren. Across the Lauterbrunnental, to your right, is a glorious line of superb mountains that culminates in the Jungfrau, Mönch, and Eiger. The trail, which is blazed, will lead you past Boganggen (2039 meters; a variant spelling is Poganggen), where there is a Berghaus, the Rotstockhütte (see Inn 17), to Oberlager. Beyond Oberlager (2050 meters) you have two options. If your destination is one of the two Berghotels at Blumental (Suppenalp and Sonnenberg, Inns 11 and 12), bear left at Oberlager and ascend to the viewpoint at Wasenegg (2155 meters). Then descend to pass the farm at Schiltalp (1951 meters) and soon reach Blumental. (Blumental is about 30 minutes above Mürren.) If you are headed directly for Mürren, from Oberlager descend on switchbacks to Brünli (2127 meters; also spelled Bryndli). You'll pass another Berghaus at Spielbodenalp (see Inn 16), then cross the Schiltbach. The trail leads through Gimmeln and then joins a paved road into Mürren.

WALK 6 • Hohtürli from Golderli over the pass to Kandersteg: 13 kilometers; 1370 meters up/1620 meters down; 9 hours.

Like the hike over the Sefinenfurke, this is challenging and should not be attempted in snow or bad weather. If done in one day, it's a long and tiring route, requiring an even steeper final ascent than the Sefinenfurke. But the scenery, especially on the Kandersteg side, is breathtaking. This hike can be broken up into segments by stopping overnight at any of several points: Berghaus Enzian at Bundalp, the alpine club's Blümlisalp hut at the pass, the little farm at Ober Bergli, or one of the Berghotels at the Oeschinensee. The final section of the trail, when you ascend on the Upper Kiental side of the pass, is more difficult than the final section of ascent on the Kandersteg side. If you are staying in the Kiental and wish to see the pass, but are in any doubt about this route, you can take the train from Reichenbach to Kandersteg and ascend from that side.

To start from Golderli (if you start from Pochtenalp, walk up to Golderli), follow the trail for Bundalp and Hohtürli (the route is signposted or blazed all the way). In 5 minutes, at Steinenberg, turn right and ascend to Bundsteg; cross the Gamchibach and then climb up to the Berghotel at Bundalp, Berghaus Enzian (see Inn 10). If you start from Griesalp, the signpost in front of the hotel will direct you to Bundalp, and this path will merge with the other trail from Steinenberg and Golderli. Beyond the meadows of Bundalp is a dark, shaley slope that becomes ever steeper as it rises toward the pass; a network of eroded tracks all switchback up to the same point. The final approach, extremely steep, has log steps set into the slope and cables to hold onto.

The view from the Hohtürli Pass (2778 meters) is grand and extensive: You seem to be perched above a sea of mountains. The SAC Blümlisalphütte is about 150 meters to your left, above the little notch of the pass. If you walk out a little beyond the hut, you'll have an impressive, close-up view of the Blümlisalp group of mountains and of the deeply crevassed glacier below you. This cluster of mountains includes the Blümlisalphorn (3663 meters), the Weisse Frau (3650 meters) and Wilde Frau (3260 meters; the "white wife" and the "wild wife"), the Morgenhorn (3627 meters; "morning peak"), and still more—all glistening with ice and snow. The Blümlisalphorn was first climbed in 1860 by Leslie Stephen, a Victorian don and the father of Virginia Woolf.

The descent begins steeply down a wall of scree, then along some rocky ledges to the green and gentler slopes below. You'll descend through the meadows of a narrow valley with a breathtaking sight to your left: a magnificent wall of mountains glittering with the ice and snow of hanging glaciers. Beyond a bridge you'll reach the alp at Ober Bergli, which sells simple refreshments and offers Matratzenlager. As the trail branches, bear right (north) for the scenic route that continues high above the turquoise Oeschinensee, giving splendid views down onto the lake, set magnificently below sheer cliffs. You can also bear left to descend to the alp at Unter Bergli and then along the lakeshore to reach the cluster of inns at the western end of the lake (see Inns 6 and 7).

A signpost will point you to Lager and the Sesselbahn (chairlift) by which you can descend to Kandersteg. The chairlift runs until 6:30 PM during the summer. You can also walk down to Kandersteg by a signposted trail that you'll find to your left as you reach the chairlift station.

THE LAUTERBRUNNENTAL

The Lauterbrunnental is one of the grandest valleys in the Alps, not only in the Swiss Alps but anywhere in the European Alps. It is cut deep and clean between massive, continuous walls of sheer rock, and myriad waterfalls—glistening silver bands—drop plumb to the valley floor below.

One of these cascades, which are among the highest in Europe, is the Staubbach Falls, the delicate plume of which Lord Byron likened to "the tail of a white horse streaming in the wind, such as it might be conceived would be that of the pale horse on which Death is mounted in the Apocalypse." (Lunn 1973, p. 96) More impressive yet is the thunderous force of the Trümmelbach Falls, which drains the Eiger, Mönch, and Jungfrau:

Compressed into a narrow channel within the rock, from which they can be viewed from special platforms, the glacial waters burst forth with propulsive force.

Nearly facing each other, perched atop high vertical rock walls, are Mürren and Wengen, two of Switzerland's best-known ski resorts. Towering above the eastern side of the valley are some of Europe's most famous peaks—the Eiger, Mönch, and Jungfrau—and above the valley's west wall is the Schilthorn.

Most travelers never venture farther up the valley because the Upper Lauterbrunnental is accessible only to hikers. Yet its scenery is superb, and it is home to three attractive and very charming mountain inns. Indeed, the two uppermost would surely be on any connoisseur's list of Switzerland's most appealing Berghotels.

Lauterbrunnen, a village on the valley floor that can be reached by rail and road, is a point of departure for both Mürren and Wengen.

WENGEN 1275 M

Wengen is a resort set on a terrace above the eastern wall of the Lauterbrunnental. It offers a superlative, close-up view of the Jungfrau—no resort has a closer view—but from this location the rest of the great trio is cut off. No cars are allowed in Wengen (or in Mürren).

Getting there: Wengen is reached by cog railway from Lauterbrunnen or from Kleine Scheidegg (from which there are connections to Grindelwald). Another interesting way to reach the resort is via the Männlichen cable car, which originates below Grindelwald and rises to its upper station at 2229 meters—you can hike up the little Männlichen peaklet (2343 meters) for the view, then ride down on the other side from the Männlichen station to Wengen.

Walks: The finest walk from Wengen is the one to Kleine Scheidegg, taking about 3 hours. This route passes Wengernalp; unlike Wengen, where a panoramic view is somewhat cut off, from Wengernalp you can see the Eiger and Mönch. After Lord Byron passed through in 1816 (he wrote part of his poem "Manfred" here), trailing the aura of his romantic glamour, a number of his countrymen followed after him. You can also take the cog railway to Kleine Scheidegg (see p. 99); the train makes an intermediate stop at Wengernalp. There is one Berghaus at Wengernalp that functions as an attractive restaurant in summer but as a hotel only in winter.

Alp in the Blumental

From Kleine Scheidegg, you can climb the little peak of the Lauberhorn (2472 meters) in about 1½ hours for a good view of the region (see p. 101). To return by foot to Wengen from Kleine Scheidegg, you can take a very scenic but long route by walking south to Biglenalp and then northwest through Mettlenalp. The trail winds through meadows that contour around the great cliffs below the Jungfrau and part of the Mönch. You hike alongside this splendid, rugged facade of mountain walls topped with glaciers, waterfalls plunge over the cliffs to the green meadows below, and you may see and hear—from a safe distance—icefalls crashing down. The sight and sound of these avalanches are impressive; in 1838, *Murray's Handbook* advised its readers that "in fine weather there is not a more interesting or exciting journey among the Alps than that over the Wengern Alp, or Lesser Scheideck [Kleine Scheidegg]. . . it is from the summit of the Wengern Alp that the avalanches are seen and heard in greatest perfection and no one should abandon the expedition without an effort." (In Murray's day, before the cog railway, one could ride up to Wengernalp by mule or on horseback in 7 hours, and some ladies were carried up by *chaise à porteurs*.) As you approach Wengen, the trail back via Café Oberland is easier than the one via

Stalden and Staubbach, the latter involving a steep forest path with many roots underfoot, an invitation to trip at the end of a long, tiring day.

MÜRREN 1638 M

Mürren, like a sort of eagle's nest, is built on a broad ledge above the western wall of the Lauterbrunnental, standing nearly 800 meters in an almost direct vertical line above the valley floor. Upon this perch, it directly faces the Mönch and Jungfrau, with a view of the Eiger as well. Although Wengen offers a closer view of the Jungfrau, Mürren presents a dazzling and more extensive panorama—indeed, the best view of the famous Oberland trio in its entirety that can be seen from any resort village. More charming and less closely built than Wengen, Mürren has more of a village air. Mürren's attractiveness is enhanced by the absence of automobiles: It's one of several Swiss resorts (including Wengen) in which cars are not allowed.

Now one of Switzerland's best-known resorts, famous for skiing, Mürren was discovered by the British as they fanned out across the Swiss Alps in search of mountains to climb or just to gaze at. A certain Frederic Harrison claimed to have discovered Mürren and to have "'founded' it as a station.'" He wrote that in 1853–54 at Mürren "there was neither inn, nor hut, nor so much as a glass of milk to be got in the two or three poor chalets there . . ." (Lunn 1973, p. 82) Harrison evidently admired the view so much that he was not put off by the lack of accommodations and sang Mürren's praises to everyone he met: "The next year if I remember, I found a small Gasthaus installed in the noble plateau . . ." Some of his countrymen responded to the noble landscape with very Victorian solemnity. Visiting Mürren in 1880 with his father (the Archbishop of Canterbury), E.F. Benson reported: "My heart . . . went out to the snow mountains, and has never yet come back. We passed through Mürren on the way down, and there saw English people playing lawn-tennis on one of the hotel courts, and never shall I forget my father's upraised eyebrows and mouth of scorn as he said, 'Fancy, playing lawn-tennis in sight of the Jungfrau.'" (Lunn 1973, p. 84)

Mürren is at one end of the grand route over the Sefinenfurke (see p. 76), and several other walks can be taken from it as well.

Getting there: Take the funicular from Lauterbrunnen up to Grütschalp and then the little cog railway that runs along the top of the cliffs to Mürren. (Lauterbrunnen is reached by a train that originates in Interlaken.) You can also reach Mürren by using the first stage of the cable car to the Schilthorn, which starts at Langwald (the bus from Lauterbrunnen to Stechelberg stops at Langwald).

BLUMENTAL 1836 M

The slope above Mürren is known as the Blumental, or valley of flowers—a fitting name for its meadows, which are filled with a stunning profusion of wildflowers in all their brilliant colors. One section of the slope is known as Mürrenberg, and because that name appears on some maps, it may seem that the two names are interchangeable, but that is not strictly accurate. Blumental, moreover, is the name you'll see on local signposts. Two guest-houses in Blumental, sited near each other (but which are quite unlike each other), offer simple and less expensive accommodations than those that are available in the village.

Staying in Blumental one summer evening, we strolled after dinner through silent meadows filled with purple, pink, and yellow wildflowers, and watched two little golden red foxes gamboling in the grass, tumbling and pouncing. Turning to face the mountains, we saw the alpenglow flush the snows of the Eiger, Mönch, and Jungfrau with pink. After attempting to describe the scene in my journal that night, I could only write: "Words fail."

Getting there: From the train station in Mürren, walk east to the town's big sports center or down the main shopping street, then follow any of several signposts up the slope to Pension Sonnenberg and Pension Suppenalp. Reach Sonnenberg first, where a sign points you left for Suppenalp, another 5 or 10 minutes farther. From Mürren: 1.2 kilometers; 200 meters up; 25 minutes.

11 • PENSION SUPPENALP • 1850 M

A simple wooden chalet, dating from about 1910, is set at the edge of the meadows, just before the slope steepens to close off the Blumental meadows. It is off the main trail, quite by itself except for a very modest little farm next door with a facade hung with cowbells—home to nine cows and one farmer. Together, these two buildings constitute Suppenalp. They are set at the edge of a small notch, a V-shaped depression, framing an excellent view of the Eiger, Mönch, and Jungfrau. A small terrace in front of the inn faces the mountains.

The old Gasthaus has been very modestly renovated; it is plain and unassuming, simple rather than lovely. The long, narrow dining room, wood-paneled and rather dark, with a traditional low ceiling, is its social center, although there is another room upstairs, also very plain, where one can sit and read. The food, however, is not plain, but strikingly good. Our mushroom soup was clearly Hausgemachte (homemade), not canned, with thick slices of fresh mushroom, after which we were served a large mixed salad, turkey with mustard sauce, Rösti, and a fine apple tart. Likewise, breakfast was unusually good, with a choice of Muesli or cornflakes, sliced cheese, yogurt, and a dish of blackberry jam. Ms. Judith Wicki, who runs the inn, is congenial and also well traveled, having worked for many years in Tunisia and India. (Both she and the young farmer next door rent from the owners, a local family that owns the Suppenalp.) The cook, however, comes up every day from Wengen.

Our simple room was paneled in the traditional pine, with broad floor boards. It had a striking view of the Jungfrau. A shower is available (towels are provided) with toilet and cold-water sink in the hall. The dormitory is not crowded and has a warm-water sink.

There are nine private rooms, one with five and one with three beds, and 20 Matratzenlager places. The inn is electrified, but cooking is done with wood. Normally, and especially when there are several guests, there is one evening menu, but substitutions can be arranged if you phone or ask ahead. Along with the usual fare on the à la carte menu are a few unusual dishes: trout with horseradish sauce, Knödel (dumpling) soup, and among the desserts, panna cotta with strawberries.

The inn is open from June 15 or July 1 (depending on the season's weather) until about October 15, and from December 20 to about April 20 or one week after Easter, when many skiers stop here. Tel. 033/855 17 26; 3825 Mürren.

Getting there: See directions to Blumental.

12 • RESTAURANT-PENSION SONNENBERG • 1836 M

The old Berghaus here burned down and was rebuilt in 1976. The dining room is cheerful and bright, in the standard, contemporary, and informal style found in dozens of other new Swiss "sport" (generally for skiers) restaurants. Some may find this attractive, others conventional, impersonal, unindividuated. Sonnenberg offers more amenities than Suppenalp, but less individual character: Except for the absence of private bathrooms, it seems more of a modern hotel than a Berghaus, although it is up at an alp.

From the large terrace in front of Sonnenberg there is an excellent view of the Jungfrau, although not of the Eiger. The food is tasty, and along with the standard dishes the menu offers tortellini with mushrooms and chicken with mushrooms. A young couple, Hansruedi Meier and Monika Schmid, rent and manage the place.

There are nine double rooms, one room for three people, and one single, all with sinks, and two Matratzenlager rooms for 20 people each. The rooms are comfortable and pretty, with warm-water sinks and towels and shower available. It is open from mid-June to mid-October and from mid-December to mid-April. Tel. 033/855 11 27; 3825 Mürren.

Getting there: See directions to Blumental.

Walks:

WALK 1 • Sefinenfurke: round-trip 16 kilometers; 800 meters up; 7 hours.

Starting from Blumental rather than Mürren saves a little altitude, although not much—about 100 meters of ascent. For this route, walk past the farm at Schiltalp and then up to the viewpoint at Wasenegg, from which the trail descends to join the one heading up from Mürren to Boganggen and the Sefinenfurke.

WALK 2 • Schilthorn (2970 meters): round-trip 9 kilometers; 1200 meters up; 7 hours.

You can hike up to the top of this small mountain or hike partway and then ride the cable car to the top. From the summit there's an extensive view of the Bernese Alps and especially of the Jungfrau. The Schilthorn formed part of the setting for the James Bond film *On Her Majesty's Secret Service*. It is famous not only for its view but also for the circular, revolving restaurant on its summit; it turns slowly, and by spending 55 minutes at your table you can see the whole panorama revolve around you. Among several famous ski races held near Mürren is the Inferno, from the top of the Schilthorn down to Lauterbrunnen—a plunge of 2170 meters.

From Blumental, head first for the farm at Schiltalp, to the southwest, which you can reach in about 40 minutes. From there, keep to the right (west) for the trail to the Schilthorn. As you reach the stony bed of the Schiltbach, you may have to go upstream a little to pick up the trail on the other side, which is marked by blazed rocks. Climb rather steeply to a bleak little lake, aptly named the Grausee ("gray lake"), which lies below a stony wall in a rather harsh landscape. To continue by cable car to the summit, turn to your right and in 30 minutes climb to a junction and

the Birg lift station; to continue instead on foot to the summit of the
Schilthorn will take another 1 hour, 10 minutes.

First cow encountered on the descent from the Sefinfurke towards Mürren

WALK 3 • The Sulsee from Grütschalp: round-trip 7 kilometers; 430
meters up; 5 hours.

For this hike, it's easier, as well as shorter, to take the cog railway to
Grütschalp and start from there (to walk from Mürren to Grütschalp adds
4 kilometers). Several trails extend northward from Blumental (and from
Mürren), high above the Lauterbrunnental; hiking in this direction, as
far as you choose to go, gives you spectacular views of the Eiger, Mönch,
and Jungfrau. As you traverse the long slope the ground undulates, rising
and falling slightly, but there is not much ascent. At Suls there is a little
mountain tarn, the Sulsee, a quiet, unfrequented spot. You can hike to the
little Suls lake—it's a long walk from Blumental—but it may be difficult
to find the right way (our innkeeper told us to always take the higher of
two paths at any junction, meaning take the one to the left, but we missed
the way).

From the Grütschalp station (1489 meters), take a path through the woods and emerge into a meadow with a few alps at Floschwald/Sausmatten. Turn right at a signposted junction. There are blazed rocks along the trail, which leads to the Sausbach; you'll pass a little alp on your right. Cross a bridge, turn right, cross a rivulet, then double back so the little alp is on your left (but do *not* cross the river again and head north). The going becomes rough, over rocks that can be wet or muddy. At Kühbodmen take the path to the left toward the alp at Suls, and in a few minutes reach the Sulsee (1920 meters). There's a good view of the Wetterhorn, Eiger, Mönch, and Jungfrau. The small SAC Lobhornhütte is a little higher to the right (you must obtain the keys to the hut in advance in Lauterbrunnen or Mürren if you wish to stay overnight). To return, retrace your steps to Kühbodmen. There you can walk down—cross a road but continue down on the path—to Sulwald (1530 meters), where a small Selbstbedienung (self-operated) lift can be used to descend to Isenfluh (1081 meters). To ride down, open the door of the lift, turn the crank, and lift the telephone receiver to request descent. From Isenfluh you can take a little bus that goes down to Lauterbrunnen, or you can walk to Lauterbrunnen on the road in an hour or a little less. You can then return to Mürren by train. The total walk without using the Sulwald-Isenfluh lift will take about 7 hours from Blumental, 5 hours from Grütschalp.

UPPER LAUTERBRUNNENTAL

In contrast to the lower valley—home of such well-known attractions as the Schilthorn and Trümmelbach Falls and the site of two highly favored resorts, Mürren and Wengen—the upper part of the valley, undeveloped and unspoiled, receives few visitors. It has been preserved not only because it culminates in a nature reserve, but also because it is accessible only to hikers. The road up the Lauterbrunnental ends at the pretty and very quiet little village of Stechelberg (920 meters), beyond which you must walk. Although the most famous Oberland peaks cannot be seen from the upper valley, the scenery is magnificent. Strung out along the trail that climbs beside the left bank of the Weisse Lütschine are three of Switzerland's most engaging mountain inns.

The first British travelers to make their way to the upper valley found the accommodations less attractive. John Murray, in 1838, mentions a group of "miserable chalets" near "Trachsel-Laune" and, farther on, a single chalet, Steinberg—"a desolate and wild spot, pent in by abrupt rocks and glaciers, and might truly be termed The World's End." (Murray 1970, pp. 74–75) Things had improved by 1884, when Robert Allbut could write that at "Obere-Steinberg, accommodation for the night, in primitive style, may be obtained, six beds being provided in a building adjoining the chalet." (Allbut 1884, p. 143) One well-marked trail leads from Stechelberg to all three inns. Although there is also a trail along the right bank of the stream, keep to the one on the left bank.

Berghaus Trachsellauenen, pleasant and attractive as it is, is down in the woods, but considerably higher up the valley are two quite wonderful old inns that are above tree line and offer a view. The fame of these inns has spread by word of mouth. You will certainly need to telephone ahead if you want a private room on a weekend, perhaps even for weekend Matratzenlager places. Hiking up, you come first to Hotel Tschingelhorn and then, 20 minutes farther up the trail, to Hotel Obersteinberg. (I would not attempt to choose between them.) In an informal sampling of opinion, I have heard some hikers say that Obersteinberg has the finer view because of its slightly higher and more open position—the view is more extensive—while others prefer the view from the Tschingelhorn as well as its setting at the edge of the forest. From Hotel Tschingelhorn you can see the Jungfrau and most of the mountains as far as the peak of the Tschingelhorn, but from Hotel Obersteinberg you can see the glacier above the valley and the Breithorn, as well as the other mountains. Hotel Tschingelhorn is smaller and cozier. But both are old, simple, and charming, and give about as good an idea of the essence of a traditional Berghaus as you can find.

The grandest part of the upper Lauterbrunnental is above these two hotels; you can walk up from Stechelberg, drop off your extra things at whichever hotel you'll be staying in, then hike up to enjoy the stunning country above. Vicki von Allmen, a young American woman who came to work in the Obersteinberg dairy and ended up marrying into the family (she still works in the dairy), has tried to unearth some of the history of the upper valley. It is fragmentary and the date of origin of both inns is uncertain, but there is some evidence that in 1776 there was a village or hamlet, Ammerten, that was destroyed by an avalanche on or near the site of the present Tschingelhorn. Travelers began to come to the upper valley for its splendid scenery by the end of the 18th century and then more frequently by the 19th century. Vicki von Allmen told us she has read that Goethe mentioned in his diary that he stayed at Obersteinberg in 1779.

13 • BERGHAUS TRACHSELLAUENEN • 1200 M

This pretty inn is quite close to Stechelberg and is thus the first one you encounter as you ascend the upper valley; you'll see its half-timbered back about 1 hour beyond Stechelberg. It's in a lovely spot, built close enough to the stream so that you can hear the rushing water as it tumbles down its rocky bed. The house was built in 1886; the present owners, Ferdinand Gertsch and his family, bought it in 1966. You step in through a little terrace on the uphill side of the house into a sort of cozy Gaststube, with tile floor and wood walls. The dining room, however, is upstairs; instead of the usual pine it combines wood with white plastered surfaces, a pretty yet simple room, old-fashioned, airy, and light. There's a little fireplace.

The bedrooms have the traditional washstands with pitchers and basins. Toilets and a warm-water sink are in the hall and showers are available (no charge). There are nine double rooms and two single ones in the house, with two more rooms in a very old house beside the main one; the old house has a toilet but no sink.

Trachsellauenen has no Matratzenlager. It's open from June to the end of September. Tel. 033/855 12 35; 3824 Stechelberg.

Getting there: Take a PTT bus to Stechelberg, where the road ends and the signposted trail to the upper valley begins, then walk 2.3 kilometers; 280 meters up; 1 hour.

14 • HOTEL TSCHINGELHORN • 1685 M

You know at once that you are in an old house. And indeed, this house took its present form in 1898 as an enlargement of an older, smaller house that may have dated from 1890 or earlier. A little glassed-in porch faces the trail; behind it is a small, charming dining room with an old black iron stove, a sofa, and a case full of books and children's games and puzzles—it also serves as the parlor. The rather low ceiling makes the room look snug. Everything is pine: walls, ceiling, and the floor of broad planks. This was once an alp and the family still keeps 11 heifers, mainly to crop the grass, we were told. Until about 1990 they used a mule to bring provisions up, but now a small cable way brings up supplies. The hotel is run by Katherine and Erika von Allmen; it was their grandfather who enlarged the house in 1898. These two sisters now do all the work, with only one helper. (I can remember the first time we stayed here, in the 1980s, when their mother, a kindly old lady who looked like the grandmother I only dimly remember from my childhood, urged us in a most grandmotherly way to have yet another helping of soup.) They grow their own lettuce for the salads—you'll see the the vegetable bed outside the house—cook on a woodstove, and bake in an oven outside the house when bread runs short. They generate electricity from their own hydro turbine.

Berghaus Trachsellauenen

As at some other older Berghotels, there is a guest book you can sign. The Tschingelhorn guest books go back to 1907 and include a number of amusing entries. Clearly, the early visitors were largely, as one would expect, from the United Kingdom, which is apparent even before you see their home addresses: "Never had such a ripping wine before," wrote G. Clifford from Dublin, while Alison Lennox Carver from Cheshire wrote simply, "Topping!" And Alfred Lloyd, from London, put "Clerk in Holy Orders" beside his signature.

There is an à la carte menu for lunch and snacks, but one dinner menu for all evening guests. On a recent visit we had vegetable soup (seconds are always available), chicken in curry sauce, rice, salad, and a dessert of vanilla pudding with a canned peach and caramel syrup. The bedrooms are neat and simple, with huge down covers. There is a toilet and cold-water sink down the hall. A shower room is a new addition, and there is a minimal charge for the shower (4 Sfr). There are eight private rooms, one of which has four beds and one has three, and there are Matratzenlager places for 12.

The hotel is open from June to the end of September or a little longer in fine weather. Tel. 033/855 13 43; 3824 Stechelberg.

Getting there: From Stechelberg, 3.5 kilometers; 765 meters up; 2¼ hours.

15 • HOTEL OBERSTEINBERG • 1778 M

The house is similar to Hotel Tschingelhorn: small, cozy, and Victorian in appearance. No one is quite sure anymore when it was built—they think perhaps in the 1860s. It came into the von Allmen family (this is a common name in the valley and they are distinct from the Tschingelhorn von Allmens) in 1882.

Its pretty little parlor, separate from the dining room, is a snug, cozy room with an oil lamp, a tile stove, a few books, and old photos on the walls. A framed letter from a group of British visitors, dated August 1914, expresses thanks to the hotelkeepers for their kindness and hospitality during a period of "unavoidable detention" and to the Swiss people for their sympathy.

Guest books have been preserved from as early as 1894, although some of the very oldest have holes in their pages, having been eaten by mice. On September 13, 1894, Mr. and Mrs. Raymond of New York opined that this place is "lovelier than Madison Square" and declared the beds to be satisfactory. Barely a week later, Miss Isabel Louise Johnson of Boston praised the kind hostess, the hot milk, and the "unexpected luxury of a hot water bottle" found in her bed. In 1899, following several terse notes by English guests who had climbed with local guides and to describe their tours wrote "snow good," a visitor who identified himself only as an Irishman complained that " 'good' is not a proper description of the snow in these parts. Why will A.C. [sic] gentlemen talk slangily? They are worse than cockneys."

Besides the dining room, which is rather plain, with white paper cloths on the tables, there is a little Stübli, where guests can order snacks or drinks

Vicki von Allmen—cheese making at Obersteinberg

before or after meals, and a small outdoor terrace for lunches and afternoon refreshments.

Obersteinberg still functions as an alp. They keep thirteen cows (five are their own, the rest are only pastured here) and four pigs, and make their own Bergkäse ("alp cheese") and butter in a little dairy beside the hotel. Vicki von Allmen, the American dairymaid, works here with her husband, whose sister, Dori von Allmen, now owns and manages the inn. They still keep a mule, which goes down to Stechelberg every day for provisions, supplemented by a weekly helicopter drop.

One evening meal is served to all guests. On one visit we had soup (ravenously hungry, we had two bowls each), beef stew with mashed potatoes, lettuce salad, and canned pears with chocolate sauce. (More recently, after soup—no seconds this time—and salad, there was minced chicken in curry sauce, then crème caramel.) At breakfast there was cheese from their own dairy, a saucer of cherry jam, and a bowl of delicious dark honey.

Only a few mountain inns today remain as old-fashioned as Obersteinberg. Unlike Tschingelhorn, which now uses a generator to light a few lamps in the evening, Hotel Obersteinberg still relies on candles on the dining tables and in the private rooms and petrol lamps in the hall (cooking is done with gas). And it is one of the few mountain inns that have not installed a shower.

There are 14 private double rooms and 30 places in the Matratzenlager, which along with some of the private rooms is in a second house beside the hotel (this annex was rebuilt in 1956 after its predecessor was destroyed by an avalanche). Private rooms are simple, with light pine walls and floors, huge down covers, and basins and pitchers on the washstand. Two tiny towels are provided. Guests in private rooms use an indoor toilet and cold-water sink, but Matratzenlager guests use an outhouse and a sink outside the dormitory. The hotel is open from June 1 to the end of September. (If you stay for a week, they will bring up your baggage on the mule.) Tel. 033/855 20 33; private line: 855 33 01; 3824 Stechelberg.

Getting there: From Stechelberg it is 4.5 kilometers; 858 meters up; 2 hours, 40 minutes.

Walks: From any of these three inns, Trachsellauenen, Tschingelhorn, or Obersteinberg, you can hike up to a beautiful turquoise mountain tarn, the Oberhornsee, with a splendid backdrop of mountains and glaciers. Simply continue up the trail beyond Hotel Obersteinberg. From Obersteinberg:

2 kilometers; 287 meters up; 1¼ hours.

From the Oberhornsee (2065 meters), a blazed path continues to an alpine club hut, the Schmadrihutte, set in even greater scenic splendor. To reach the hut, continue past the lake on a path leading down to the river beyond. Turn left and follow the path along the riverbank to a plank bridge. Beyond that, the trail ascends to a mound (even from here, should you go no farther, the view is spectacular), then descends again to a second river and another plank bridge. The trail leads across meadows, then climbs up a moraine to reach the hut at 2262 meters, almost 2 hours beyond the lake.

THE SEFINENTAL

Above the main body of the Lauterbrunnental are two higher valleys. The Upper Lauterbrunnental rises directly south of the Weisse Lütschine, the northward-flowing river that drains the main valley. To the west is another high valley, the Sefinental, which climbs to the Sefinenfurke, a pass that connects the Kiental with the Lauterbrunnental. Although the pass is steep and the hike is long and challenging, it is a highly scenic and popular route. It extends from Mürren at one end (see Inns 11 and 12) to Griesalp/Gold-erli/Pochtenalp in the Upper Kiental at the other end (see Inns 8, 9, and 10). It is often done in one day, but a number of inns on the Sefinental side of the walk provide alternative stopping places that hikers can use to break up this long hike into shorter segments. Two of these options are Spielbodenalp and the Rotstockhütte. If you're walking westward to the Kiental, a stop at either one of these inns will shorten the climb to the pass, and if you're heading eastward will reduce the long descent to Mürren.

16 • RESTAURANT-PENSION SPIELBODENALP • 1800 M

If nearly utmost simplicity will soothe your soul, come to Spielbodenalp. Accommodations here are among the plainest to be found at almost any mountain inn, apart from the very few that still offer Heulager (hayloft sleeping). But simplicity does not mean a dreary setting: You'll see a house of weathered, velvety brown wood with a row of great cowbells hung across its facade, brightened with flowers.

The house was built in 1897, when Spielbodenalp was only a summer farm, an "alphütte" that sold milk, cheese, bread, and butter to hikers. It's still an alp, with five cows and five calves that provide the milk and butter for guests. The place was bought by the Gertsch family in 1970. Anna

Gertsch runs the Berghotel now with her husband, Christian Stäger. Herr Gertsch, Anna's father, lives above the barn and tends the animals. Beside the farmer's quarters is the house with sleeping quarters, and attached to that is the restaurant—the newest structure—built in the late 1920s. In front of this little cluster is an enclosed grassy area, really a small pasture, in which a couple of goats, some chickens, and a few of the cows wander around (you may also hear a couple of pigs squealing behind the barn) and the Stäger children tumble about. Facing this domestic and pastoral scene is the grandeur of the peaks above the Lauterbrunnental, a wall of rock topped with snowfields.

Spielbodenalp

There are three private rooms: one for two people, one for three people, and one for four. Unlike the rooms in most inns (furnished with a big double bed, washstand, and clothes cupboard and perhaps a little table and chair), these few rooms are small and severely plain, quite spartan. Our room had two little beds, a tiny table, a shelf, and a splendid view. There are 30 places in the Matratzenlager. All guests, in private rooms and dormitory alike, wash outside at a cold-water tap above a wooden trough—you can contemplate the stars while brushing your teeth—and use a couple of pit toilets built behind the house. There is no electricity; they use a diesel generator for the washing machine and milking machines, kerosene lamps for illumination, and wood and gas for cooking.

Most of their business comes during the day as thirsty, tired hikers descend from the Sefinenfurke or other points and stop here to sit at a table outside for lunch or refreshments. There are few overnight guests, who gather in the rather plain dining room when the evening turns cool. Dinner is à la carte. Seeking a vegetarian meal, we ordered pea soup, mixed salad, and Rösti with red cabbage, which was very filling.

The hotel is open from May or June to mid-October. Tel. 033/855 14 75; 3825 Mürren.

Getting there: From Mürren, 2.25 kilometers; 262 meters up; 40 minutes.

17 • ROTSTOCKHÜTTE • 2040 M

Despite its name, this is not an SAC hut. It is privately owned but run just like a club hut. Its location makes it useful, as nothing on the Sefinental side is closer to the Sefinenfurke pass. Built in 1946 by a ski club, this snug little building of dark gray stone with red shutters resembles a club hut in being compact and very simple. The site (the hut and an alp right beside it) is known as Boganggen, set on high meadows quite close to the pass, with a spectacular view of rugged rock walls capped with snow. The cows you may see ambling around provide the hut's milk but belong to the alp, which is under separate ownership.

If you stay here, you'll find conditions pretty much the same as at many older SAC huts, although the newer club huts have indoor toilets and some even have solar-powered showers (for which there's a charge). The Rotstockhütte has no private rooms, but club-hut-style accommodations: sleeping shelves in two large dormitories (a sleeping pad, pillow, and two folded woolen blankets at each place). Outside the hut are latrines and a washhouse with a cold-water trough sink.

These are quite basic accommodations, but many Swiss and European hikers consider a night or two (many Swiss can get to the mountains on weekends) in a Matratzenlager to be fun, like summer camp—they associate it with youth and carefree wandering. Even for a hut like this, lacking most amenities, you should phone ahead for a place on weekends. When we stayed here there were, besides Swiss, a few Germans, a young Englishman, and a group of 14 middle-aged French friends who hike together every summer for 4–5 days and who were exceedingly jolly, laughing as they scrubbed themselves briskly with cold water and washing down the meal (the food was plentiful, though indifferent) with copious amounts of wine.

As you would expect, there is no electricity up here. Anni and Andreas Feuz, the young couple who run the inn, cook with gas and wood, and use solar power for the refrigerator and lamps. Andreas cooks and Anni hands out food and drinks. It's hard work, but Anni has happy childhood memories of this place, and they both love the view. Anni places bowls and tableware on the tables and guests lay out their own settings; she serves various drinks from the little counter. For the evening meal, each table gets a tureen of soup, then platters of food: We all used our big soup dishes for the next course of spaghetti, meat sauce, and green beans; dessert was custard sprinkled with canned fruit. Far from any village and up on the high meadows, the inn is provisioned weekly by helicopter, like an SAC hut.

There are 52 Matratzenlager spaces. The hut is open from about June 1 to the end of September. Tel. 033/855 24 64 or 855 30 28; 3824 Stechelberg.

Getting there: From Mürren, 5.25 kilometers; 400 meters up; 2 hours.

Walks: From here either up to the Sefinenfurke Pass or down to Mürren takes about 2 hours.

If you wish to visit both the Upper Lauterbrunnental and then the Sefinental consecutively, it is not necessary to return first either to Mürren or to Stechelberg in order to start up the other valley. Two alternative trails connect the two high inns of the Lauterbrunnental, Hotels Tschingelhorn and Obersteinberg (Inns 14 and 15), with the Sefinental (Inns 16 and 17), linking the two valleys.

WALK 1 • Tschingelhorn to Gimmelwald: 4.5 kilometers; 570 meters down, 270 meters up; 2½ hours.

From Hotel Tschingelhorn, do *not* take the trail down to Trachsellauenen and then Stechelberg, but instead follow the one that leads to the Sefinental and Gimmelwald. This descends through a forest, but openings in the trees yield a splendid view of the line of mountains just across the narrow valley. There are numerous tree roots underfoot that would be slippery if wet. The trail descends to Wasserbrücke, a bridge across the Sefinen Lütschine, after which signs point you up to Gimmelwald. At Gimmelwald you can turn left (southwest) to reach Spielbodenalp in about 2 hours (or, if you wish, the Rotstockhütte, a walk of 3½ hours), or you can turn right (north and then northwest) for Blumental or Mürren.

Rotstockhütte

WALK 2 • Obersteinberg to Gimmelwald: 6 kilometers; 730 meters down, 380 meters up; 4 hours.

The second, alternative, route starts just behind Hotel Obersteinberg. It leads higher on the slope separating the two valleys, with a more extensive view. It passes Busenalp (a side trail climbs a little higher to the viewpoint at Tanzbödeli), then descends extremely steeply to a bridge about 1 kilometer west of Wasserbrücke; from there you can turn left (west) and climb up to the Rotstockhütte, a walk of about another 3 hours, or you can turn right (east), to join the trail up to Gimmelwald (from which you can reach Spielbodenalp in 2 hours or Blumental in about 3 hours).

GRINDELWALD AND SURROUNDINGS

Grindelwald (1050 meters), set at the foot of the Eiger—one of the mythic mountains of the Alps—is among the stellar attractions of Switzerland. Other ski resorts, such as Gstaad and Davos, are more chic (and some are certainly more ostentatious: namely, St. Moritz); other summer resorts offer overall a greater number of hiking trails (Zermatt is first in that regard); but Grindelwald enjoys one of the most scenic locations to be found anywhere in the Alps.

It lies in a deep, narrow valley facing a colossal wall of rock—nearly 15 kilometers in length and cleft by several icefalls—which forms the base of the Wetterhorn, Mättenberg, and Eiger. It was described thus by the distinguished alpinist Leslie Stephen, a Cambridge University don, famous in his day as a man of letters but perhaps most remembered now as the father of Virginia Woolf: "No earthly object that I have seen approaches in grandeur to the stupendous mountain wall whose battlements overhang in mid-air the villages of Lauterbrunnen and Grindelwald. . . ." (Stephen 1871, p. 70) The slope behind Grindelwald rises steeply to a terrace of high meadows with an even more extensive view, one of the grandest in the Alps. From this high balcony you can see across the valley to a constellation of peaks that seem to spring from the glaciers. These mountains include the fearsomely named Schreckhorn ("peak of terror"), which Leslie Stephen, who made the first ascent, called "the most savage and forbidding" of all the Oberland peaks; the Wetterhorn ("peak of tempests"); the Finsteraarhorn (at 4274 meters, the highest peak in the Bernese Oberland, as sharply pointed as a spear); and three of the most famous mountains in Switzerland—the Eiger, Mönch, and Jungfrau—almost personified by their names, like characters in a fable: the Ogre and the Virgin, separated by a Monk hooded with a cowl of white snow.

The Ogre well deserves the title. From its notorious North Face or Wall (Nordwand in German), ravaged by avalanches, many climbers have plunged to their death; some, dead from injury and exhaustion, have remained frozen against its ice until falling rocks dislodged their bodies. But there are easier routes on the Eiger, as well as on neighboring peaks, and Grindelwald is an important mountaineering center.

A major attraction in this area is the Jungfraujoch railway, an extraordinary feat of engineering, constructed between 1896 and 1912. The Jungfrau Express begins from Interlaken although you can pick up connecting trains in Grindelwald, Lauterbrunnen, or Wengen. All passengers change trains at Kleine Scheidegg (2061 meters), beyond which a cog railway corkscrews up through a tunnel blasted out inside the Eiger and Mönch, emerging at the Jungfraujoch, the snowy notch between the Mönch and the Jungfrau. The station, at 3475 meters the highest railway station in Europe, is now a small complex, with an ice cave, restaurant, tiny post office, and shop. Visitors step outside onto a balcony from which they can look down upon the Konkordia Platz—Place de la Concorde— a grand space like the conjunction of Parisian boulevards that is its namesake. Instead, here five glaciers pour into a central ice field, among them the Grosser Aletsch glacier, the biggest glacier in Switzerland. In the other direction, visitors can gaze across the Grindelwald Valley and the Thunersee to the very borders of Switzerland at the distant blue horizon. You can also ride a small elevator up to the Sphinx, a tiny perch above the glaciers, between the nearby Mönch and the Jungfrau.

A sidenote: Owing to a peculiar historical circumstance, under a charter dating from 1540, the Grindelwald region is divided into seven sections or Bergschafts, each with its own president and council. Of the inns mentioned in this section, only the Faulhorn and the restaurant next to the Pfingstegg upper lift station are privately owned; the rest belong to their Bergschaft and are run as concessions.

KLEINE SCHEIDEGG 2061 M

From this high saddle separating the Grindelwald Valley (the Lütschintal) from the Lauterbrunnental, the view is stupendous, extending from the Eiger to the Jungfrau and beyond. From Kleine Scheidegg you can also walk out toward the base of the North Wall of the Eiger, or as close as you care to get. Indeed, climbers begin their ascent of this man-eater from the meadows beyond Kleine Scheidegg. You can study the great North Face, pick out the various routes (diagrammed in books about Eiger climbs), and watch and hear an astonishing display of avalanches that occur generally in the afternoon, when the sun's warming loosens ice and rock and sends them thundering down the face.

Long before the death of young men on the North Wall made the Eiger famous, British travelers began coming to Kleine Scheidegg, following in the footsteps of Lord Byron, who passed through here in 1816 and described his impressions. At that time, travel through the Alps was something like a trek to a remote part of the Himalayas. The first visitors slept on straw and could obtain only soup and milk for dinner.

At Kleine Scheidegg there is no village, only the station where Jungfrau Express passengers board the cog railway before it enters the tunnel and a few hotels and refreshment stands. The area around the station is noisy and crowded, abuzz with tourists, but the throngs melt away after the last train of the day departs—and the scenery, of course, remains.

Near the station is the historic **Hotel Bellevue,** first built in 1854. At that time, the hotel operated in summer only; today, Kleine Scheidegg is much esteemed by skiers, and its hotels are open winter and summer alike. From a telescope on the Bellevue's terrace, anxious friends and families have watched their loved ones on the Eiger wall; from here, in 1966, a British journalist looked on in horror as the great American climber John Harlin fell to his death. Fritz von Almen, the hotel's proprietor during the years of the first famous Eiger climbs, befriended many climbers and helped organize rescue teams. Today his widow, Mrs. Heidi von Almen, runs the hotel. The Bellevue has character to match its history: a huge sitting room with a parquet floor and Oriental carpets, overstuffed chairs, and Victorian writing desks; a big formal dining room; and photographs of some of the first North Face climbers. But Frau von Almen, who has the reputation of an eccentric, was unwilling to let us see a room.

August 1, Swiss National Day at Alpiglen

Getting there: Take the cog railway up from Grindelwald or Lauterbrunnen, via Wengen. If you walk, the trail is more attractive on the Wengen side (see Wengen, p. 79).

Walks:

WALK 1 • Round-trip 4 kilometers; 420 up; 1½ hours. Climb a small peak, the Lauberhorn (2472 meters), for a panoramic view.

WALK 2 • Walk to Wengernalp and Wengen (see Wengen—Walks)

WALK 3 • From Kleine Scheidegg to the top of Männlichen (2343 meters): 4½ kilometers; 300 meters up; 1½ hours. The return to the lift station is ½ kilometer; ½ hour. Männlichen is another peaklet with a panoramic view extending from the Eiger to the Jungfrau and along the peaks of the upper Lauterbrunnental. From here, you are much closer to the Eiger North Wall than at First and the Bachalpsee, and the Wall is not foreshortened: You seem to be at eye level with it, instead of looking up at it as you do from Grindelwald, Alpiglen, and even Kleine Scheidegg. Männlichen is connected to both Wengen and Grindelwald by cable cars.

    Berghaus Männlichen (2227 meters), near the upper station for the Männlichen cable car, is an old inn that has been recently renovated. Although not slick, it lacks the cozy appeal of other inns that may not be as old but have been less modernized. Rooms are comfortable. It is open June to October. Tel. 033/853 10 68.

ALPIGLEN

This quiet and beautiful place is nothing more than a Berghaus and a little alp surrounded by meadows in a setting of startling contrast: Towering above the peaceful green pastures is the grim North Face of the Eiger. Next to Kleine Scheidegg, this is the closest one can get to the base of the North Face, and many who have come to challenge the Eiger have camped in the meadows of Alpiglen and begun their climb from here. But in contrast to Kleine Scheidegg, which is swarming with crowds, very few people come here. Perhaps because of the fitting silence of the Alpiglen meadows—or because from this place so many set forth on their last climb, never to return—these meadows were chosen as the site of the monument to the North Wall dead. The memorial stone was unveiled in 1988 at ceremonies marking the 50th anniversary of the wall's first ascent.

In this sunny, lovely, peaceful spot, it's hard to imagine the desperate struggles and for some the agony that occurred on the wall just above.

Getting there: Alpiglen is quite easily reached because there is a small station here on the cog railway line connecting Grindelwald to Kleine Scheidegg. You can also hike up to Alpiglen from Grindelwald.

18 • HOTEL DES ALPES • 1616 M

If you have just come down from Kleine Scheidegg, this old hotel will appeal to you at once. It is not only attractive but also isolated and very quiet. The house, built in 1893, was renovated in 1994 but retains its charm—it has not been overly modernized. The view is splendid, extending from the Eiger looming right above you across to the Wetterhorn. From a charming little terrace, bright with flowers, you can sit outdoors and contemplate the mountains, and in fine weather guests may eat dinner or breakfast outdoors. Inside, there is a rather plain, wood-paneled Gaststube. The hotel has been run since 1960 by the Nebiker-Lüthi family, friendly, pleasant people: Plump, genial Lydia and her son do the cooking. This place bears out the general principle that much at a Berghaus depends on the personality of the owner.

In the main house there are six private rooms. Our room was pleasing and old-fashioned, with head- and footboards on the beds; the traditional pitcher and basin; and broad, honey-brown floor planks. Besides toilets and warm-water sinks in the hall, there is a large new bathroom (incongruously located downstairs, outside the dining room) with showers, toilets, and more sinks. In a separate building there is a large Matratzenlager with about 40 places (it has, however, a very high ceiling, so it is at least airy) and a smaller one for eight. Dormitory guests use the new toilet/shower room attached to the hotel.

The Hôtel des Alpes is locally famous for its Käseschnitte, a dish found on many restaurant menus but made here to perfection. Frau Nebiker-Lüthi makes each order herself, using six or seven different kinds of cheese: These are cubed, slivered, and laid on a thick slice of bread that is pancooked with white wine, then baked in the oven until golden, and finally sprinkled, according to your preference, with any of these: chopped parsley, onion, paprika, garlic, tomato, or even fruit. The smell is irresistible, redolent of cheese, wine, and herbs. Even if you're watching your diet and avoiding cheese, consider breaking your rule for this delectable dish

(Raclette is nothing compared with this); you can share one with a partner. Ask what kinds of cheese go into this dish, and the cook will smile: It's a family secret.

Half-pension is available, or overnight guests may order à la carte. With soup and a salad, even a shared order of Käseschnitte makes a full dinner, but other dishes are available as well, including ravioli, Braten with grat-inéed potatoes and vegetables, house-made sausage or Bratwurst with Rösti, and more. At breakfast you're given a wooden platter with three different kinds of cheese, a slab of butter, and a bowl of jam.

The hotel is open from the end of May or early June until the end of October, depending on the season. Tel. 033/853 11 30.

Walks: From here, you can walk to Kleine Scheidegg in 1½ hours, to Mannlichen in about 2½ hours, or down to Grindelwald, depending on which trail you choose, in nearly 3 hours or by a steeper trail in 1½ hours. The last part of the standard walk to Grindelwald is on paved road. (At a junction, a sign points to STEILER ABSTEIG NACH GRINDELWALD, meaning steeper descent: This path, when muddy after rain, will be slippery.)

19 • BERGRESTAURANT STIEREGG • 1700 M

The massive wall of rock that looms above Grindelwald is cleft by hang-ing glaciers at two different points. The Unter Grindelwaldgletscher, the one nearer to Grindelwald, fills the deep notch between the Eiger and the Mättenberg, which is actually the base of the Schreckhorn. This lower glac-ier is the tongue of a conjoined group of higher glaciers that sweep around the eastern side of the Eiger and hug the curve of the Schreckhorn wall. Perched on a bit of shelf upon the rock wall above this cleft is Bergrestau-rant Stieregg, a solitary little wooden chalet with a magnificent view of the glacier; it is, moreover, the only place from which a nonclimber can see the east face of the Eiger.

Stieregg is very small, pleasant, and snug. There has long been an alp with sheep here, rather than cows, and there are still sheep: When we arrived they were just being let out of a stone pen near the inn. An older hotel (perhaps the same inn that is mentioned in the *Baedeker Guide* of 1893) near the site was destroyed by an avalanche in 1940; some of its dishes have been preserved and are used at the present inn, which was built in 1951 and renovated in 1982. Everything, although simple, is nicely done, with thoughtful and pleasant details, as the family has done the best it can with a small house and limited facilities. The little wood-paneled dining room, with only seven tables, is lit by gas lamps; there is no electricity. The tables are dressed with red-checked cloths and glasses of wildflowers.

There are no private rooms, but instead of one large Matratzenlager the inn's 18 places are divided into three separate rooms. Along with the usual alpine club hut–type of blankets, there are down quilts at each place

Evening at Stieregg

in cheerful checked covers, red-and-white alternating with blue-and-white ones for varied color, and large pillows with matching covers beneath the conventional little dormitory pillows. Our room had a small patterned carpet, a little sofa, a framed old picture, and a mirror—attractive and comfortable touches never found in such dormitories. The toilets are in a new wooden outhouse about 10 feet from the inn that is quite unlike the usual outhouse latrines: These can be manually flushed (containers of water are set out on the floor), the floors are covered with linoleum instead of bare wood, and there are mirrors. Washing is open air at a tap over a hollowed log, the sort of arrangement seen on alpine farms. (Because of low water pressure and the need for water in the kitchen, which is quite busy during the day, this tap is turned off during peak kitchen hours.) In front of the inn is a small grass terrace with a few tables and a magnificent view of the hanging glacier, torn by its own movement into fantastic shapes with teeth of ice hovering over the deep slits, glinting blue, of crevasses. The quiet of this secluded spot is broken by the thunder of occasional avalanches as chunks of the glacier sheer off and crash down.

The menu is not extensive but, as with the physical arrangements, the dishes are made with care and thoughtfulness. The homemade vegetable soup is a house specialty and it's excellent, thick and full of fresh vegetables. Our mixed salad was not the usual plate with the usual elements but a huge bowl for the two of us, with shredded cabbage, carrots, lettuce, and tomato. The fried egg I ordered on my Rösti had a dash of paprika for a touch of bright color.

Stieregg is run by several generations of the Rubi-Kaufmann family, grandmother Heidi Rubi and her daughter Maggi Rubi (who speaks English). These two ladies perform prodigious amounts of work: not only cooking but also carrying 10 to 15 kilograms of supplies up from the lift station three times a week (including bread and fresh vegetables from the garden of their house in Grindelwald) and carrying all the inn's laundry down to Grindelwald. These provisions are supplemented by a weekly helicopter drop. Besides the standard fare on the menu, with a little advance notice they can also prepare steak, lamb, and potato gratin. Another specialty of the house is Heidi Kaffee—coffee with whipped cream and schnapps.

Modest as it is, the house is often full on Saturday nights. The spare simplicity of a little Berggasthaus in such a setting may work untold wonders for harried spirits and troubled souls.

Stieregg is open from June to mid-October. This is clearly an attraction, and for a weekend stay one should phone ahead for reservations. Tel. 033/853 17 66 or Natel 077/565 31 8; 3818 Grindelwald.

Getting there: You can hike up to this inn or take the Pfingstegg cable car, which eliminates 400 meters. From the upper cable car station: 2.5 kilometers; 308 meters up; 1 hour, 10 minutes. To reach the Pfingsteggbahn, follow Grindelwald's main street eastward, past the First lift station and the church. A sign for the lift station directs you to the right, downward toward the river. To walk up to Pfingstegg (1392 meters), you can take a gradual path to the left (north) through Auf der Sulz, reaching Pfingstegg in about 1¾ hours, or a steeper, more direct path that climbs through the woods and cuts off about 20 minutes of the hike. At the upper cable car station, a path continues toward the right for Stieregg, which you can reach in about 1 hour, 10 minutes from the upper station. Although there is deep exposure to one side in several sections, the path is wide and well graded, and the exposed parts are guarded by fencing.

Walks: Once you're here, you can only stroll around the small meadow area in which the inn is set, or walk forward on the little ridge in front of the inn, beyond which there's a sharp drop to the glacier (deep erosion is cutting back the shelf on which Stieregg is sited and in perhaps a century or less it will cease to exist); otherwise, you can't do much more when you're here than contemplate the view. A signpost indicates the way to the SAC Schreckhornhütte, but that route includes a difficult passage with ladders and fixed ropes, especially unsuitable for children. Therefore, the only walking opportunity here is the hike you took to get up to the inn, which was fairly short if you came up by cable car. But the view is splendid, all the more so because you are so close to the glacier.

FIRST

The steep slope behind Grindelwald rises to a high shelf of meadows, most easily reached by the First lift system. From a lower station just off the main street of Grindelwald, a cable car system using six-person gondolas ascends this slope, with intermediate stops at Bort and Grindel, before terminating at First (the German word, pronounced *feerst,* means ridge, peak or top) at 2168 meters. You can also hike up from Grindelwald, a steep climb of about 1120 meters, which could take nearly 4 hours. Trails extend along this shelf in both directions, west and east, linking the Grindelwald area with the well-known Bernese Oberland Pass route.

Walks:

WALK 1 • Bachalpsee: 5.5 kilometers; 100 meters up; 1 hour up, 40 minutes back to First.

This very scenic, easy, and popular walk is a destination in its own right, but also the first section of the walk to the Faulhorn Inn (see Inn 21). Except for perhaps a handful of people who climb up on foot from Grindelwald, most start from the top station of the First lift. From there, a well-trodden trail leads to this lovely little lake (2265 meters), which faces a splendid scene of glaciers framed by the Schreckhorn and Finsteraarhorn, and beyond them, the Wetterhorn and Eiger. Tourists in sandals and town shoes make their way along the trail, although probably not comfortably.

20 • BERGRESTAURANT WALDSPITZ • 1918 M

About three-quarters of the way up the slope to First, this newly renovated Berghaus replaces an old inn, Hotel Alpenrose Waldspitz, that dated from 1866. Before the First lift system was built, it served as a way station for people heading up to the Faulhorn by mule or on foot —and those who started up on foot and then got weary could hire mules or donkeys here. The former establishment was in such disrepair, and its sleeping accommodations so cramped, that it has been virtually rebuilt, so completely renovated in 1996–1997 that little remains of the old house—just the dining room ceiling and a small section of the exterior wall. This was the decision of the local Bergschaft (see p. 99), the community that owns the property. Consequently, what you'll find here is a bright, cheerful, new mountain inn, with certain comforts: indoor toilets, warm-water sink and shower, and carpet on the the dormitory floors. With light wood walls and a tile floor, the dining room looks fresh and new. From the inn's terrace, the view of the mountains above Grindelwald—especially of the Eiger—is extensive and fine. The place is under the very active management of Adi Bohren, a former member of the Grindelwald mountain rescue service, who emits positive sparks of energy as he hastens around, cooking, overseeing the remaining construction work, welcoming guests, and greeting old friends from the community. He explains that what he wants to achieve here is a place that's relaxed, where people feel at ease: not guest quantity (i.e., crowds of guests), but quality of ambience. He is on the job from morning until night, from preparing breakfast to cooking dinner for latecomers, serving the last evening drinks and chatting sociably with his farmer-neighbors. He has even concerned himself with the decor: Bohren himself made the handsome table near the dining room counter, a massive old tree trunk with six or seven side trunks.

Dinner is à la carte, with soup, the usual meat dishes, and chicken breast served with salads. The food is fairly good and, as Adi applies his extraordinary energy to his new job, will likely get much better. Breakfast is a buffet, with orange juice, Muesli, a big hunk of cheese from one of the neighboring alps (which also provides the milk and butter), and a bowl of good jam.

There are three Matratzenlager, with a total of 35 places, and one private double room, although more private rooms may be added (reconstruction was not quite completed in 1997). Waldspitz opens whenever the First lift does, usually early in June, until about October 20–25, then again from about December 20 until Easter. Tel. 033/853 18 61; Natel 077 35 94 25; 3818 Grindelwald.

Getting there: The inn can be reached by a private bus (Swiss Pass not valid) from Grindelwald (but not by private car, as the road is private), or by hiking down from the topmost First station above, or by hiking up from the Bort station (one of the midway stations on the First lift) or from Grindelwald itself. Walking down to Bort (on a new, rather steep but well-

Afternoon at the alps above the Waldhaus

cut forest path) will take about 40 minutes; walking up from Bort about 1 hour, 20 minutes. From First, follow the signs to all points; you'll cross in front of the lift station (that is, facing the entrance), then in about 2 minutes a sign points you down for Waldspitz, which you can reach in 40 minutes. A nice evening stroll from Waldspitz is to follow the road for about 20 minutes toward First; the road ends at a group of working alps.

21 • BERGHAUS FAULHORN • 2681 M

This inn sits atop a protuberance that is considered a little peak in its own right, although it seems a hill compared with the mountains around it. The path up is quite smooth and there is no scramble at all. The original structure was built in 1830 or 1831, making this one of the oldest Berghotels in Switzerland. One of its first guests was Felix Mendelssohn, who spent a night here in 1831 during an alpine walking tour; he was deeply impressed by the scenery and wrote, "That Goethe could write nothing in Switzerland but a few weak poems, and still weaker letters, is to me as incomprehensible as many other things in this world." Richard Wagner slept at the Faulhorn in 1852, and Franz Liszt may also have slept here.

It's easy to see why an inn was established soon after the first wave of hikers began to frequent the Alps. Up on its little peaklet, this spot commands a majestic view across the Grindelwald Valley of the giants of the Oberland with the Eiger, Mönch, and Jungfrau as the centerpiece. Many a guest spends the night here in order to watch the sunset or sunrise, if not both, as the alpenglow flushes the snowy peaks with rose, then gold.

The Faulhorn is mentioned in some of the earliest guidebooks for British travelers. One such traveler, John Carne, wrote in his 1840 account, *Journal of a Tour Through Switzerland and Italy:* "The view enjoyed from the Faulhorn is the most bold and brilliant in Switzerland. That from the Righi [*sic*] is tame in comparison . . . Its peculiar excellence arises from all the great mountains being closely seen in the form of a splendid amphitheatre . . ." Visitors rode up to the Faulhorn on mules and horses and ladies could be carried up on a Tragstuhl, which required four porters who charged (in 1838) 6 francs each. Mules also hauled up the hotel's provisions, descending to Grindelwald and returning to the Faulhorn in one day. After the First lift was built, the mule only had to go as far as the upper station to pick up provisions. But the days of supply-by-mule are gone, and the Faulhorn is now provisioned by helicopter twice a week. Other modernizations have also occurred: The restaurant was enlarged and renovated in 1964. The hotel is run by Frau Claire Mangott-Almer, whose father bought it in 1930.

The sleeping quarters are in a separate building dating to about 1832, adjacent to the restaurant. *Murray's Handbook* (1838) refers to "3 very tolerable apartments, and one or two lofts; still it is but sorry sleeping accommodation, the *désagrémens* of which are hardly compensated to ladies by the 'uncertain' beauty of the early view of the glaciers: for gentlemen the quarters are good enough." The private rooms have a great deal of charm; they are furnished with old-fashioned, dark wood bedsteads (made up with sheets and blankets as well as down quilts in pretty covers); walls, floors, and ceilings are pine. Along with the customary washstand with its basins and pitchers, some rooms have old pictures on the walls, and some have old sofas as well. No less important, the rooms smell fresh and sweet.

There are two rooms with three beds, five rooms with two beds, and two large Matratzenlager rooms with a total of 84 places. The toilets for private rooms and the dormitories are separate, both indoors. Dormitory guests use a washroom with cold-water sinks; guests in private rooms are supplied with full pitchers of water and basins. Guests are asked to use water sparingly, as it must be pumped up from the glacier (all water used for cooking is boiled). A bottle of mineral water costs 4 Sfr, so you might want to bring up a full water bottle. Dinner is à la carte, although there is a daily special meal. The menu includes Erbsensuppe (yellow pea soup) among the standard dishes.

Among Swiss mountain inns, this is perhaps the one where it is most difficult to get a private room, especially on a weekend. You must telephone well ahead (at least eight days), and it is no less advisable to call in advance for a Matratzenlager place—even for a weekday. Tel. 033/853 27 13 or 033/853 10 25; 3818 Grindelwald.

Getting there: From the upper First lift station: 6.5 kilometers; 515 meters up; 3 hours. From First, walk out to the Bachalpsee (see Walk 1 above) and continue on the trail heading eastward beyond the lake. Then climb a rocky slope, following red-and-white blazes, to the saddle above. At the saddle you'll see the little peak of the Faulhorn clearly to your right, with the inn atop it, reachable in another 15 minutes; from the Bachalpsee it will take 2 hours at a slow pace.

Walks: The chief walks from the Faulhorn Inn are to Bussalp and to Schynige Platte.

WALK 1 • Bussalp from Faulhorn: 4.5 kilometers; 890 meters down; 2½ hours. Most hikers take a bus down from Mittelläger; walking back down to Grindelwald will add 2 hours to this hike.

From Faulhorn, start westward back to the Bachalpsee, where there are actually two lakes, and walk down to the lower of the two lakes. Continue along the west shore of this lower lake. A signpost points to Bussalp, to the

Eiger, Mönch, and Jungfrau from the Faulhorn

right. (At a junction here, you'll see a trail marked for Spielmatten and Grindelwald, but it's steep and eroded.) The trail leads up through a little gorge that cuts through a rock, then descends a slope of grass and rocks. The meadows and views are lavishly superb. At a junction marked for Mittelläger or Bussalp Oberläger, stay left for Mittelläger if you wish to take a bus back to Grindelwald.

WALK 2 • Schynige Platte (2067 M)

This is one of Switzerland's grandest hikes, on which the great chain of Oberland mountains—with the Eiger, Mönch, and Jungfrau at its center—unfolds before your eyes as if a scroll were unwinding. The highest point on this walk will be the Faulhorn Berghotel, and even the saddle (2546 meters) below the inn is higher than any other point on the hike. Nevertheless, it's not all downhill, as the trail rises and dips continually. It's often done in one day, between First and Schynige Platte (or the reverse), but an overnight stop at the Faulhorn can break it up.

From the Faulhorn Inn, descend to rejoin the main trail at the base of the little Faulhorn peak and head westward. A short stretch, which may take about 15 minutes, runs along the top of a very narrow ridge. The trail drops to Mandlenen, where there is only a tiny cabin, the cozy little **Weber Hütte Gast Stübli,** where you can get a meal or a snack; simple overnight accommodations are also available. Beyond the little hut is a section with some black rock that can be slippery. The trail, which is always clear (sometimes SP is painted on a rock), turns west to enter a long, high valley, then crosses to the right into another high valley. Just at the end, when you're ready for a break, you must ascend a last and fortunately short slope, above which is Schynige Platte and the station from which you can take a cog railway down to Wilderswil.

Getting there: From Faulhorn: 8.5 kilometers; 614 meters down; 3½ hours. The figure for descent is misleading, as the trail undulates and you'll be climbing several hundred meters as well as descending them. (Grindelwald to Schynige Platte: 6½ hours, not the 5½ hours listed on trail signs.) From Schnynige Platte you can also hike down the steep trail to Wilderswil. Most hikers take the cog railway down to Wilderswil, from which there are frequent rail connections to all points in the region.

SCHYNIGE PLATTE

It's difficult to pin down a definition for Schynige Platte: A rounded bump on the edge of a rocky crest, it's essentially a viewing point, one of the best in the Bernese Oberland. Upon the site are an alpine garden, an old hotel, and a cog railway station. Schynige Platte is close to Interlaken, which was described in *Murray's Handbook* (1838) as virtually an English colony—"two-thirds of the summer visitors, on a moderate computation, being of our nation, who have converted the place into a sort of Swiss Margate"—and thus very accessible. Many people ride up just for the view, others to hike. Schynige means "shining," perhaps referring to the way light glints off the shaley rock of which the ridge is composed, and Platte refers to the form of the rock.

The very narrow-gauge cog railway is a delight: Some of the cars are nearly antiques, made of wood with slatted seats and open sides, although there are canvas shades to pull down in case of rain. The newer cars are much in the same style. The descent to Wilderswil is about 1400 meters, and it takes the little train an hour to wind its way down to the valley floor. Originally run on steam, it is now electric, but four or five times a year they still run a steam engine for the public's enjoyment.

22 • HOTEL-RESTAURANT SCHYNIGE PLATTE • 1970 M

This old hotel is a historical curiosity—it would not have been preserved in any country but Switzerland—one of several such included in this book. Perched up high like an aerie, with a truly eagle's view of the mountains above Grindelwald and the Lauterbrunnental, this spot began attracting travelers by the mid-19th century. Toward that century's end, before the opening of the Jungfraujoch cog railway and well before the advent of cable cars, Schynige Platte was virtually a requisite stop on tours of the region. It is still a popular attraction, easy to reach because of the cog railway, and a favorite spot for weddings.

Hotel Schynige Platte predates the cog railway, which was inaugurated in 1893; the present management is not sure how old the hotel is but thinks it may date from the 1860s. Before the railway, people rode up on mules and some ladies were carried up on Tragstuhls by porters. The cog railway company bought the hotel at the end of the 19th century, and it has been privately leased by the Brunner family since 1963. The hotel continues to function, mainly as a restaurant, because of brisk business during the day from tourists who ride up on the cog railway. Overnight guests are few. Because Schynige Platte has not been developed for skiing (perhaps its slopes are too precipitous), the hotel is closed in winter. If this were a ski area, the hotel would surely have been modernized (and the charming, old-fashioned little train would have been replaced by something that could move greater numbers of people at higher speed). But that is not the case.

Upon arriving at the hotel you will see what looks like a new structure—although it only looks new because of its facade, which was added in 1963—and a large terrace full of people eating ice cream on sunny afternoons and admiring the splendid view. Walk up the broad steps, past a glassed-in dining terrace, to a grandly spacious interior dining room, with proportions that are distinctly premodern. The kitchen and restaurant were also modernized in 1963. But step upstairs and you will see at once that this is indeed a holdover from the 19th century. The stair landings are decorated with a few stuffed marmots and chamois (some have their horns on askew or even backward) and old prints, tinged with foxing, of mountain scenes. Massive wooden chests are set out along the hallways, which are broad and high ceilinged. There are 16 private rooms and 40 Matratzenlager places in a separate building. Guests in the private rooms use a toilet and sink (cold water) in the hall or may use the pitchers and basins provided in each room for a sponge bath. Wooden towel racks hold several small linen towels. Matratzenlager guests must use the public washroom in the hotel. There are no showers. Indeed, there is no source of water on the ridge, and all the water used at the hotel comes from collected rainwater or is brought up by the cog railway. The hotel obtained electricity only in the 1950s.

The hotel is down-at-the-heels—there are cracks in the plaster in the hallways—but it is not a dump. Our room had been freshly painted and was clean and well aired.

Dinner is à la carte, although half-pension may be possible. The menu offers soup, salad, a variety of meat dishes that may include veal Schnitzel, steak or chicken, Rösti, noodles, cooked vegetables and salads, and fruit salad and freshly baked cakes. There's a nice breakfast buffet with orange juice and Muesli or cornflakes, as well as loaves of good bread and bowls instead of packets of jam. Hotel Schynige Platte is open from the end of May through mid-October. Tel. 033/822 34 31; 3800 Interlaken.

Getting there: By foot, from Faulhorn or First (see Inn 21—Walks); by cog railway from Wilderswil.

Cog railway from Schynige Platte to Wilderswil

Walks: The chief walk is the hike to the Faulhorn and beyond to First (see Inn 21—Walks), but shorter walks may also be taken near the hotel. Schynige Platte is the end of a ridge along which there are several pinnacles, all good viewpoints. A signposted trail behind the hotel leads to these points, as well as to the Faulhorn and First (and thus to Grindelwald).

The closest viewpoint is the Daube (2076 meters), from which there's a panoramic view extending northward to the lakes, which can't be seen from Schynige Platte. The Daube can be reached in about 30 minutes. If you continue along the ridge, you'll come to the next viewpoint, the Oberberghorn, at 2069 meters; a little round-trip route, the Kleiner Rundweg, has been laid out that circles the Daube and Oberberghorn and takes about 1½ hours. From the Oberberghorn you can continue on the Panoramaweg, a trail that snakes along the narrow ridge northeastward to a third viewpoint at 1990 meters; this third point can also be reached by another trail cut lower on the slope that bypasses the Daube and Oberberghorn, or the two trails can be combined to make a round-trip taking about 2½ hours.

REICHENBACHTAL

Like a great earthen dike, the Grosse Scheidegg ridge is slung across the eastern end of the Grindelwald Valley, separating it from the Reichenbachtal, a higher valley to the northeast. This "large" Scheidegg, at 1962 meters, is actually about 100 meters lower than the small one (Kleine Scheidegg), but is a broader saddle. Unlike the Kleine Scheidegg, swarming with passengers for the Jungfraujoch line, the Grosse Scheidegg is much quieter, with nothing atop it but a large Berghotel and a bus stop. The view at Grosse Scheidegg (and for some distance on either side of it) is dominated by the massive base of the Wetterhorn, in breadth the most formidable rock wall to be seen anywhere in the Alps. From the equally huge system of glaciers couched above this base emerge innumerable waterfalls, which streak the vast wall with ribbons of silver.

The best known of all long-distance hiking routes in Switzerland is the traverse of the Bernese Oberland, from the very westernmost edge of the canton near Gstaad to Engelberg in the east (from there, one can continue even farther east, to Altdorf). The three mountain inns in the Reichenbachtal—Grosse Scheidegg, Schwarzwaldalp, and Rosenlaui—are found along this route. A paved road, connecting Meiringen and Grindelwald, extends through the valley, but traffic is very light, as connecting access is limited to local inhabitants and to the bus service. There is also a trail, mainly separate from the road, but which cuts across loops of the road in a few places.

23 • BERGHOTEL GROSSE SCHEIDEGG • 1961 M

The house is said to be 100 years old, but has been enlarged and renovated. Before this Berghaus was built, travelers found the most basic sort of accommodation here: *Murray's Handbook* (1838) refers to a chalet, "weathertight, affording one or two beds for such travellers as are driven to sleep here; and a cup of coffee or hot milk for those who desire to warm themselves after their cold morning's ride over the mountains."

In the 19th century, *Murray's Handbook* was the standard guide—the traveler's bible—for Switzerland. The Reverend Jones noted cynically how innkeepers, once their establishment was listed in the *Handbook,* presumed upon their reputation: "A man gets his name well in *Murray's Handbook,* keeps it there by his deserts till it appears in several successive editions . . . and then, with travelers flocking to his door, begins to think of raising his price or reducing the entertainment offered." (Jones 1866, p. 187)

Behind the hotel is a terrace, where meals are served in fine weather. The dining room, bustling when we were there, is rather modern. We came up here once during an Älpler Fest on the last Sunday of July—a sort of Swiss outdoor summer festival; these events are held in various locations throughout the country. Long tables were set up, as is customary at these affairs, and crowds of people sat outside enjoying beer, soft drinks, and plates of grilled Wurst with Rösti, while a band in traditional dress (men in short-sleeved black velvet jackets with embroidered lapels) played folk music—lively polkas and other dances. To one side a space had been set apart for the various games typically held at these festivals. We watched contestants line up to see who could hurl a huge rock farthest with one hand. Later in the afternoon there would be an open wrestling event, folkstyle, out on the meadow behind the hotel.

There are only two private rooms, quite pleasant ones with three beds each, but there are several Massenlager (Matratzenlager) with spaces for 130 people. Warm-water sinks are in the hall. The hotel is open from May into October. Tel. 033/853 12 09.

Getting there: You can reach Grosse Scheidegg by bus from either Grindelwald, Meiringen, or from Schwarzwaldalp or Rosenlaui. You must change buses at Grosse Scheidegg, which serves as a border between two private bus lines; the road eastward is private, closed to private cars. You can also walk here from Grindelwald or Schwarzwaldalp, or from a high trail that links the topmost First lift station and the trails above Grindelwald with Grosse Scheidegg.

24 • HOTEL-CHALET SCHWARZWALDALP • 1454 M

This is an inn of modest size (smaller and more attractive than the one at Grosse Scheidegg), built in 1942 to replace a larger hotel that burned down in that year. Although located beside the road, with a bus stop near its door, the inn is agreeably set in a meadow below the grand wall of the Wetterhorn. The dining room is pleasant, fairly small and simple, with traditional wood paneling. There are four double rooms with warm-water sinks in the chalet, shower available, and 61 Matratzenlager places in an old wooden house behind the restaurant with cold-water sinks.

In good weather most people sit outdoors here for lunch and refreshments. Schwarzwaldalp tries to offer a menu with more variety than at many other inns: There's a salad bar out on the terrace, and Bratwurst is grilled outdoors. The menu features homemade Gulaschsuppe; Steinpilz (mushroom) risotto; Bratwurst with onion sauce and apples; beef Stroganoff with paprika cream sauce and Knöpfli; and roast lamb with salad, among other dishes. Half-pension is available.

The hotel, operated by Moni and Andi Angst-Huber, is open from May to the end of October. Tel. and Fax: 033/971 35 15; CH-3860 Meiringen.

Getting there: You can get here by bus from Grindelwald and Grosse Scheidegg or from Meiringen and Rosenlaui. West of Schwarzwaldalp the road is private, closed to private cars. Or you can walk here from several points: from First, from Grosse Scheidegg, and from Rosenlaui. To walk from First, take the trail east, then turn left for a more gradual descent via Grosse Scheidegg, or turn right for a steeper trail down to the road and Schwarzwaldalp.

THE ROSENLAUI VALLEY

The principal feature of this valley, the Rosenlaui Glacier, is famed for the deep azure of its crevasses and séracs (huge upright blocks of ice) and its exceptionally pure white surface. The Gletscherschlucht (entrance fee) permits you to enter a gorge hollowed out within the glacier for a closer view.

Otherwise, the best view of the glacier is from Gschwantenmad, a pretty meadow about 15 minutes up the road from Hotel Rosenlaui toward Meiringen. Nearby are the Engelhörner (angels' peaks), a cluster of 28 rocky spires, a challenge to rock climbers. Indeed, pure rock climbing as a sport in its own right (rather than the classical "mixed" climbs involving rock, ice, and snow) is said to have first become popular here. It was because of the Engelhörner, as well as the adjacent Rosenlaui Glacier and the Wellhorn, that the area became known as a mountaineering center, with Arnold Glatthardt's famous climbing school at Rosenlaui. Gertrude Bell, a fearless Englishwoman and one of the prominent climbers of her day, made the first ascent of one of the spires in 1901—it was subsequently named the Gertrudespitze—and climbed seven of the others as well.

25 • HOTEL ROSENLAUI • 1328 M

This is one of the more unusual Swiss mountain hotels. After a mineral spring was discovered at Rosenlaui in 1771, a first simple inn was built there in 1795 and slightly improved in 1826; guests came to drink the waters and to bathe at the Baths of Rosenlaui, although *Murray's Handbook* described only "a homely inn . . . erected over a source of mineral water, which supplies 5 or 6 rude tubs of wood, serving as baths. The number of guests who resort hither for the use of them is very limited." John Carne, who published his travels in 1840, had a better impression of the baths of Rosenlaui: "It is strange to meet with so lovely a spot rising, as if by enchantment, in such a place. One dwelling only is there, but that is neat and well-arranged . . . " (Carne 1840, p. 110) The old inn burned down in 1860 and was rebuilt in 1863.

Replacing the old wooden chalet, the present Hotel Rosenlaui was built in 1904 with a flourish of Victorian elegance: four stories high, with pointed roof, little wrought-iron balconies, and a grand salon with parquet floors. But secluded, isolated Rosenlaui in its undeveloped, pastoral valley never became much of a spa—it stopped functioning as a Kurhaus by 1914—and an avalanche destroyed the mineral spring around 1950. (The older hotel of 1863 still exists, next door to the present one; it housed the climbing school that flourished here in the mid-20th century but now serves as a sports center for young people.)

Rosenlaui was taken over by the Kehrli family in 1960, and they left their stamp on it in remarkable ways. Ernst Kehrli was more than an innkeeper—painting was his passion, and his large, abstract modern canvases, looking incongruous in this Victorian spa hotel, were hung in the parlor, the halls, and guest bedrooms; his widow made the hotel almost a museum of his work. A new generation of Kehrlis have now taken over, with their own taste and style, and have wrought great changes, including the creation of one of the most remarkable of all Berghaus dining rooms, with respect to both appearance and cuisine.

Anyone who visited the hotel in former years will not recognize the present dining room, although it is the same room. The coffered ceiling,

Between First lift station (above Grindelwald) and Rosenlaui

once dark brown with age, has been sandblasted and restored to its original pale golden color, and all its beautiful carving can now be seen. Confining, waist-high partitions were removed, creating a large, open space, whose parquet floor is now also more visible. The effect is of relaxed elegance: tables set with white linen, handsome silver napkin rings, engraved slender goblets, candles, and pretty little ceramic pots of plants or flowers. In agreeable contrast to the formality of white napery and silver are the handsome, contemporary metal lights, made by a friend for the young

Kehrlis. Classical music plays softly. Clearly much thought went into every detail, because Andreas and Christina Kehrli say that you can't have nice food with ugly tables, and vice versa: Everything has to work together.

One menu is offered to all overnight guests (although they may choose to order à la carte). We were served a tureen of homemade vegetable soup, a large mixed salad, chicken breasts in a pastry crust with little boiled potatoes and steamed vegetables, and a caramel brûlé pudding, and spent 2 hours at the table—unheard of for a Berghaus meal. (The à la carte menu includes chicken cordon bleu and risotto.)

Our room was also attractive, newly repapered, pretty, light, and airy. And spacious. Andreas Kehrli does not like small rooms: He says that when you enter a room, you should have space on either side of you. He remarks that when many hotels were renovated to add private bathrooms (this does not apply to mountain inns, which almost never have private baths), the rooms were chopped up into small units; as a result, he says, "you have no space to turn around in," except for the few hotels that made every other room into a bath, in between two bedrooms. (At Rosenlaui, toilets, showers, and warm-water sinks are in the hall; towels are provided.) A more difficult task for Andreas is deciding what to do about his father's paintings, the strong, sometimes harsh colors of which do not suit the hotel's style. He has removed many from the bedrooms and continues to struggle with this aspect of his legacy.

On the hotel's second floor is a huge elegant parlor, a period piece and historical curiosity: polished tables, chaise longue, carpets on the parquet floor, and displays of china and old silver. Beside that is a large room that was used as a gallery for Ernst Kehrli's paintings but now displays an exhibition about the Alps: the geologists and botanists who studied them, the first artists who painted them and so helped launch the cult of wild beauty and made it fashionable to go to the Alps, and photographs and notes about early climbers and guides.

The hotel has 12 private rooms and 60 Matratzenlager places distributed in another 12 rooms, none with more than 6 places; the Kehrlis try to enable dormitory guests to have a room to themselves. The hotel is open from mid-May to the first week in October. Tel. and Fax: 033/971 29 12; 3860 Rosenlaui.

Getting there: The hotel is on a paved road, with a bus stop at the door from which one can take a bus eastward to Meiringen or westward to Schwarzwaldalp and Grosse Scheidegg, and from there to Grindelwald.

There are also trails connecting to these points. To walk here from Schwarzwaldalp takes 35 minutes.

Walks:

WALK 1 • The Hochmoor: round-trip 7 kilometers; 350 meters up; 4 hours.

The Hochmoor is a sort of high moorland above Rosenlaui. Turn left from the hotel and walk to nearby Kaltenbrunnen, in the direction of Meiringen, and continue uphill on the road for a minute or two to the trailhead, which is signposted. A sign directs you southwest to Kaltenbrunnenalp, Wandelalp, and Seilalp. Follow a gravel road for a few minutes, then turn left (northwest), again signposted for the same points. You'll ascend to meadows, with lovely views of the Engelhörner and the Rosenlaui Glacier. Signposts will direct you again to Kaltenbrunnen, Wandelalp, and Oberstafel. Follow the blazed trail, cross over a stile, and then ascend through meadows; the way is blazed. You'll pass a large rock with the names of various destinations painted on it. The way ascends through a few pine

Traditional Emmental barn at Ballenberg open air museum

trees, then emerges onto the Hochmoor, a distinctive terrain covered with low junipers, heather, and grass, and boggy in places. Follow along the side of the slope to Gyensprung, heading north to a little hill and to an alp at Krauternlager. Descend on a gravel road, and follow signposts back to Rosenlaui. Ask Andreas Kehrli about other hikes.

26 • GRAND HOTEL GIESSBACH • 675 M

There is something improbable about this hotel, an isolated, grand confection on a forested slope overlooking the beautiful lake of Brienz. We had heard of it from time to time over the years and finally decided to investigate. Including it in a guide to mountain inns may seem like something of a stretch, but it is in its way a Berghotel, a hotel in the mountains, and reminds us that the golden age of mountain hotels included a breadth of different types, from utmost simplicity to luxury. In a general sense, Grand Hotel Giessbach looks a little as if Mad King Ludwig of Bavaria (the castle-building fanatic) had decided to create a hotel in the Swiss Alps.

The hotel began because of the Giessbach Falls, a spectacular series of waterfalls that plunge in several steps, about 150 meters in all, into the Brienzersee. The falls were "discovered" by 18th- and 19th-century Swiss painters. Tourists followed in their tracks, a path was cut alongside the falls, and a small Gasthaus opened to provide refreshments. By the later 19th century, this humble inn had been transformed into a luxurious "palace hotel," with turrets, terraces, and balconies. In 1879 a funicular, said to be the first in Europe, was constructed to bring up the visitors, among them industrialists, financiers, and aristocrats, including British royals and members of the czar's family. Here they could variously starve or stuff themselves. The hotel offered various "cures"—a water cure, a whey cure, and thermal and "electrical baths" (whatever they were)—as well as elaborate meals with every culinary delicacy. The falls were (and still are) illuminated at night, and the path alongside them was extended to include bridges over the falls and a gallery behind one of them, where you stand sandwiched between the cliff and the tremendous jet of water.

The hotel fell into decline during the Depression and the two World Wars and changed hands several times. The previous owner tried to make the hotel look modern, then decided to tear the building down but was blocked by a Swiss government commission for the protection of landscapes and monuments, as a hotel in such a setting—on a forested slope beside a great waterfall, overlooking one of Switzerland's finest lakes—

was deemed unique and the building itself of historic importance. To the rescue came a certain Franz Weber, a prominent financier whose organization, Helvetia Nostra, campaigns on environmental issues. He started a foundation to save the hotel, raising private and public money, but there is no doubt that Herr Weber is the decisive force behind the hotel today. Elaborate restoration was effected, removing false ceilings and stripping off inauthentic trim and colors. Today the decoration is once again authentic, and everything is fresh and bright. The plaster angels and cameo heads, previously covered over, smile down from the ceilings, amid wreaths of plaster vines and flowers. The fin-de-siècle grand salon is furnished with marble-topped tables and plush chairs. But the black coats and velvet gowns of the 19th century have been replaced by sport shirts, slacks, and cotton dresses.

The hotel has one restaurant for those on the pension plan and another for those who wish to order à la carte, and a terrace where you can dine beside the falls. The menu contains many elaborate and expensive dishes as well as others within the normal price range of most Swiss country inns and, as Herr Weber is a great campaigner against brutal treatment of animals, a large selection of reasonably priced vegetarian dishes. There are 70 private rooms, all with bath, and no dormitories. A room facing the falls or the lake costs more than a room facing the forest.

The hotel opens the last weekend of April and closes the last weekend of October. Tel. 033/951 35 35; Fax: 951 37 07; 3855 Brienz.

Getting there: Of the several ways to reach Giessbach, the most delightful is via one of the steamers that ply the Brienzersee; you can board a boat at Interlaken, Brienz, or one of the intermediate stops, and get off at Giessbach. Ride up to the hotel on the little funicular (4 Sfr) beside the dock, or take the trail (signposted) and walk up in 15 minutes. From the rail station in Brienz, a van will drive guests to the Grand Hotel Giessbach for 7 Sfr. You can also take a PTT bus from Brienz that stops just above the hotel on its way to Axalp, or you can walk from Brienz, following the road along the lake, to reach Giessbach in about 1¼ hours.

Walks: From Giessbach, there are walks in several directions.

WALK 1 • From the hotel you can walk up the path alongside the falls, reaching the top in just over an hour; about 315 meters up. Farther up this slope is Axalp, 3.5 kilometers; 860 meters up; 3 hours.

At Axalp there are a few inns that are much simpler than the Grand Hotel Giessbach, alternative stopping places for this area: **Bärghus Axalp** (inexpensive: Matratzenlager, cook your own food), 033/951 19 18; and the larger **Sporthotel Axalp** (inexpensive: double rooms and Matratzenlager, meals available), 033/951 16 71. The Axalp postal code is 3855 Axalp or Brienz. (Several buses a day run between Axalp and Brienz.) Beyond Axalp, you can follow a trail that continues to the Tierwang, between the Schwarzhorn and the Faulhorn, to cross over to the Grindelwald side; you could continue westward to the Berghaus Faulhorn (see p. 109) or southeastward to the First lift station and from there ride down to Grindelwald. Note that you can also reach Axalp by bus from Brienz.

WALK 2 • Alternatively, instead of heading up the slope from Hotel Giessbach, you can follow a trail westward above the lakeshore to the village of Iseltwald: 2.5 kilometers; 105 meters down; 1½ hours. There you can pick up the lake steamer.

Recommended visit: One of Switzerland's most delightful attractions, **Ballenberg,** is located near Brienz, and you could easily combine a visit there with a stop at Giessbach. Ballenberg is a remarkable open-air museum of Swiss rural life, with more than 80 authentic examples of traditional houses from almost every part of Switzerland. It occupies a large park with the houses sufficiently separated so that visitors feel they are really strolling through the countryside; there are fields of grain beside some houses, kitchen gardens or woodland beside others. There are sheep in the pastures, cows in the barns, and authentic furnishings in the houses. Every day there are exhibitions of traditional crafts such as weaving and carving and special events on Sundays. Visitors can watch blacksmithing, cheesemaking, and traditional ways of doing laundry. Every day you can buy bread made from homegrown wheat and baked in a traditional oven or meat smoked on the premises.

You can bring a picnic lunch or eat at one of three restaurants, all in traditional style and set in different parts of the park—this avoids the crowding and unpleasant ambience that would be produced if Ballenberg had only a single, institutional cafeteria. Ballenberg is charming, tasteful, and unpretentious; one is not met at every corner by attendants in period dress, although there are a few of these at special exhibitions. Count on spending about 5–6 hours, pick a sunny day, and wear good, comfortable shoes, as there's a lot of walking.

The park is open from mid-April to the end of October, from 10 to 5, or until 6 from July to September during fine weather. Admission is 12 Sfr per adult, 6 per child. Horse-drawn wagons can be rented by the hour or half hour. A shuttle bus connects the Brienz rail station with the park. Guided tours are possible if you phone in advance. Tel. 033/951 11 23; 3855 Brienz.

ENGSTLENALP

The Gental is a high valley near the eastern end of the chain of mountains that constitute the Bernese Oberland. In the heart of the valley is a lake, the Engstlensee, and near its shore is Engstlenalp (1835 meters), a cluster of summer farms with a Berghotel in their midst. The setting is alpine, a U-shaped valley cut between two rocky walls. Above the lake to the north is the rocky prow of the Graustock (2661 meters), and the long ridge opposite—the Wendenstocke (3042 meters)—is frosted with glaciers. To the east, above the upper end of the valley, is the snowy summit of the Titlis (3238 meters), and to the west there is an impressive view of the Wetterhorn, the edge of the great Oberland wall.

There are other places in the Swiss Alps that face higher mountains and more famous ones, but few of such gentle loveliness. The blue-green lake is pristine, utterly clear: Looking into the shallow water near the shore, you can watch the fish dart about. The deeper water reflects the Wendenstocke, broad and steep, streaked with snowfields and small glaciers. It is stunning, and we have reflected sadly that such a lake in such a setting elsewhere would probably have been "developed" and spoiled.

Engstlenalp exudes tranquility; a sort of well-being seems to be in its very air. Bring a book, lie down in the grass, listen to the birds and the wind—no one will disturb you. If your nerves are jangled, your spirits ruffled, and you are in urgent need of physical and psychical repair, consider Engstlenalp. It's the kind of place where you can feel the tension ebbing from your shoulders almost as soon as you arrive.

A road leads up to the door of the inn, but goes no farther; however, the road does not substantially disturb the ambience of the place. Traffic is very light, consisting mainly of a bus that comes up a few times a day and local people who drive up for an afternoon's fishing or a picnic. Many guests, moreover, arrive on foot.

27 • BERGHAUS ENGSTLENALP • 1835 M

An inn at Engstlenalp, as mentioned in this book's introduction, was established in the 19th century. As noted there, John Tyndall, the distinguished Victorian physicist and alpinist, called it "one of the most charming spots in the Alps" (he also singled out its charming hostess for mention) after a visit in 1866. In 1884, Robert Allbut called Engstlenalp an "oasis in the desert, with fine stone pines and magnificent views," and went on to note the "comfortable inn, at which, if time permit, travellers should rest for the night, enjoying the pleasant surroundings more at leisure." (Allbut 1884, p. 153) The 1893 *Baedeker Guide* called Engstlenalp a "beautiful pasture, with fine old pines and Alpine cedars" and recommended the inn, which charged a "reasonable" 6 Sfr for full pension.

The original inn, a small wooden building, now serves as an annex, housing Matratzenlager. Beside it is the "new" hotel, built between 1890 and 1893; after the wind blew off the roof in 1993 and snow fell into some of the rooms, the inn was partially renovated in 1994–1995. Engstlenalp was once considered a Kurhaus because of its Wunderbrunner, or "miraculous spring" (praised by Baedeker for its "excellent water; temperature 40–42 degrees Fahrenheit"). Until 1960, when the paved road was extended to Engstlenalp, guests and their luggage could arrive on mules.

If you arrive after a long hike, stretch out in the meadow, and perhaps doze off, you'll be awakened in late afternoon by an orchestra of bells and the cries of cowherds, driving the cows in for the evening milking. As the cows wear bells of various sizes, they ring in different tones: The combined effect is melodic.

Soon you'll be following the cows back, to your own dinner and night's shelter. The inn has been owned by several generations of the Immer family and is now run by Fritz Immer and his wife, Marianne Immer-Schild, who directed the renovations. There are two public rooms: a new Gaststube just off the kitchen and the lovely old dining room, with high windows to catch the light of long summer afternoons. Its coffered ceiling and large, gilt-framed mirrors faintly suggest an old-style French country hotel. But the pine walls, floor, and ceiling, not to mention the menu and the sound of cowbells through the windows, place you firmly in Switzerland. Dinner is à la carte. Marianne Immer has extended the old menu, which besides such standard fare as soup and salads, Bratwurst, Schnitzel, and Rösti now includes steaks and trout. And as at other alps sited beside a Berghotel, the farmers use the inn as a pub, gathering there companionably in the evening for a drink: beer or Kaffee-Zwetschge—coffee with plum schnapps. Hands have been washed and rubber barn boots exchanged for shoes, but otherwise they are in farm clothes, sleeves rolled up and very much at home. The Nidlete, the festival celebrating the new cream, is still held here, occurring on either the first or second Friday in August.

The renovations have been limited to an addition on one side of the building, where there is a new entrance, a new kitchen, and a small wing with six new double rooms that have private baths. The new rooms make no pretense at being old; they are in contemporary style, but handsome and

Tannalp, on the high route from Meiringen to Engstlenalp

tastefully designed. The "old-style" rooms have been preserved—Frau Immer is fully aware of their charm and means to keep them intact—with only two changes: Carpet has been laid on the pine boards, and new shared showers and toilets have been installed on each floor. Guests can therefore choose between the new and the old. It seems inevitable and indeed reasonable for some modernization to be introduced at these old hotels, as long as they retain the essential character of a mountain inn—otherwise they become museum pieces. (Those inns inaccessible by road and still beyond the reach of electricity, such as Obersteinberg, cannot, of course, install modern comforts.) The new rooms at Engstlenalp—simple, clean, and spare—do no violence to the style of this old inn. Frau Immer has managed it with great taste. And, she says, she never liked the fact that until she and Fritz took over the inn, there was only cold water for guests to wash in and that the old toilet/sink areas were open on one side to the air and quite cold at night.

The old rooms have a sweet simplicity. We stayed in a room with two carved wooden beds, a painted chest, and a clothes cupboard. Small towels were provided, as well as the customary pitchers and basins.

There are 13 Nostalgiezimmer (old-style) double rooms, 2 rooms with three to four beds, and seven singles, as well as 50 Matratzenlager places. The rates for these old-fashioned rooms are lower than for the new ones, remaining in the medium-price range. There is also a reduction for all guests who stay for several days. Berghaus Engstlenalp is open from May 1 to October 31. Tel. 033/975 11 61; Fax: 975 13 61; 3862 Innertkirchen.

Getting there: Engstlenalp can be reached by bus or car from the west, and by foot from either west or east.

The western approach to Engstlenalp begins near Meiringen, a pleasant, quiet town in the Aare Valley. The church of Meiringen, although not a grand structure like the Engelberg Kloster, has several old frescoes, and sections of an older, Romanesque church have been uncovered. Other local attractions include the Aareschlucht, or gorges of the Aare, where the river flows through a narrow chasm sunk deep between walls of vertical rock, and the Reichenbach Falls, which so impressed Sir Arthur Conan Doyle that he selected it for the site of the death struggle between Sherlock Holmes and the evil genius Professor Moriarty. The falls, no thin wisp of spray but a full volume of water, shoot over a precipice with such force that you can hear the distant roar in Meiringen across the valley. A small funicular leads to a viewing point for the upper falls. After witnessing this thunderous cascade, it is hard to believe in Holmes's survival, but his devoted fans at the time would not allow it to be otherwise.

A bus from Meiringen goes through Innertkirchen, a village a few miles southwest of Meiringen, then up the Gental to Engstlenalp. The road is private and a toll of 6 Sfr is charged for private cars.

You can also reach Engstlenalp by foot from Innertkirchen with a choice of routes. Three trails—low, middle, and high—extend up the valley from the west and join at the inn. The least interesting trail runs alongside the road, in the center of the valley. For the middle and upper routes, you can use the Hasliberg lift system to ascend the mountain behind Meiringen. This series of lifts rises through several intermediate points, Reuti and Bidmi, and then to Mägisalp, from which you can take a chair lift to Planplatten (2245 meters) at the top. If you get off at one of the lower stops, signposts direct you up to Planplatten.

For the middle route, take the Hasliberg cable car up to Reuti, where signposts will direct you past a few scattered farms at Hinderarni, Underbalm, and Baumgarten to Engstlenalp. The middle trail offers good views, but as the high route is more scenic (and the low route easier), you'll meet the fewest hikers on this loneliest, middle route.

For the scenic upper route or Höhenweg, from Planplatten to Engstlenalp: 9.5 kilometers; 10 meters up/520 meters down; 4 hours. It is, however, misleading to give ascent/descent figures because the trail rises and falls considerably along the ridge. Take the series of Hasliberg lifts to Planplatten. (If you walk up, the ascent from Meiringen is 1645 meters.) The trail is well signposted. From Planplatten, descend at first to the Planplatten Sattel, then follow the trail along the crest of a ridge, rising to the little peak of Balmeregghorn (2255 meters). Some sections are rather exposed (this route is inadvisable in snow or bad weather). The trail leads to Tannenalp (also called Tannalp), where there's a small lake and Berghaus Tannalp. From there, a path descends rather steeply to Engstlenalp.

From the east, only a single trail leads to Engstlenalp. From the Jochpass: 2 kilometers; 372 m down; 1 hour. The approach begins at the attractive little resort town of Engelberg, which has a Benedictine Abbey, or Kloster, that was founded in the 12th century but rebuilt several times after fires; the church is Baroque in style. Above the town stands the rounded, snowy head of the Titlis (3238 m); a close view of the summit is available to nonalpinists by a series of three lifts to the top of the Klein Titlis (3028 m). Hikers can use that lift system for a substantial boost to the Jochpass (2207 m), the saddle leading to the Gental. The first stage is a funicular to Gerschnialp, from which you take a gondola to Trübsee and then a Sessellift (chairlift) to the Jochpass. (Trübsee is the point of departure for the cable car to the Klein Titlis.) From the Jochpass it's all downhill to Engstlenalp on a well-marked trail, and it takes about 1 hour.

Walks: If you decide to linger for an extra day at Engstlenalp, you can walk up to Tannalp at 1976 m, which takes an hour. From there, a small road leads in another hour to Melchsee-Frutt (1902 m) and a third lake, the Melchsee, from which a lift descends to Stockalp in the Melchtal.

CHAPTER 6

THE VALAIS

The Valais (Wallis in German), in the southwest of Switzerland, is home to the country's highest and grandest mountains. Among the Valaisian Alps are the Dom (4545 meters), the highest mountain entirely within Swiss borders; and the Monte Rosa (4634 meters) and the Matterhorn (4478 meters), which are both along the Italian border. And there are many others: There are more 4000 meter mountains in the Valaisian Alps than in any other mountain chain in western Europe. Many have the classic alpine profile: sharply edged ridges and pointed summits. Some of these "horns" have such steep slopes that snow cannot adhere to the rock at the top.

The Valaisian climate is comparatively dry and sunny; when it is raining in the Bernese Oberland, it may be clear and bright in the Valais. Switzerland's excellent wines are grown in the Rhône Valley. But despite the drier climate, there are green meadows on the high slopes and abundant wildflowers.

The canton is divided between a French-speaking western and a Germanic-speaking eastern part. Tucked away in their high, remote valleys, people developed dialects of French and German that are incomprehensible or nearly so to outsiders. Therefore, in each of these two sections, people speak not only their own dialects but also standard French or, in the east, Schwyzer Dütsch and High German.

VAL DE BAGNES

The Val de Bagnes is the gateway to the Grand Combin, the first great peak on the western side of the Valaisian Alps. That mountain is not only one of the "four thousanders" (measured in meters), as the great alpine peaks are called, but also one of the most splendid to see—a complex, visually interesting mountain with several summits. It is therefore an agreeable surprise that its approach should be an undeveloped and relatively unfrequented valley.

Chemin des Planètes on the way to Hotel Weisshorn

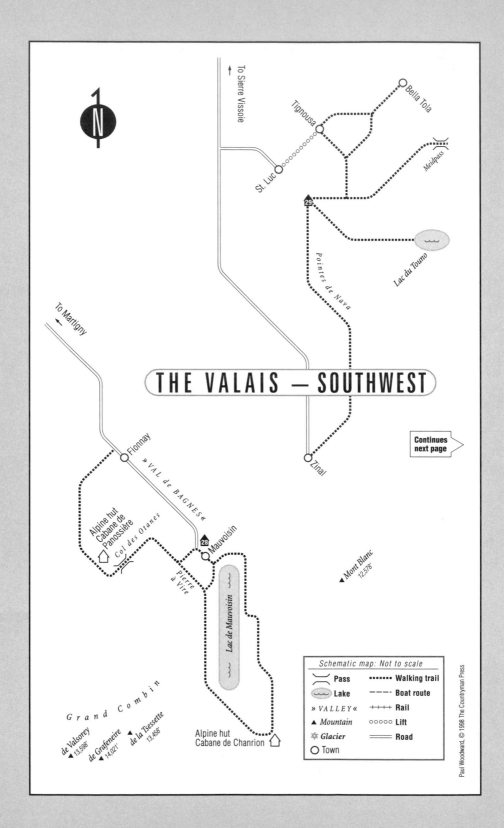

THE VALAIS — SOUTHWEST

N

To Sierre Vissoie

Bella Tola

Tignousa

Meidpass

St. Luc

29

Pointes de Nava

Lac du Tourno

To Martigny

Continues
next page

Zinal

Fionnay

» VAL de BAGNES «

Alpine hut
Cabane de
Panossière

Col des Otanes

28 Mauvoisin

Pierre
à Vire

Mont Blanc
12,578'

Lac de Mauvoisin

Grand Combin

de Valsorey
▲ 13,598'

de Grafeneire
▲ 14,021'

de la Tsessette
▲ 13,458'

Alpine hut
Cabane de Chanrion

Schematic map: Not to scale

⌣⌣	Pass	•••••	Walking trail
⬭	Lake	– – –	Boat route
» VALLEY «		++++	Rail
▲	Mountain	ooooo	Lift
❋	Glacier	━━━	Road
○	Town		

Paul Woodward, © 1998 The Countryman Press

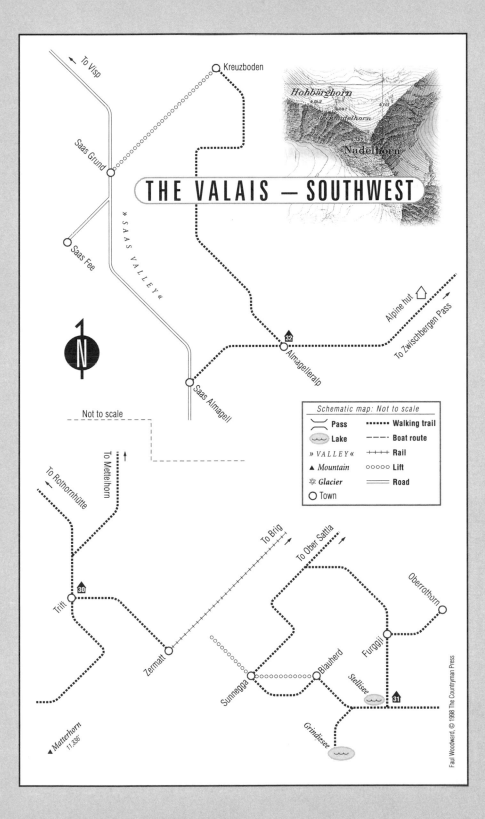

THE VALAIS — SOUTHWEST

To Visp

Kreuzboden

Saas Grund

Hohbärghorn

Nadelhorn

Saas Fee

S A A S   V A L L E Y

Alpine hut

To Zwischbergen Pass

32
Almagelleralp

N

Saas Almagell

Not to scale

To Mettelhorn

To Rothornhütte

Schematic map: Not to scale

Pass   Walking trail
Lake   Boat route
VALLEY   Rail
Mountain   Lift
Glacier   Road
Town

To Brig

To Ober Sattla

Oberrothorn

30
Trift

Zermatt

Furggji

Sunnegga

Blauherd

Stellisee

31

Grindjisee

Matterhorn
11,336'

Paul Woodward, © 1998 The Countryman Press

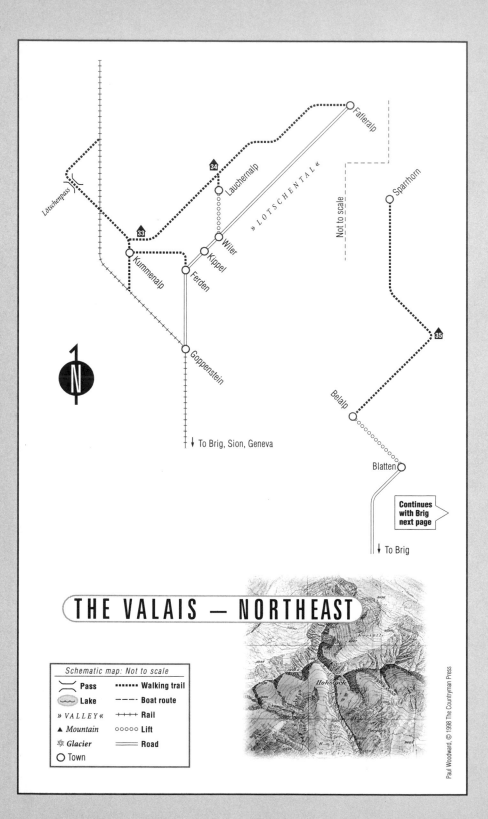

Falleralp

Sparrhorn

34

Lauchernalp

»LÖTSCHENTAL«

Not to scale

33

Wiler

Kippel

Lötschenpass

Kummenalp

Ferden

35

Goppenstein

Belalp

↓ To Brig, Sion, Geneva

Blatten

Continues with Brig next page

↓ To Brig

N

THE VALAIS — NORTHEAST

Paul Woodward, © 1998 The Countryman Press

Schematic map: Not to scale

⌣	Pass	▪▪▪▪	Walking trail
⌒	Lake	− − −	Boat route
»VALLEY«		++++	Rail
▲	Mountain	○○○○○	Lift
☼	Glacier	═══	Road
○	Town		

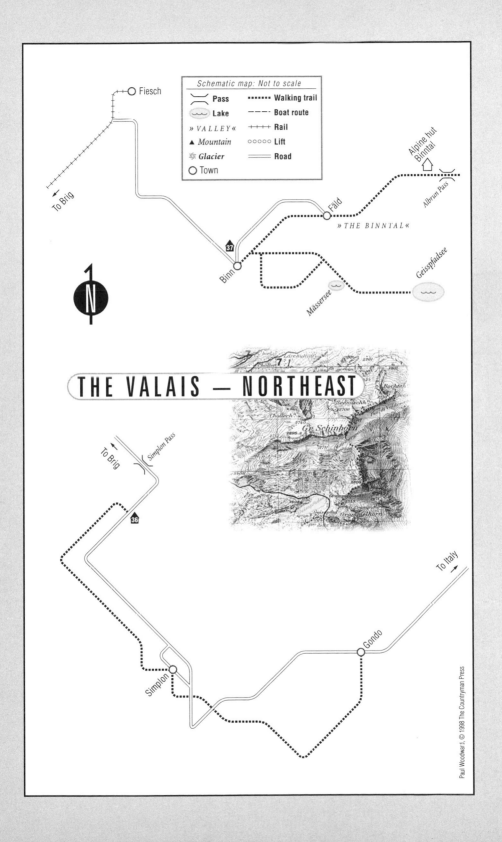

Schematic map: Not to scale

⌣ Pass	••••••• Walking trail
◯ Lake	– – – Boat route
» VALLEY «	+++++ Rail
▲ Mountain	ooooo Lift
❋ Glacier	━━━ Road
◯ Town	

Fiesch

To Brig

Alpine hut
Binntal

Albrun Pass

37

Fäld

» THE BINNTAL «

Binn

Geisspfadsee

Mässersee

THE VALAIS — NORTHEAST

To Brig

Simplon Pass

36

To Italy

Gondo

Simplon

Paul Woodward, © 1998 The Countryman Press

The Val de Bagnes runs almost parallel to the Val d'Entremont, its immediate neighbor to the west, which leads to the Grand St. Bernard Pass. Unlike that valley, which is on a major road connection to Italy, the Val de Bagnes gets few visitors and very little traffic. The upper Val de Bagnes has been a federally protected nature preserve since 1906. Its slopes are glorious with wildflowers, growing in profusion and immense variety, and include some rare species.

Getting there: Martigny is the starting point for the westernmost Valaisian valleys, a pleasant little town with something of a French air to its central square, lined with trees and cafés. It's so close to the French border that it can be used to approach the Tour de Mont Blanc, the popular hiking route that circles the great mountain. From Martigny you can take a little cog railway to Vallorcine in France, and from there a train to Chamonix; you can start the tour from either place. Martigny is the home of a notable museum, the Fondation Pierre Gianadda, which mounts exhibitions of major artists every year and often succeeds in obtaining the loan of paintings from private collections that one would never otherwise see. It also displays a permanent collection of Gallo-Roman objects.

On a shelf above Le Châble, at the entrance to the Val de Bagnes, is Verbier, one of Switzerland's most chic ski resorts. But the rest of the valley bears no resemblance to Verbier, in which scarcely an old building can be seen. The valley's few villages are very small, modest, and old-fashioned, with traditional Valaisian wood chalets. As for Mauvoisin, it consists of nothing but the hotel and a great dam above. If you plan to stay for several days, the hotel will provide you with bread for your picnic lunches, but you can bring in your own picnic and snack supplies. The last village in the valley, Fionnay, has a small food market and a simple, modern, very adequate hotel, the Hôtel du Grand Combin. But the really interesting establishment is the inn at Mauvoisin (it's listed in the telephone directory under Fionnay).

People come up to Mauvoisin for the hikes and the marvelous scenery or sometimes just to view the dam and climb up to its top (250 meters high). Before its construction in the 1950s, the valley was subject to numerous floods; in June 1818, "la Grande Débâcle" occurred when an ice dam from the Gietroz Glacier broke, sending tons of water and debris down the valley and killing 40 people.

The valley's most interesting native son was a peasant, Jean-Pierre Perraudin, a man of keen observation. Perraudin figured out the principal elements of the theory of glaciers ahead of the work of scientists by 15 or 20 years. A Swiss savant who passed through the Val de Bagnes in 1815 noted that he had met in a cottage a local peasant who expounded his opinion—based on long observation and thought about his native landscape—that it was glaciers that had transported the huge blocks and other debris strewn about the valley, because these boulders were too big to have been carried there by the river. This learned visitor recorded Perraudin's hypothesis (which scientists now accept), rejecting it as extravagant and impossible. A Swiss clergyman met the same peasant in 1818 and reported another of Perraudin's theories: that the glaciers had formerly extended far beyond their present positions. Perraudin deduced this because the striations on rocks always run in the direction of the valleys, which made him think they were caused by the passage of glaciers that had later retreated.

The Grand Combin was the lure that first brought a few visitors to this very poor valley. It was first climbed in 1857; a second ascent of one of its peaks was made in 1857 by William Matthews, who several months later founded the British Alpine Club. Not only were the local people poor, but mountaineers in those days could count on only very simple accommodations and few comforts. Matthews described his delight when his guide, Auguste Simond, produced "before our charmed eyes" iron spoons with which to eat their dinner, which consisted of bowls of boiled milk. (They had borrowed a copper cauldron from a shepherd and brought two buckets of milk, which they carried, suspended, from their metal staffs.) Simond reminded Matthews that on their previous outing they had not been able to find any spoons, so he had decided this time to be better provisioned.

The Grand Combin became notable. In 1865, eight days after making the first ascent of the Matterhorn, Edward Whymper climbed La Ruinette, one of the Grand Combin's peaks. An inn was established at Fionnay in 1862, and another at Mauvoisin about a year later by a local man who had obtained from the commune of the valley the concession for a hotel and enough pastureland to keep one or two cows and several sheep. The Hôtel du Glacier de Gietroz Mont-Voisin was built in 1862–1863, but later changed its name to Hôtel de Mauvoisin. It was renovated in 1946 and slightly enlarged in 1952. The hotel has remained within the family for four generations; it is owned and run today by Christophe Florey-Perraudin, a descendant of the hotel's original builder.

28 • HÔTEL DE MAUVOISIN • 1850 M

It is the intention of Christophe, as everyone calls him, to retain the character, ambience, and friendliness of a simple mountain inn while introducing a few modern conveniences. Christophe, who speaks very good English, is very much on the scene, greeting guests and eating meals in the same room where guests are served. He is the ideal host and the whole place is stamped by his friendly, cheerful nature: He has the *esprit* of the Suisse Romande, a Gallic gaiety and lightness. Despite an almost fatal road accident in Algeria that deprived him of an arm, he carries guests' luggage and helps in various other ways: When we missed the bus after one hike down the valley, he drove his specially equipped car to Fionnay to pick us up.

The hotel, three stories high, has a little terrace on which day visitors sit for lunch or drinks. There is a cozy, old-fashioned parlor with wing-backed chairs, an old piano, pictures, books, and games, and only one 20th-century intrusion, apart from the electricity: a television set. Dinner is usually served in the little café—what the Swiss-Germans call a Stübli—a pine-paneled room with wooden tables and benches, because it is cozier and more intimate than the very spacious dining room. This larger room is more formal, but in the relaxed style of a French country hotel, and somewhat old-fashioned: The walls are adorned with paintings and an antlered deer's head, and there are white cloths on the tables. Breakfast (a buffet with orange juice, cornflakes, whole loaves of bread, and bowls of jam) is served in the dining room.

One rainy, misty morning we sat in the café along with a group of men on their way to the Cabane de Chanrion, an alpine club hut farther up the valley. One of the men was the hutkeeper, and they were waiting for the weather to break (which it did after lunch). A glass or two of wine and the group, convivial to start with, took up songs of the hunt and the mountains; one, possessed of a beautiful tenor, sang solo verses.

There are eight private rooms, each with a little sink with hot water, soap, and small towels, and big down comforters on the beds. A bathtub and shower room are available in the hall for all guests for no extra charge. The *dortoir,* or dormitory, is in a separate building, with 36 places. There are also showers available for dorm guests, free of charge.

The kitchen here is quite special for an *auberge de montagne* or Berghaus; meals are delicious and interesting. One evening meal is prepared for all dinner guests, although you may order à la carte. On one evening, after soup, we were given thinly sliced turkey in curry sauce, rice, salad, and apricot tart. On another, when we requested a non–red meat alternative to sauté de boeuf, we were served chicken stuffed with sautéed leeks and a variety of vegetables including tomatoes stuffed with herbs and bread crumbs, followed by fresh berries with crème Chantilly. On still another evening, we had broiled chicken legs and spaghetti in a tangy brown sauce enlivened with bits of lemon. There's an outdoor grill on the terrace, and the à la carte menu includes several *grillades* of chicken, pork, or steak; one of the specialties of the house is *croûte aux champignons forêts* (mushrooms in puff pastry).

Hôtel de Mauvoisin is open from June 15 to the end of September. Tel. 027 778 11 30; Fax 027 738 11 30; 1931 Mauvoisin.

Note: Some of the walks in the upper valley may be taken from Fionnay, a pretty, unspoiled village, where you can get accommodations at the **Hôtel du Grand Combin,** a simple and modern hotel that was built to house some of the workers when the Mauvoisin dam was being built. Its 20 private rooms have private showers, and there are also dormitory places with showers available.

Getting there: To reach Mauvoisin, take a train from Martigny to Le Châble and change there for the PTT bus that goes to the hotel at the end of the road.

Walks: Several spectacular walks may be taken from Mauvoisin or in its vicinity, and it is worth spending a few days here. The easiest and the most difficult hikes have a common beginning, then diverge.

WALK 1 • Tour de Pierre à Vire: 5 kilometers; 680 meters up and back down; 4½ hours.

This is a lovely, wild, high walk—a sort of Höhenweg. Walk upward on the road across from the hotel; a yellow sign to your left is a notice for the Cabane de Panossière. A few steps beyond that, a red blaze mark on a rock will indicate the trail, which is to the right. The first 50 meters are very steep: This is the worst part of the entire trail and will take about 15 minutes. One hour 15 minutes after starting, come to a signed junction at Pâzagnou (there is nothing else here but a signpost), and turn left in the direction of Les Rosses; PIERRE À VIRE is also painted in red letters on a low rock. The trail climbs gradually and is narrow but good. After about 2 hours of climbing, it levels off. You'll have beautiful views of the Glacier de Gietroz across the valley and of the lake below, as well as up and down the valley in both directions. In another 45 minutes, after crossing a brook (no bridge, but the crossing is easy), at a junction where the signs have fallen and may still be lying on the trail, turn left and begin the descent for La Lia and Mauvoisin. Soon you'll reach the road below; this is La Lia. To return to Mauvoisin you must turn left, but consider first turning right, where in a few minutes you'll see an old *écurie,* or stable, of dry stone with a pitched roof; this will give you an idea of the sort of farm buildings that once existed here.

Approaching Mauvoisin from this side, you must walk through a rather long tunnel, lit by fluorescent lights; the ceiling may be dripping. At one point there's a view of the astonishingly powerful spout of water that shoots into the lake. You'll emerge near the dam wall, then follow the trail that descends to Mauvoisin.

Note: You can walk up by this descent route and return the same way. Do not, however, descend by the ascent route described above; the first section is too steep.

WALK 2 • Cabane de Chanrion: 16 kilometers; 730 meters up and down; 5½ hours.

This alpine club hut is at 2462 meters but the high point of the approach is 2572 meters. The hut is quite close to the Italian border, and in 1943 the hutkeeper received Signor Luigi Einaudi, future president of the Republic of Italy, who was then fleeing from the Germans. The route described here follows the *rive droite* (or right bank) and returns along the *rive gauche* (left bank); you can reverse this, or walk out and back along the same bank. From the hotel, walk up to the dam and turn left, crossing along the dam wall, and then go through a series of tunnels, which have enough light through windows so you can see your way; this may take 30 minutes. Emerging from the tunnels, follow the trail, which gently switchbacks through meadows to a shelf above. After this climb, the trail descends slightly to two small blue tarns (one is the Lac de Tsofeiret); the views are very fine. Descend a steep stretch on scree and a little rock, with some fixed chains to hold onto—there's an exposed section—this takes about 20 minutes. Then the trail becomes more gradual, with a few sections of boulders, and crosses a turbulent stream on a good bridge. It leads over a stony moraine and intersects a jeep road, then descends a grassy slope to the cabane. The hut is in a bowl of folded green meadows, facing rugged mountains of dark rock streaked with glaciers.

To return by the *rive gauche,* head down steeply at first. You'll intersect the jeep road and then walk along the left shore of the lake. Toward the end you'll pass through the long tunnel described for Walk 1, electrically lit and rather drippy in spots, then emerge near the dam wall.

WALK 3 • Cabane de Panossière: 10 kilometers; 1100 meters up/1370 meters down; 9 hours.

The hut is at 2670 meters but the high point for this route is 2880 meters. From Mauvoisin, it should take about 4 hours to reach the hut. You can reach this hut from either Mauvoisin or Fionnay, or make a loop

Approaching the Cabane de Panossière

trip, as described here. If you take this walk from Mauvoisin, you must cross the Col des Otanes, a very challenging, rather difficult route—it's an easier walk from Fionnay, but also quite long: Leave as early as possible. It leads to a scene, however, that is one of the finest in the Swiss Alps.

If you start from Mauvoisin, begin as for the walk to Pierre à Vire. However, turn right instead of left when you reach the signposted junction at Pâzagnou. The trail traverses a slope, contouring above the Val de Bagnes, rising and falling a little and crossing some streams—all but one are unbridged, but there are good rocks on which to place your feet. At a couple of junctions follow the signs, which will all point left for Panossière; there will also be rocks blazed CAS (for Club Alpin Suisse), or sometimes just P.

The ascent gets steeper, and there is one short, rough section on scree (about 10 minutes) as you climb into a high, upper valley. This side of the Col des Otanes faces toward the north and you're likely to find snow in it, even in August. Sections of boulders will be visible even if there is snow on the approach to the pass; look for the blazes on the rocks. These will eventually lead you to the right side of this upper valley. Follow the blazes on a long, steep section of tumbled boulders; a couple of cairns also serve as markers. You may have to use your hands to steady yourself as you scramble over the boulders—this is really a route, not a path. There is a sort of false col: You'll think you've reached the top of the ridge only to discover that there's a little more to go. Leaving the boulders behind, follow a trace of path on some reddish earth, and then cross over another section of boulders with blaze marks. Finally you'll reach the col and a signpost. The view is one of the most spectacular in the Alps: the monumental sweep of the Glacier de Corbassière, like a vast river of ice, and to your left, the majestic form of the Grand Combin, dominating the scene. Unlike some of the grand viewpoints in the Alps, such as the Gornergrat, which can be reached by cog railway, or the meadows behind the Fluhalp Hotel, which can nearly be reached by lift (both above Zermatt), people must get up here entirely on their own exertion, and very few come. The scene is unspoiled and wild, which still further enhances its splendor.

A dirt path switchbacks down to the hut, occasionally crossing a small section of rock slide. To your left you'll see the remains of the old hut, which was destroyed by an avalanche; the new hut, to your right, is a substantial stone structure, built farther out on the moraine in a less exposed position. From the pass, it will take about 30 minutes or more to get down to the hut. To continue to Fionnay, walk on past the hut down the long Corbassière Valley. As you descend, you'll see the snout of the glacier on your left. The trail keeps to the right side of the valley, descending to a green bowl, crossing some shallow streams, then ascending again to a higher section of moraine before resuming the descent. Toward the end there's a steep descent through woods, then you'll cross a meadow to reach Fionnay, about 2½ hours past the hut. If you wish to return to Mauvoisin by bus, check the current schedule (posted at Mauvoisin) before you leave; the last bus leaves Fionnay for Mauvoisin at approximately 4:50 PM, but the schedule may change.

If instead you take this hike from Fionnay (1490 meters), from which the approach to the cabane is easier, look for the signpost at the bridge in Fionnay, beside the road and the bus stop. Cross the bridge, look for CHEMIN PÉDESTRE (footpath) signs and a white/red/white blaze, and cross the meadow behind the village on a visible track. At the end of the meadow, follow the trail up steeply through woods; as you emerge above tree line, the grade becomes less steep and the high upper valley opens before you. The trail threads along the left side of the valley, bringing you up to the hut. The ascent to the hut is 1180 meters and will take about 4 hours; the Col des Otanes is another 210 meters steeply up.

VAL D'ANNIVIERS

ST. LUC

At the upper end of the Val d'Anniviers, high above the Rhône Valley, is a very pleasing village, St. Luc—small, quiet, and attractive. The road goes no farther. Above the village there is good summer rambling and winter ski touring.

29 • HOTEL-RESTAURANT DU WEISSHORN • 2337 M

Some Berghotels are tucked away in a grove of trees or into a fold in a mountain slope or blend into their surroundings because of their gray stone or weathered wooden walls. But the Hotel Weisshorn is unmistakable and visible from afar. You can see it while hiking almost anywhere in its valley and even from St. Luc, the village below. A big white building, it stands foursquare and tall on a promontory high above tree line, seemingly in the middle of nowhere, and with nothing to block its presence.

The hotel was built in 1882, which was quite an undertaking as the road was not extended to St. Luc until 1930. Because of its clientele, it was then called *l'hôtel des anglais*. By the mid-1960s it was more or less abandoned, when the Swiss army proposed to buy it for shooting practice. Rather than see this happen, a group of six friends with an attachment to St. Luc bought it in 1969, built a jeep road for access, and began repairs. In the winter of 1990 a violent windstorm tore off the roof, which was then rebuilt with a copper cover and more solid carpentry. Hydroelectric power was also installed, which permitted running water even in winter, as well as toilets and showers on each floor.

Even in the 1980s the hotel was still markedly run-down, but now it's a different story. All the rooms have been redecorated and furnished with new beds of Arolla pine; they look nice and, just as important, smell fresh and clean. The corridors, decorated long ago with murals and trompe l'oeil patterns resembling rusticated stone, are being renovated bit by bit.

The old Salon (so labeled), a step into the Victorian era, has been preserved, furnished with green velvet sofas and armchairs and patterned carpets on the old floor of wide pine boards. When the hotel was first opened, it took six men two days to carry up the piano, which was requisite for an elegant evening in a 19th-century parlor. And for their baths, the guests used a device then known as an English douche, a tall cylinder with a shower head and faucet, built atop a stove and standing above a small tin tub; one of these antiques is now displayed in the salon. Another room, separate from the salon, was the fumoir, where the gentlemen—who had to wear jackets and ties—smoked after dinner. (It is no longer maintained.)

Bedroom in the Hotel Weisshorn

The old dining room is now used mostly for serving light meals and after-dinner coffee or wine; dinner and breakfast are served in a new glassed-in terrace with windows that look out over the Rhône Valley as far as Les Diablerets and the Plaine Morte and the edge of the Bernese Oberland. From behind the hotel there are distant views of the Weisshorn and Dent Blanche.

Provisions are brought up by jeep in summer and by snow-cat in winter, which also brings skiers back from the slopes (there are several teleskis in the direction of Tignousa). Every year, on the second Sunday in August, the Sierre-to-Zinal footrace is run on the trail passing the hotel, which may then be full. The 30 kilometer course has 2000 meters of ascent: Some hero with iron legs and lungs to match has run it in 2 hours, 40 minutes.

The hotel is open from mid-June through mid-October and again from Christmas to Easter for cross-country and downhill skiing. There are 22 private rooms and 20 dormitory places. Tel. 027/475 11 06; 3961 St. Luc.

Getting there: 3 kilometers; 180 meters up; 1½ hours from the upper Tignousa funicular station. The approach to Hotel Weisshorn is from St. Luc. From the town of Sierre in the Rhône Valley, take the PTT bus to Vissoie and change there for the bus to St. Luc. The bus ride is dramatic, as the road was carved high into a steep slope that seems perpendicular to the valley floor.

From St. Luc (1650 meters) you can hike up to the Hotel Weisshorn, or you can ride up to Tignousa (2200 meters) on a funicular and then hike to the hotel on a trail that's nearly on the level. For the funicular, follow St. Luc's upper street, the Route du funiculaire (there are signs), which is just past the east or higher end of the village. If you prefer to walk, the trail starts at the northeast end of the village and is signposted for Chalet Blanc (a farmhouse) at 2179 meters.

The approach to Hotel Weisshorn is something of an astronomical experience. The new François-Xavier Bagnoud astronomical observatory is just above the upper Tignousa funicular station. It houses several telescopes and may be visited. And a *chemin des planètes* (planetary walk) is laid out along the 6 kilometer trail between Tignousa and the Hotel Weisshorn: A sculpted sun and planets, representing the solar system, are set out in the same proportional scale and size as they are found in the heavens, with 1 meter on the walk standing for 1 million kilometers in space and 1 centimeter of the sculptures' diameter equaling 1000 kilometers. The installation was made in 1989.

From Tignousa, the trail curves in a broad semicircle to Hotel Weisshorn, designated as H.W. by several blazes on rocks. Near a white farmhouse, the Chalet Blanc, the path that ascends from St. Luc joins this quite level traverse. Only the last section of the approach to the hotel is uphill. From Tignousa it will take about 1½ hours; hiking up from St. Luc will add another hour to that.

Walks: Several walks in various directions can be taken from the Hotel Weisshorn.

WALK 1 • Bella Tola: 12 kilometers; 1050 meters up and down; 5½ hours.
   This small peak (3025 meters) offers a panoramic view from its summit, and the Victorians loved to climb it before dawn and see the sunrise from the top. From the hotel, walk back toward Tignousa but turn right at the signposted junction at Chalet Blanc; the trail will lead northeast to the peak, climbing through meadows and growing steeper. (Blazes may read B.T.) It leads you up to a ridge connecting the Rothorn and the Bella Tola. The Rothorn is the peak to your left, but stay on the path to your right (southeast) for the Bella Tola. The trail traverses this ridge and is very exposed; this route is inadvisable in fog or snow. Several rough trails switchback up the rocky cone that leads to the summit; the one to the left is generally better.

WALK 2 • Meidpass (2790 meters): 8 kilometers; 700 meters up and down; 5 hours.
   This pass connects the Val d'Anniviers with the Turtmanntal and is the line dividing the French-speaking Valais from the Swiss-German part of the same canton (called Wallis in Swiss-German). Walk back toward Chalet Blanc but turn right off this main trail and follow signposts for the Meidpass or blazes for M.P. The trail climbs generally eastward on broad switchbacks; only the final section is steep.

WALK 3 • Pointes de Nava: 9 kilometers; 450 meters up; 5–6 hours.
   The landscape east of Hotel Weisshorn is open and wild. Several itineraries in this direction require considerable trailblazing, but in clear weather you can see for a great distance, and experienced walkers should be able to make their way. Behind the hotel to the south is a long rocky ridge, the Pointes de Nava. The Tour des Pointes de Nava loops around this ridge. You will be wandering off trail across open country (the Pointes de Nava Ridge is a landmark), so this should not be done in misty weather. This is a full

day's hike. You could start by walking south, with the ridge to your left, toward Zinal (see Walk 6 below). At Alpe Nava a sign points you left to Pas de la Forcletta; this curves around the edge of the ridge with the Pas (or Col) de la Forcletta on your right (east), and you will return by bearing northward on the other (eastern) side of the Nava ridge. This is a full day's hike, 5 or 6 hours.

WALK 4 • Lac du Touno: 8 kilometers round-trip; 350 meters up and down; 3 hours.

A small mountain tarn, this lies just south of Le Touno, the mountain you can see behind the hotel, directly east. A track starts out from the hotel, southward, along the east side of the Pointes de Nava, then diverges to the left past Vijivi to reach the lake in 1½–2 hours—it takes nearly the same time to return. (For this walk and Walk 5, you will wander across open meadows, so they should not be done in misty weather.)

WALK 5 • Lac d'Armina and Lac de Combavert: 6 kilometers round-trip; 300 meters up and down; 2½ hours.

These two lakes lie on either side of the trail up to the Meidpass (see Walk 2 above), Armina just north of the trail and Combavert just south of it.

WALK 6 • Zinal: 16 kilometers; 900 meters up and down; 6 hours one way—return by bus to St. Luc.

One of the giant peaks above Zermatt is the Zinalrothorn, named for this village, now a ski resort. A signpost behind Hotel Weisshorn points you south toward Zinal. On your way to Zinal you'll see a number of other snowcapped peaks, including the Grand Cornier and Besso, that separate the Val d'Anniviers from the Zermatt Valley. The country is nearly empty; you'll pass only a farm or two. At Alpe Lirec there's a steep descent to Zinal; from Hotel Weisshorn, it's about 3½ hours. (*Note:* The view from Zinal is blocked by low ridges, and you have to continue walking south of the village to see the high mountains.)

TRIFT VALLEY

Zermatt's name for more than a century has been linked to the Matterhorn—not only one of the highest of Swiss mountains and arguably the handsomest, but also a legendary one. The drama and tragedy of its first ascent has been told many times. It made young Edward Whymper as famous in his day as Sir Edmund Hillary became in ours, and it still lures people from all over the world, some of whom have no plans to climb any other mountain, to try their skill or luck on its rock, ice, and snow.

The Matterhorn, however, is not the only great peak nor even the highest mountain above Zermatt: More 4000 meter mountains—17 of them—surround the Zermatt Valley than can be seen or climbed from any other point in the Alps. Among these, the Weisshorn, Dom, Täschhorn, Lyskamm, and Monte Rosa are all higher than the Matterhorn.

Some of those who flock to Zermatt come for only a day or two, or even less, to ride the cog railway up to the Gornergrat and perhaps take a cable car to some other viewpoint. But leave behind the cog railway or cable car stations and you'll be in the company only of hikers. The Trift Valley, a high tributary valley above Zermatt, has no lift of any sort and can be reached only on your own two feet. It is the starting point for several spectacularly scenic walks.

30 • HÔTEL DU TRIFT • 2337 M

Hôtel du Trift is a Berghaus that has, as it were, come back from the dead. For many years, hikers and climbers on their way to higher points passed the abandoned, derelict old hotel with barely a glance: There was nothing to glance at. The plaster walls were cracked, peeling, and faded, and the inside was a wreck. But pass the hotel today and you'll see people sitting at tables outside on the grass, refreshing themselves with cold drinks or wolfing down plates piled with food, while a couple of waitresses fly in and out of the kitchen. The exterior walls have been repaired, newly plastered, and painted (restored to their original soft pink), and new green shutters have been attached to all the windows. Inside everything is spick-and-span.

The original Trift Hotel was built in 1886 or thereabouts but was destroyed after only one year by an avalanche. The present hotel was constructed between 1898 and 1900 and business was good. Nearly half a century later, in 1948, the SAC Rothornhütte was built much higher up the valley and could place climbers near the base of the great mountains that crown the Trift Valley. After the alpine club hut was built, business fell off at the Hôtel du Trift, and eventually it was closed.

A young idealist, a former student and child of the 1960s, came up to Trift in the late 1970s with dreams of reopening the hotel. He and his friends camped inside, made some repairs, hauled provisions up on their backs, and began to start the enterprise again—but they belonged to the youth and drug culture, and soon things were adrift. Eventually the people who own the property closed them out. Then a young Zermatt native, Fabienne Aufdenblatten, entered the scene: Her great-grandfather had built the hotel. She wanted to restore the place because of family ties and because she loved it. Her energetic young husband, Hugo Biner, a ski teacher and mountain guide (occupations he still practices in winter), threw himself into the work, and they took over in 1994.

Matterhorn from Höhbalm

Hugo repaired the outside walls: He sanded the facade, replastered and painted the walls, and hung new shutters on all the windows. He renovated the dining room (having restored the handsome old wooden floor dating from 1898), cleaned up the private rooms, whitewashed the walls, laid linoleum on the floors, and put in new bedding. Understandably, given its history, you will not find antique bedsteads and washstands here, but the rooms are clean, bright, and simple—indeed, rather spare, but that accords well with the Berghaus ethos. There are indoor washrooms with cold-water sinks and toilets. (Towels are not provided.) Hugo is working on still further improvements. They use diesel fuel and solar panels for power;

there is now electric light in the dining room and in the sleeping rooms until 11 PM. Provisions are brought by helicopter.

Hugo and Fabienne cook the meals as well, with the help of a very small staff (who also help look after the couple's young children). Their specialty is ice tea, a mixture of different kinds of tea with lemon and orange juice and sugar.

One four-course menu is served to all guests in the evening and Hugo, as if he does not have enough to do, is studying cookbooks as well. On a recent evening, with the hotel full (with a large party of Dutch hikers), he served soup, salad, spaghetti bolognese, and vanilla pudding. Besides all that, he makes sure to greet all new guests personally, to know their names, and to make sure that all are comfortable and well fed. Not only has the hotel been structurally restored and repaired in its appearance, but Hugo and Fabienne have also rekindled here the spirit of the true Berghotel, where the personality of the owners stamps the inn with a distinctive character.

When we stayed overnight, many guests rose early to watch dawn touch the mountain snows with a rosy flush. Then we stepped inside for a breakfast buffet with Muesli and cheese along with the traditional bread, butter, and jam.

The restoration of the Hôtel du Trift has proved a boon to hikers, for reasons beyond the fact that you can get a cold drink there after a long hot climb. The hikes in the Upper Trift Valley are among the most spectacular in the Zermatt area but also long and tiring, and they are not really served by the Rothornhütte. It is now possible again to break these hikes up with a night at the Trift Hotel.

There are, so far, five private (double) rooms and 32 Matratzenlager places; rather than huge dorm rooms, as in some inns, there are several smaller dormitories, each holding six or eight maximum. Hôtel du Trift is open from July 1 to the end of September. Tel. 077/28 18 14 or Natel 027/967 68 59.

Getting there: 2.3 kilometers; 740 meters up; 2¼ hours. To reach the hotel, start on the main street of Zermatt. From the train station, walk toward the Matterhorn, past the Hotel Mont Cervin: The next paved through-street on your right leads to Trift. Look for a trail sign placed high above this corner. Walk up the lane past the Hotel Romantika; you'll soon pass the last house and find yourself on a dirt path that rises to the Triftbach, which you cross on a bridge. The river is used for a major hydroelectric project, and signs warn that wading in this torrent is very dangerous, because water levels can fluctuate suddenly.

Beyond the bridge the path switchbacks steeply. About 1 hour after leaving Zermatt you'll reach little Café Edelweiss on a small shelf overlooking the town. Beyond this the trail levels out briefly, then climbs steeply again. You'll cross the Triftbach on another bridge. There is no shade in this steep gorge and it's a warm climb on a sunny day. You'll reach the Trift Hotel 1¼ hours beyond Café Edelweiss.

Walks: Although these walks can be done in one day, you can also break them up by staying overnight at the Hôtel du Trift.

WALK 1 • Höhbalm: 16 kilometers; 500 meters up/1250 meters down; 6 hours.

This is one of the grandest hikes in the Alps. Starting at Hôtel du Trift, cross to the left just beyond the hotel (there's a signpost) and follow the trail across the meadow to the slope opposite the hotel. The trail traverses up this slope; when you reach the shoulder at 2610 meters, nearly all your climbing is done. The trail swings around the shoulder and a spectacular view opens: In the course of this hike you'll see nearly all the 4000 meters peaks above the Zermatt Valley. The trail, always distinct, leads southwest and then west to make a long traverse (up to 2 hours) on the slope of the Gabelhorn massif: Directly opposite, to your left, is the magnificent north face of the Matterhorn. You'll cross some boulder slides and a few sections of trail are exposed. Then the trail descends through meadows to join another trail below. Turn left for Zermatt (or right for the SAC Schönbiel-hütte). It takes another 2 to 3 hours to reach Zermatt.

WALK 2 • Mettelhorn: 10 kilometers; 1100 meters up and down; 5 hours up/3½ hours down.

This small, 3406 meter peak with a panoramic view can be climbed by hikers and is also used as a training climb for the Matterhorn (for endurance, not technical climbing skills—no rock climbing is required). It offers splendid, close views of the Zinalrothorn and Weisshorn and their glaciers and much more. Note that the views are also superb from the high meadows partway up to the peak, and we have often hiked up to there and no farther just for the magnificent scenery. Although often done in one day, this is a long, tiring climb, greatly eased by spending a night at Trift. Just below the peak is a small glacier, usually snow-covered. This is one of the very few glaciers considered safe for unroped parties, but there may be crevasses: Check at the Guides' Office on the main street of Zermatt (or ask Hugo Biner at the Trift Hotel) before you take this trip to inquire about conditions. You can rent an ice ax in Zermatt for this route and should also consider renting crampons. If you climb in the early morning, the snow may still be frozen hard. Although it is important to start early for this hike, you should not get to the snowfield too early, when the snow will be frozen hard, unless you have crampons. From Trift, start at about 8 AM.

From the Trift Hotel, follow the sign pointing right for both the Rothornhütte and the Mettelhorn. Cross a bridge below a waterfall and when you reach a junction, turn right (east)—the trail to the left is for the Rothornhütte. Climb a steep slope; the grade eases above to rise more gradually through high meadows. If you stop here, you'll still enjoy a view that is pure visual joy, enhanced by the silence and loneliness of these wild meadows.

The trail occasionally grows indistinct, but there are cairns, and you must continue up through this narrowing valley toward the saddle ahead; keep to the right. It seems that you are heading for one of the gray rock peaks you can see to the right of that saddle, but neither of these peaks is

Hotel Fluhalp

the Mettelhorn. Traverse left up a stony slope, then traverse right to the top of the saddle. From there you'll see the snowfield and the cone of the Mettelhorn to your right (east). Cross the glacier—avoid the thin lines and discolorations in the snow that indicate crevasses—and switchback up the steep, shaley cone to the summit. It takes 2¼ hours to return to the hotel.

WALK 3 • Rothornhütte: 5 kilometers; 850 meters up and down; 5 hours up/3½ down.

This alpine club hut at 3198 meters is used for climbs of the Zinalrothorn, Ober Gabelhorn, Wellenkuppe, Trifthorn, and a few others. This is a tiring walk, but the hiker can enjoy breathtaking views from the hut. From the Trift Hotel, walk up to the junction for the Mettelhorn, but turn left at the signpost. The trail is very clear; it leads along the narrow crest of a moraine, then steeply up to the rock shelf on which the hut is perched.

31 • HOTEL FLUHALP • 2616 M

The Hotel Fluhalp is sited on the massif that borders the Findel Glacier, one of several great ice floes above Zermatt. Fluhalp still serves as the only hut for climbs of the Rimpfischhorn, Strahlhorn, and Adlerhorn and for the crossing of the glacier-covered Adlerpass to Saas-Fee. The only other building on all this slope is the original hotel, in the meadow just behind the present hotel.

Before Fluhalp was built there was nothing here at all, not even a farm. The old house, dating from 1890, proved too small, and the new inn was built between 1937 and 1939. Of striking appearance, its solitary four-story structure dominates the slope: Its colors are warm, with walls of velvety, dark brown weathered pine and cheerful red shutters. The handsome stone terrace in front offers a good view of the Matterhorn.

As in a Swiss Alpine Club hut—which in a loose sense it is—a list of licensed mountain guides hangs on the dining room wall. Old photographs of local peaks and guides are also displayed. The dining room is snug and old-fashioned; its walls and ceiling are dark brown wood rather than the light-colored pine often seen. Diners sit on wooden benches or old-fashioned carved wooden chairs. The bedrooms, also of dark brown wood, are simple and spare—just a wooden bedstead and a table. The Matratzenlager are unusual: A group of beds fill the room instead of the usual sleeping shelf or bunk beds. The beds in the dormitory are fitted with mattresses only, no sheets, but the customary blankets and pillows are provided. No smoking is allowed in the private rooms or the dormitory. You can get a hot shower for 3 Sfr, and there's a warm-water sink in the hall. No towels are provided.

The hotel produces its own electric power with a hydro and a diesel generator (the rooms are lit at night by hydroelectric power) and cooks with gas. Provisions, once carried up by mule, are now brought by helicopter and jeep.

Owned by a Zermatt family, Fluhalp is currently being run by a young Austrian, Hauni Haunschmid, and a Swiss-Austrian kitchen crew. One menu is served to all guests in the evening. When we last ate there dinner began with potato soup, served in attractive pottery bowls, followed by mixed salad, poulet cordon bleu, parsley potatoes, peas and carrots, and vanilla pudding with whipped cream and chocolate sauce. Fluhalp does a brisk lunch business, and there is an extensive menu, more interesting than the usual Berghotel fare. Among these unusual dishes are potato soup with ham and marjoram; salad with avocado, mango, and shrimp; chicken salad with ham, mushrooms, and lettuce; pasta with pesto or eggplant; and pancakes with berries.

There are 20 private rooms, with two to four beds each, and 35 places in the dormitory. Private rooms cost 11 Sfr more with bedsheets: Except for the Hospice du Simplon, we have never encountered this price distinction at any other inn.

Fluhalp is open from about June 20 to mid-October and again, for meals only, from mid-December to the end of April. You need to phone about one week in advance to reserve a room on a weekend. Tel. 027/967 25 97; Fax: 967 54 26; 3920 Zermatt.

Getting there: 4 kilometers; 360 meters up; 1½ hours from Sunnegga. Fluhalp is easily reached with the assistance of the Sunnegga-Blauherd lift system. From Zermatt, an underground funicular, the Sunnegga Express, takes you quickly up to Sunnegga at 2288 meters. From there you can hike to Fluhalp or continue by gondola to Blauherd at 2522 meters. (The third stage of this lift system is a cable car to the top of the Unterrothorn, 3103 meters.) You can also walk up to Fluhalp from Zermatt.

From Sunnegga, take the signposted trail that rises at a moderate gradient eastward, below a band of cliffs, then along a grassy stretch to the Stellisee. This little lake is a popular picnic site. The alternative walk from Blauherd is the shorter and easier approach, with an ascent of only 60 meters. From Blauherd follow the jeep road, signposted for Fluhalp, which descends to join the path up from Sunnegga, and reach Fluhalp in about 30 minutes. The walk up from Zermatt takes you through the hamlet of Findeln (2069 meters), with its old wooden barns and houses. Walk south from Zermatt to the adjoining hamlet of Winkelmatten, where a signpost in front of the little white church points left for Findeln. Follow the paved road up to a waterfall, turning left just before it. Cross the cog railway tracks and continue uphill. The trail forks: Both branches lead to Findeln, but the path straight ahead is more direct. The ascent to Findeln is 460 meters; you'll reach it in 1½ hours and Fluhalp in another 2 hours.

Walks: Several excursions can be taken from Fluhalp. The shortest is one of the most beautiful.

WALK 1 • This walk is to a place that has no name, which I'll call the Findel Glacier Overlook: 4 kilometers; 300 meters up and down; 1½ hours.

Simply walk out behind Fluhalp, past the abandoned 19th-century hotel. A trail eastward passes two small aquamarine lakes, then climbs about 300 meters to a grassy promontory overlooking the grandeur of the Findel Glacier. No sign marks this place, but note this: It takes about an hour to reach it. Moreover, if you go farther and higher, the trail will become very steep and cross several boulder slides, with no place where you can lie down on the grass. (This route climbs up to the Pfulwe, a pass leading to the Täsch Valley, but the way is rough and indistinct and crosses the edge of a small glacier.) Few come past here, and you'll have this wild and lovely place pretty much to yourself.

WALK 2 • The Grindjesee: 4 kilometers; 280 meters down and up; 2 hours.

Unlike the much more popular Stellisee, this pretty lake is rather out of the way; it cannot be seen from the main trail, as it's concealed in a very narrow, small valley just before the moraine of the Findel Glacier. (If you are hiking up from Sunnegga, the milky-green lake visible below to your right is not the Grindjesee.) It's a charming spot for a lazy afternoon, and perhaps it's just as well that it's not so well known. Sheltered from the wind, trees grow along the shore, although the lake is above tree line. It also has a view of the Matterhorn. At a junction just below (west) of Fluhalp, bear left and then left again, following a trail that descends into the valley of the Grindjesee at 2334 meters.

WALK 3 • The Tufternkumme: 4 kilometers; 380 meters up and down; 4 hours.

The high ridge above the Stellisee and Fluhalp rises to two small peaks, the Unter- and Oberrothorn, separated by a saddle known as the Furggsattel or Furggji. The wild, uninhabited valley slung between the two peaks is the Tufternkumme, and descending it makes a nice hike. To reach the Furggsattel from Fluhalp you can take the trail back up toward Blauherd, but a more direct, although steeper, trail ascends just behind (east of) the hotel. It intersects a trail coming from Blauherd for this same destination. At that junction, bear right and continue up to the saddle, which you can see clearly above you. Reach this Furggsattel in about 1½ hours, or slightly less from Blauherd. Note that maps but not signposts use the name Tufternkumme or -chumme. As you reach the saddle, you'll see the Tufternkumme trail on the right, cut slightly above the center of the valley. You can reach Zermatt by descending the farther side of the Tufternkumme. The trail will switchback more steeply down to intersect the broad trail between Tuftern—a small cluster of old wooden houses (and a simple restaurant) to your left—and the Ober Sattla to your right. Turn left and head southward for Tuftern, from which a trail leads down to Zermatt, or continue a little farther for the funicular station at Sunnegga, from which you can ride down to Zermatt.

WALK 4 • The Oberrothorn: 12 kilometers; 850 meters up and down; 5½ hours.

This route is inadvisable in snow. Like the Mettelhorn, this little 3145 meter mountain is used for endurance training for higher mountains (but not technical rock climbing). The excellent views from the summit make it a popular route for hikers, most of whom greatly reduce the effort by taking one of the series of lifts that ascend this massif (whereas there are no mechanical boosts for the Mettelhorn). You can take the cable car from Blauherd to the top of the Unterrothorn at 3103 meters. From there, you could walk down to the Furggsattel, then climb up the Oberrothorn. The disadvantage of this last option is that by riding up to 3000 meters so quickly, you'll feel the altitude and get out of breath just when you need your wind. From Fluhalp, ascend to the Furgsattel (as if for the Tufternkumme), but just before the saddle bear right onto a narrow path. This path climbs the mountain's south face on a diagonal, then switchbacks more steeply on a narrow path up the shaley east ridge.

WALK 5 • Ober Sattla: 13.5 kilometers; 1000 meters down/650 meters
up; 6 hours.

On some signposts, this appears as Über Satteln. This 2686-meter viewpoint, on a shoulder overlooking the Täsch Valley, gives a perspective that
can't be obtained from any other point around Zermatt, providing close
views of the beautiful and impressive Weisshorn, the Dom (the highest
mountain entirely inside Switzerland), Täschhorn, and other peaks in the
Mischabel Range. (Note that Täsch is a village on the valley floor, but that
Täschalp, a little cluster of dairy farms, is a different and much higher place.
The Täschhutte, used for climbs of the Täschhorn, is higher still.) From
Fluhalp, walk back to Sunnegga and follow the broad track, signposted for
Täschalp but not for Ober Sattla, north past the cluster of old wooden
houses at Tuftern. There, take the upper path to the right for Täschalp and
the Täschhutte. Continue northward as the shelf narrows and the wide
track becomes a path, ascending through a narrowing green valley. (Watch
for—but please do not pick—edelweiss; this is one of the few places where
you are sure to find it.) Eventually you'll reach a junction with ÜBER SAT-
TEL on the signpost, which points to your right. In places there are red
arrows blazed on rocks; at an unsigned junction, where some arrows point
down (marking a trail that descends to Täsch Village), instead follow the
arrows pointing up. You may also see the word ALP painted on a rock. This
refers to Täschalp, to which this trail leads beyond the Ober Sattla. You must
then traverse a stony slope with several sections of boulder slides, where
you must watch your footing. This climbs steeply at the end (there are fixed
cables that you can hold) and emerges onto the grassy promontory of the
Ober Sattla and its glorious views. The return to Sunnegga, where you
can either descend to Zermatt or take the Blauherd lift back to Fluhalp,
will take about 1½ hours.

SAASTAL

The grandest mountains in the Valaisian Alps, indeed, the highest in all
Switzerland, are clustered around the Saas and Zermatt Valleys. Both these
valleys extend from the Rhône southward to the Italian border, which runs
along the summits of some of the highest peaks, including the Matterhorn
and Monte Rosa. One group of these mountains, the Mischabel Range,
separates the Saas and Zermatt Valleys; among the great Mischabel peaks is
the Dom (4545 meters), the highest mountain entirely on Swiss territory.

Along the Saas (pronounced *Sahss*) Valley is a string of villages: Saas-Balen, Saas-Grund, Saas-Fee, and Saas-Almagell, of which the best known now is Saas-Fee; it alone is referred to as Saas. All the Saastal villages can be reached by PTT bus from the rail stations at Brig or Stalden. Saas-Fee, once the poorest and most obscure of the villages, owes its prominence to its spectacular location: perched on a shelf above the Saastal at the foot of a cirque of glaciers crowned with the Mischabel peaks. (An important mountaineering center and ski resort, although known mainly among Swiss and Germans, Saas-Fee retains much of its village charm.) Saas-Almagell, quiet and small, is the last village in the valley, at the foot of a higher tributary valley, the Almagellertal. This valley is uninhabited except for the little inn at Almagelleralp and an alpine club hut, much higher.

32 • BERGHAUS ALMAGELLERALP • 2200 M

The inn is now owned by the Burgergemeinde or Commune of Saas-Almagell, and its manager, Marietta Anthamatten und Zurbriggen, rents it as a concession from the village. It was built between 1904 and 1910, at which time it was a working alp with as many as 40 cows; by 1970, when the farm ceased to exist, only 15 cows were left. In 1987, after a great storm, part of the roof collapsed and the inn was closed for a year. The villagers then decided not only to repair the roof but also to renovate the hotel. When we first came here, in the 1970s, we used to see a mule plodding up the trail, cases of soft drinks tied to its back, and later we would see the unburdened mule rolling about on the grass outside the hotel. The mule and its bearded master, who ran the hotel for many years (and was the uncle of the present manager), are memorialized in a painting in the dining room. Provisions are now brought by helicopter.

The house, dark gray with red shutters, looks pretty much as it did years ago, but inside all is new and clean. The small dining room is now modern in style, and in a little alcove there's a television set, an unusual thing to find in a Berghaus. Broad granite steps lead to the bedrooms on the two upper floors. The rooms are attractive, with old-fashioned beds, newly sanded floors, and electric light. Both the second and third floors have cold-water sinks, and there is also a hot-water shower on the third floor—no charge for its use. Bath and hand towels are provided in the private rooms. A pleasant terrace outside the hotel receives a merry crowd at midday or in the early afternoon. Most of the people you'll see on the terrace have come down from one of the walks listed below or from a climb; most are gone by late afternoon and the place is very quiet in the evening.

One menu is served to all overnight guests, although substitutions can be made if requested a little in advance. A typical dinner consists of soup, mixed salad, meat and Rösti, and meringue with whipped cream. Along with the customary jam and butter, sliced cheese and meat are served at breakfast.

The hotel is open from June 15 until the first or second week of October, depending on the weather. As the inn uses a radio-phone, its number changes every year; therefore, call the Saas-Almagell tourist office for the current number.

Getting there: There is no lift in this valley, so you must walk up from Saas-Almagell: 3.5 kilometers; 530 meters up; 2 hours. From the village square, walk eastward across the village and follow a path that switchbacks up beside a waterfall and through some woods. Above tree line the trail becomes comparatively level. Cross a bridge, walk upstream, and soon reach the hotel. To return, follow the sign to Oberer Dorfteil to reach the village square.

Walks:

WALK 1 • Zwischbergen Pass: 9 kilometers; 1100 meters up and down; 6 hours round-trip.

One of the grandest panoramas in the region, with the Mischabel Range spread before you like a banner, is seen from the very highest part of the Almagellertal. The SAC Almagellerhütte is sited up there, close to the Zwischbergen Pass on the Italian border. To walk up to the pass from the village of Saas-Almagell and return in one day is a very long and tiring haul—a climb of 1700 meters over some 16 kilometers, requiring nearly 9 hours. A night at Almagelleralp (or at the alpine club hut) breaks up the hike and makes it more manageable. From the Berghaus, continue eastward on the trail along the stream. The trail then turns to climb in broad switchbacks up a long, steep slope to your left (north). As you mount this slope, even before you reach the SAC hut, the view becomes glorious, and should you go no higher it will be worth the effort. The hut is at 2900 meters, positioned for climbs of the Weissmies, the big snow-covered mountain (4023 meters) just above, or for climbs on the Dri Horlini Ridge. To continue to the Zwischbergen Pass, at 3287 meters, follow the track northeast. The valley becomes narrow and rocky. Watch for blazes, and head for the lowest point in the saddle above you. It should take about 3½ hours from Almagelleralp.

WALK 2 • Alpenblumen Promenade: 10 kilometers; 200 meters up/900 meters down; 3 hours.

This popular walk, also called the Höhenweg Almagelleralp, is a much longer approach to Almagelleralp than the standard direct approach from Saas-Almagell. It's usually begun from Saas-Grund: Take the Kreuzboden-Hohsaas lift to the first station at Kreuzboden (2397 meters) and follow the sign for Höhenweg Almagelleralp (times posted on the signs are inconsistent). The trail winds around the shoulder of the Weissmies; along the way are numerous informative signs about a great variety of wildflowers, examples of which are (or were) growing beside the trail.

The trail crosses several boulder slides but is well blazed on these sections. To the south, you'll see the Mattmark Dam and its lake. After rounding the slope, the trail descends into the Almagellertal to join the trail up that valley, and you'll see the Hotel Almagelleralp directly ahead to your left.

THE LÖTSCHENTAL

Tucked into a deep fold between the Gasterntal and the Rhône Valley, the Lötschental is at the edge of the border between the Bernese Oberland and the Valais. Elements of a folk culture medieval or older have survived in this formerly remote valley. The carved wooden masks made for centuries in the Lötschental, grotesque faces decorated with animal hair and teeth that were intended to scare away winter, are famous throughout Switzerland. At the lower end of the valley is Goppenstein, at one end of the Lötschberg tunnel (Kandersteg is at the other end); with the opening of this tunnel in 1913, providing the first rail link between the Oberland and the Rhône, the Lötschental became more directly connected with the world around it. As it has no resort, the valley has been spared a great influx of tourists, but has long been attracting hikers, not only for its picturesque, traditional Valaisian houses, but also because of its Höhenweg, a high trail extending the length of the valley.

33 • BERGHAUS KUMMENALP • 2083 M

This simple inn is located on the western, less frequented half of the Höhenweg. Kummenalp, beside it, is a small settlement of 10 to 15 houses that seem to grip the steep slope. As is the Valaisian custom, these few farmhouses are clustered together rather than spread apart among their pastures.

Berghaus Kummenalp is among the plainer inns, an L-shaped gray stone building with red shutters and a little terrace in the crook of its arm.

This is one of those inns where the friendliness of the owners compensates for the modesty of the setup. It was built in 1936 as an inn and surely has changed little. The small pine dining room has no bar or counter: The family, cooking and washing in the kitchen on the other side of the door, and the one waitress take orders for drinks and snacks. Dinner is served family-style, one menu for all, at long, shared tables, and for all that the room is so plain, the rows of cheerful, hungry hikers are, in a way, the room's decoration. Our dinner began with a tureen of vegetable soup, followed by mixed salad, then a platter of pork cutlets, spaghetti, and cooked vegetables. Vegetarians were given extra heaps of spaghetti. Perhaps someone from the inn once visited Mexico, because the à la carte menu includes Mexikanische Pfeffersuppe and chili con carne, along with the usual dishes.

Some of the private rooms are oddly located just off the Matratzenlager, which you must walk through to get to your room. But the private rooms are pleasant and attractive: Ours had a cheerful, blue-and-white-checked quilt and matching pillow, a little table, a mirror, and pitcher and basin. Small towels were provided. Both the toilet and a fountain-trough (cold water) for washing are outside.

There are five double rooms and one single, and 28 Matratzenlager places. The inn is open from July 1 to the end of September and is run by Irene Werlen and her husband, who have taken over most of the duties from her parents. Tel. 027/939 12 80 or 939 11 78; 3916 Ferden.

Getting there: From Fafleralp: 10 kilometers; 320 meters up; 5½ hours.

34 • BERGGASTHAUS LAUCHERNALP • 2106 M

Near the upper Lauchernalp lift station (1969 meters), the Höhenweg trail splits into an upper and lower section; this Berggasthaus is above the upper trail. There is no sign announcing its presence, but it's the wooden chalet built on a stone foundation you'll see high on the slope, with a terrace built out upon a deck. This terrace affords a good view of the Bietschhorn. Within, the dining room is small but quite attractive. The inn is under new ownership and looks as if it has been modestly and tastefully renovated. Lauchernalp has comforts not available at Kummenalp, such as indoor toilets, sink, and shower.

It has only two double rooms, both newly furnished, but one of these rooms has no window. There are 41 Matratzenlager places, which are separated into several different rooms instead of one huge dormitory. Among these Matratzenlager rooms are one that is essentially a double room and another that has two bunk beds. It's open from mid-June to the end of September or mid-October. Tel. 027/939 12 50; Fax: 939 24 50; 3918 Wiler.

Getting there: From Wiler, take the Lauchernalp cable car, then walk 137 meters up; 25 minutes.

Walks: The chief one is the Lötschental Höhenweg, along which both these inns are found. The Höhenweg can be walked in its entirety in a long day (about 6½ hours) or broken up into two segments if you stay overnight at one of the two inns along the route. There is also the option of walking only part of the route, as the new Lauchernalp lift enables hikers to eliminate half the walk. Some hikers on the Höhenweg are bound for the Lötschenpass or have crossed over it; this pass connects the Lötschental with the Gasterntal (see p. 55). From the rail station at Goppenstein many hikers take a PTT bus to Fafleralp, the last stop at the upper end of the valley, and start their hike there. (The bus actually stops at Gletscherstafel, a parking area just below Fafleralp.) Others get off the bus at the lift station in the village of Wiler, ride up on the Lauchernalp cable car, then walk back to Fafleralp and take the bus back from there. Only a few hike the entire length of the Höhenweg. The trail is a good one, well graded and well marked, and along the way the panorama changes, from the view of the Fafleralp Glacier at the eastern end of the Lötschental to the Mischabel Range, which comes into sight as you approach Kummenalp and the western end of the valley. For much of the walk your visual companion will be the Bietschhorn, whose great snowy triangle can be seen from the Zermatt Valley as a marker beyond which lies the Bernese Oberland.

If you start at Fafleralp (1763 meters), note that you will not see the name Kummenalp on any trail sign until you reach the Lauchernalp area. From Fafleralp, it takes about 5 hours to reach Kummenalp. From Kummenalp you can walk back to Lauchernalp and take the lift down to the road. Alternatively, you can follow a trail that descends to Ferden (which takes 1½ hours), or continue past Restialp to the end of the Höhenweg at Faldumalp and then walk down to Goppenstein (between 2½ and 3 hours from Kummenalp). Note that from Restialp you can hike across the Restipass to reach Leukerbad, which takes nearly 8 hours.

ALETSCH REGION

35 • HOTEL BELALP • 2130 M

On a grassy knoll in a beautiful, lonely meadow with sweeping views to the south of the Rhône Valley and of the Aletsch Glacier stands a tall stone monument bearing the name of John Tyndall. Belalp, a quiet, rather obscure place, will always be associated with Tyndall, an eminent Victorian scientist, president of the prestigious Royal Society (it was he who first explained why the sky looks blue), and also a great alpinist. In 1861 Tyndall and two Swiss guides made the first ascent of the Weisshorn, today still reckoned a difficult climb. He combined his professional interests with his passion for mountains by studying the movement and composition of glaciers, which he observed at some peril to himself, and published his findings on the movement and the structure and properties of ice. His memoir, *Hours of Exercise in the Alps* (1898), remains exciting to read.

Tyndall loved Belalp from the first time he went there, finding "health in the air and hope in the mountains . . ." When his climbing years were over, he retired there, building a house from which he could gaze at the Weisshorn across the Rhône Valley, and the community of Belalp made him an honorary citizen of the village. The stone monument, known as the Tyndall Denkmal, stands on the slope above the house (now privately owned). His wife dedicated the monument "to her all beloved . . . to mark a place of memories." Tyndall died because of a tragic error when his young wife mistakenly gave him the wrong dosage of his heart medicine. (Louisa Tyndall never remarried.) The memorial is 230 meters above Belalp, and you can reach it in about 25 minutes.

Belalp is poised just above the tongue of the Grosser Aletschgletscher, the longest glacier in the entire Alps. From this vantage point there is a frontal view of the great sinuous river of ice, banded with the curving, dark stripes of medial moraines.

Here a solitary hotel was built in 1852. From this "excellent little auberge," Tyndall wrote, he set forth at 5:30 one August morning to climb the Weisshorn. (He added this footnote: "Now a substantial hotel which merits encouragement.") There is little to do here except venture forth onto the mountains or the glacier, or just contemplate them. One annual event of interest (the Schäfersonntag) occurs on the last Sunday in August or the first Sunday in September when the approximately 2000 sheep that graze on the surrounding meadows throughout the summer are driven up to Belalp, arriving in a train 1 kilometer long in late afternoon, to be separated the next morning and sent home to their respective owners.

The hotel was bought by the community of Naters in 1992 and extensively renovated in 1993–1994. It is now completely modern (rooms have private bathrooms), an attractive, comfortable place bearing little resemblance to the traditional Berghotel except for its history and associations—and the fact that guests cannot drive to it, although it is at the end of a jeep road. Just behind the hotel is a little chapel that once served its British guests. One menu is served to all overnight guests. Its manager, Bea

Tyndall Memorial, Belalp

Schwyzer, keeps a good kitchen: Our dinner began with an excellent green salad, followed by a choice of seafood with green noodles (very tasty) or curried Schnitzel. The menu includes many varieties of Rösti. At breakfast there are cornflakes in addition to the bread and jam.

It has 65 Matratzenlager places and seven private rooms with traditional wood paneling. Owned by the J. Eggel family, it's open from mid-June to November and from mid-December to the end of April. Tel. 027/924 24 22; Fax: 924 43 20; 3914 Blatten/Naters.

Getting there: From the town of Brig, take the PTT bus through Naters to Blatten, then take a cable car up to the hamlet of Belalp (2094 meters), which is closed to nonresident motor traffic. As you get off the lift, turn right; Hotel Belalp is a 30-minute walk, nearly on the level. *Note:* Next to the lift station is the Pension-Hotel Aletschhorn (2100 meters), a simpler old hotel that has not been modernized. Tel. 027/923 29 80; 3904 Belalp/Naters.

Walks:

WALK 1 • The Sparrhorn: 7 kilometers; 920 meters up; 5½ hours.

High on the slope above Belalp is a small peak, the Sparrhorn (3021 meters), offering a panoramic view of the glaciers and the mountains on both sides of the Rhône. Tyndall described the view from the summit as "perfectly unexpected and strikingly beautiful ... The sweep of the Aletsch glacier is also mighty as viewed from this point, and from no other could the Valais range seem more majestic. It is needless to say a word about the grandeur of the Dom, the Cervin [Matterhorn in French], and the Weisshorn, all of which, and a great deal more, are commanded from the Sparrenhorn [sic]." (Tyndall 1898, pp. 89–90)

This climb has no technical difficulty and the mountain is very popular with hikers. It is often climbed by day hikers coming directly from the cable car station. (A signpost at the lift station directs you onto the trail.) From the Hotel Belalp, however, take the unsigned path just to the left of the chapel, which will lead you to the Tyndall Denkmal. Aim for the long rocky ridge that tops the slope above Belalp; the Sparrhorn is not the high point in the middle of the ridge but another high point on its right side. Just to the north of the Tyndall Denkmal is a junction with no blaze or sign, but bear right toward the hump at the right end of the high ridge. Along parts of the trail you'll see a few yellow blazes as you make for that ridge to your right (it is between you and the Aletsch Glacier). Cross a stream on easy rocks. The way will lead you up onto the hump of that ridge and then along it, over tumbled boulders. Cairns mark the way, and there's a very small section, only two or three steps, where you'll need to use your hands to steady yourself. The route winds behind that hump and then rises steeply to the nearest rock mound. There's a sort of false summit before the real one, which has a cross on it. To reach the top, climb a very steep cone of shattered rock, with traces of trail.

THE SIMPLON PASS 2006 M

Only a few great passes broach the alpine wall that separates northern Europe from the south—among them is the Simplon Pass. Of great strategic value, the Simplon road/rail route provides the most direct link between Paris and Milan; its rail tunnel, built in 1906, is the longest in the world. The scenery at the pass is dominated by Monte Leone (3553 meters) to the east and the Fletschhorn (3993 meters) to the west, both surrounded by glaciers.

36 • HOSPICE DU SIMPLON • 2000 M

The prototype of the alpine inn or refuge is the hospice, or Hospiz—a house of shelter or rest for pilgrims and strangers kept by a religious order. The first known established shelter for travelers was the hospice at the Great St. Bernard Pass, founded in the 11th century. For centuries the great passes have served as the channels for trade and pilgrimage and the routes for wayfarers, migrating workers, exiles, and fugitives. The Hospice du Grand St. Bernard continues to function as an inn, although most visitors today come not for a night's rest but as a stop on the road to Italy and to see the historic structure, its museum, and the famous St. Bernard dogs—now kenneled rather than out searching for travelers lost in snowdrifts.

Napoleon (accompanied by 40,000 men and 5,000 horses) crossed the Alps in 1800 on his way to the battle of Marengo. After struggling over the Great St. Bernard, he decided that a pass road was necessary to keep him in touch with his conquests to the south. He chose the next pass to the east, the Simplon, because it is about 460 meters lower and less snowbound in the winter. Three months after Marengo, he gave the order for work to begin at top priority. So welcome had been the refuge provided by the Grand St. Bernard Hospice that in 1801 he ordered the building of a hospice on the Simplon Pass. It was not the first shelter on the Simplon: A hospice already existed there in 1235, run by the Knights of Malta. Centuries later, when the old hospice was in ruins, travelers could find shelter at another hospice built in 1670 by a wealthy merchant trader, Gaspard (Kaspar) de Stockalper. (Stockalper also improved the rough track over the pass; there is now a hiking trail across the Simplon named the Stockalperweg.)

The Simplon Hospice begun by Napoleon (but not completed until 1831) is built like an armory, with a monumental door, massive stone walls, iron gray stone stairs, and corridors paved with huge flagstones. It is solid and solemn within, under an outer coat of pink plaster that gives the facade a deceptively lighthearted appearance. It is run by members of the Order of St. Bernard, which was created around 1050 to aid travelers and pilgrims journeying between Jerusalem or Rome and the north, merchants and traders, and migrants looking for work. Even before the new hospice was completed, three monks from the Grand St. Bernard Hospice were installed at the Simplon Pass in the old hospice to provide spiritual aid to the soldiers and the men working on the new road. (Although the public thinks of them as monks, they are actually priests, Augustinians, who live like monks but perform pastoral work.)

Simplon Hospice

The Simplon and Grand St. Bernard Hospices are the most unusual of all Swiss mountain hostels. Their raison d'être is not commercial success (although they must be commercially viable) but rather *accueil*, that is, welcome. As explained by Père Michel Praplan, the current prior at the Simplon, the purpose of the house is to give people the possibility to renew themselves and their spirituality. For this reason, the hospice has a special

dispensation: The monks are not required to make guests fill out the customary registration form stating name, address, etc. In fact, the monks never
even ask the name of their guests or their religion. They make no distinction among races and different faiths. Their stated goal is simply to welcome all travelers. Père Praplan says their work is to take the difficulties of
those in trouble and lift those people to a higher plane. Today the Simplon Hospice is staffed by four priests and a deacon, who are always available to those who need help or need to talk. Père Praplan estimates that
about half their guests come for alpine sports and to be in the mountains,
about 10 percent come for spiritual help, and the rest come for both.

The essential task of the order is to be in the mountains to help travelers, broadly understood: That term today includes spiritual pilgrims—
people who are adrift and seeking a goal for their lives, a point to life, and
who go to the mountains for that reason. Although there is a chapel at the
hospice and services several times a day, guests are neither required nor
even asked to attend them, nor is grace or any prayer said before meals.
Father Praplan is quietly eloquent about the mission of his order. The
medieval travelers for whom the monks provided shelter did not come to
the mountains in search of alpine beauty—the Alps were just an obstacle
that pilgrims and peddlers had to cross. All that has changed; tourists, busi-
nesspeople, even migrant workers drive or take the train; and the monks
understand the special role that mountains now play in the consciousness
of modern beings: Mountains, they say, require us to cast off whatever is not
necessary in our lives and encumbers us, to get rid of the detritus with
which we surround ourselves, to clear our lives for what is essential.

Although the Simplon Hospice offers travelers a filling meal and a warm
bed (at low cost), as well as an alpine view, clearly one of its special attractions is the presence of a person such as Père Praplan. Speaking with great
simplicity, unashamedly, the prior says that he personally will never find
God but that this will always be a quest. He is undaunted in the pursuit
because, he seems to say, this is our human condition: The search for God
will always be a quest, not for him alone but for all humanity.

The house is open all year. There are 20 rooms (they contain from four
to eight beds but a visitor is only charged per bed, not per room). Blankets and pillows are provided but not sheets or towels; sheet sacks (known
in French as *sacs à viande* can be rented for 3 Sfr. There are also 45 dormitory places in five separate rooms. Toilets, warm-water sinks, and showers
are in the hall. There is no television in the house.

Meals are served family-style at long tables in a large room with a coffered ceiling, beside which is a small bar where guests can order wine, beer, or coffee (you may bring your wine to the dinner table) and buy packaged snacks. A small lay staff runs the kitchen. On our visit, dinner began with tureens of soup, followed by salad, spaghetti with a separate meat sauce, and a tray of flavored yogurts for dessert. At breakfast there were slabs of butter and bowls of jam with the bread. Before the advent of tourism, guests at the Grand St. Bernard Hospice did not pay for a night's stay or, in case of bad weather, until it was safe to travel. But the hospices are financially autonomous and must charge to survive. The monks receive no pay, but along with the other expenses of running an inn, the hospice must pay government taxes. Also, it is a tradition of these houses that the religious don't pay; rates for the public are low. Meal times are fixed: breakfast at 8 AM, a substantial midday meal at noon, and supper at 7 PM. The hospice also receives many youth groups and offers summer camp programs in French, German, or English, special mountaineering courses for young people— indeed, some of the priests have been alpinists—and spiritual retreats.

Reservations are accepted and even advisable. Tel. 027/979 13 22; Fax: 979 14 79; 3901 Simplon-Pass.

Getting there: The hospice is beside the road, reachable by car, PTT bus from Brig, or footpath.

Walks: A 35 kilometer trail named the Stockalperweg, for the 17th-century merchant who maintained the "old" Simplon Hospice and constructed several imposing buildings both at the pass and in the region, extends from the town of Brig in the Rhône Valley to Gondo, a village on the Swiss-Italian border. Because there is PTT bus service between Brig and Gondo, a hiker can walk part of the Stockalperweg and ride the bus for the rest. You can, for example, take the bus to the Simplon Hospice, stay overnight, then walk to Gondo the next day and catch an afternoon bus back to Brig. The trail is well marked not only with the standard yellow hiking signs but also with special little brown STOCKALPERWEG signs. In most places it deviates considerably from the road, which is only rarely in sight.

If you start from Brig (678 meters), it should take a little more than 5 or even up to 6 hours to walk up to the pass; descending from the pass to Brig takes about 4 hours. About 2 hours south of the pass is a pretty village, Simplon Dorf (1472 meters), with a small eco-museum, a good bakery, a food shop, and a few hotels. You can take the bus to this village and start hiking there: From the village, count on about 5 hours to reach Gondo. As you approach Gondo (at 855 meters) the trail descends steeply to an attractive river with rocks sculpted and hollowed by the water. (Note that Gondo is also at the end of the Zwischbergen Pass route above Saas-Almagell; see p. 159.) The bus ride back takes you through entirely different scenery, through a dramatic gorge with steep walls of rock.

THE BINNTAL

Among the places off the beaten track that are described in this book, the track to this obscure valley is surely one of the least beaten. Not only are foreign visitors quite rare here, but few Swiss have even discovered it. Just enough visitors come to keep pleasant old Hotel Ofenhorn, which clearly dates from another era, alive and functioning. It is no Berghaus—for it stands in a village and can be reached by car or PTT bus—but it has the character and flavor of the traditional old hotels. It belongs to that era and to that school.

The Binntal is at the far eastern end of the Valais. Mountains and glaciers rise above its meadows, but none is so famous that crowds of visitors have been attracted here, and therein lies part of its charm. In fact, the village of Binn, which has long been settled, is rather anxious about its survival. The Celts had a cemetery here, and the river that flows through the village is spanned by a handsome, arched stone bridge bearing the date 1564, but these days there's little to occupy its citizens. About 130 people now live here year-round, of whom only eight are teenagers and only six schoolchildren, and the community is uncertain whether it can survive as anything other than a summer place. Some visitors are attracted by the hiking, others by its reputation for fine wildflowers or even for its peace and quiet, but the valley is best known for its exceptional wealth of varied and even rare minerals.

But a charming summer place it is. If you have ever dreamed of a sweet, simple, unspoiled village, just modern enough to have telephones and a paved road leading into it, this may be the place. It has one food store and a few shops that sell crystals and various minerals found in the surrounding mountains. There isn't even a village bakery. But visitors do come. There's a simple restaurant in the village center, a small new hotel (**Pension Albrun**) across the river, and at the upper end of Binn, old Hotel Ofenhorn.

37 • HOTEL OFENHORN • 1400 M

The Ofenhorn shows the influence of the time when France was the center of gentility, culture, and style. The sign over the dining room door reads SALLE À MANGER, and the different floors are labeled 2ÈME and 3ÈME ÉTAGE. The dining room is large and spacious, as in a French country hotel, giving an air of relaxed, easy comfort. And the exceedingly pleasant garden restaurant, with tables under the trees or umbrellas, is in the Gallic spirit. The half-pension evening meal is served only in the dining room, but you can enjoy dinner in the garden if you prefer an à la carte menu. And on a beautiful summer evening, who would forgo the pleasure? Dining on the terrace you hear the sound of the river flowing just below and the laughter of children from swings beside the hotel, and as you gaze up the slope your eye meets the green meadows that descend to the edge of the village.

When evening falls and you go inside, there's a little parlor with over-stuffed armchairs and a case full of books (also a television set, but when we were there no one ever turned it on), and a bar for an evening drink.

The hotel is now owned by an association and run by a director. It's open from June to October 20. It has 50 simple rooms with warm-water sinks, but showers and toilets are in the halls. Tel. 027/971 45 45; 3996 Binn.

Getting there: To reach Binn, take the train to Fiesch in the Rhône Valley northeast of Brig; change there to a bus (private: half-price with a Swiss Pass) for Binn.

Walks:

WALK 1 • Binntalhütte and Albrun Pass. To the hut: 18 kilometers; 870 meters up; 5½ hours. To the pass: an additional 1 kilometer; 140 meters up; 6¼ hours.

Although this is one of the most popular hikes in the valley, quite long but not steep, it is uncrowded. Note that many of the trails bear numbers, corresponding to the way they are numbered on the topographic map. The road extends beyond Binn to the bridge just below the very pretty hamlet of Imfeld (Fäld on maps). Hikers with cars drive out as far as they can; others walk, either along the road, or on a path just above the river's left bank, or on a more scenic trail (requiring a little more ascent and descent) on the slope above the river's right bank. That scenic trail begins to the left side of the hotel (the meadow side). There you turn right and follow a path that's paved for the first few meters but then becomes a narrow footpath with a WANDERWEG sign. It leads through woods and fields in 1 hour to Imfeld. Note that if you wish to shorten this hike, the people at the Restaurant zur Brücke in Binn (beside the bridge) will drive you to Imfeld for 20 Sfr.

From Imfeld (Fäld), two trails extend to the hut, one above the right bank of the river, the other along the left bank. To make a loop, head out above the right bank, following signposts for Freichi and the Binntalhütte.

Hotel Ofenhorn, Binntal

A blazed path cuts across loops of a farm road. At the alp at Freichi, a signpost directs you straight ahead for the hut. Cross a bridge to join the trail that entered along the stream's left bank; again, signs will direct you eastward. The trail now climbs by steps to successively higher shelves of meadows. Ascend a large mound dusted with powdery white dolomite, keeping to the left side, then steeply up to Blatt, where there's a ruined stone house. The trail winds around a lovely meadow, crosses another bridge, and climbs to a higher shelf, with a scenic view of several alps in a bowl of meadows surrounded by mountains. Cross a bridge below a waterfall (a higher trail crosses the cascade without a bridge); from the shelf above you'll see the hut, reached by a network of trails. The Binntalhütte (2269 meters) is about 3 hours from Imfeld (Fäld). To reach the Albrun Pass (2409 meters), which marks the Italian border, tucked between the Ofenhorn and Albrunhorn, will take another 30 minutes. Return to Binn in 2 hours. The cumulative ascent/descent (or total ascent) is 1215 meters. From Imfeld (Fäld), it's only 1100 meters.

WALK 2 • Geisspfadsee: 12 kilometers; 1045 meters up; 6½ hours.

The high point is 2445 meters, just above the lake, which is at 2439 meters; the cumulative ascent is 1030 meters. You can make this something of a loop trip, ascending by one trail and descending by another, and on the way up you can make another little loop to see the pretty Mässersee. Cross the bridge in Binn, proceed eastward, and then turn right off the road at a signpost for the Geisspfadsee and the Mässersee. Ascend the trail numbered 14, a narrow path climbing very steeply through woods for about 200 meters, then cross in front of a cascade. You'll cross a gravel road and immediately turn left onto another path. At the next signpost, near the chalet at Mässerchäller, turn left for the Mässersee. In another 20–30 minutes at a signposted junction, you'll have a choice: To make the little loop to the Mässersee, continue straight ahead on the route numbered 9; route 8, to the right, is signposted for the Geisspfadsee. For the Mässersee, ascend a steep, rocky mound and reach the little lake 2 hours, 40 minutes after starting. To continue from there to the Geisspfadsee, traverse above the valley, as directed by a signpost, and join route 8. You'll switchback up a big talus slope—a little rough, but the way is well blazed and always distinct. Emerge above and cross a brook on easy rocks. A few blazed metal wands and blazed rocks direct you up through a high, narrow valley, like a little notch, and you'll emerge just above the lake, to which you must descend a few meters. The lake is very scenic, surrounded by steep, rugged slopes; in late July, its dark blue water was still full of ice floes.

In descent you can bear left and take route 8 instead of returning via the Mässersee. This is also a beautiful trail, descending through a wild valley to a bowl of meadow. We had it nearly to ourselves. There was silence, except for birdsong and the sounds of the rushing stream and of wind waving through the grass. The meadow was thick with flowers of every color, and the views beyond were of snow-streaked mountains. If such a place doesn't bring peace to the soul, nothing will.

When you reach a four-way trail junction, you can retrace your steps to the trailhead or take the way north signed for Mineraliengrube, which you'll reach in an hour; you'll hear the sound of tapping before you see this great exposed slab, swarming with mineral hunters busily pounding chunks of rock with their hammers. The trail descends beside the quarry to a paved road, where you turn left. Return to Binn via either the road or the trail beside it, or by the higher trail from Imfeld (Fäld). Return to Binn in 3 hours.

CHAPTER 7

APPENZELL

Although it's at the eastern edge of Switzerland, beside the Austrian border, Appenzell is at the very heart of Swiss Berghaus culture. This is Berghaus country, with more inns per mile (or kilometer) of trail than anywhere else in the country. It's the only part of Switzerland where hikers don't pack a picnic lunch for a day's outing because there is always a Gasthaus, more likely several, on the route of any hike. Not only don't you need to pack a lunch, but you can also hike from inn to inn for several days.

Appenzell actually consists of two parts, Ausser Rhoden and Inner Rhoden (Outer and Inner Appenzell). The term Appenzell in this book should be understood as referring only to Inner Appenzell, which in many respects is quite different from Outer Appenzell. The topography of Outer Appenzell is gently undulating; Inner Appenzell has a core of rugged mountains. Outer Appenzell is Protestant; Inner is Catholic. Outer is home to many industries; Inner has virtually none.

Upon first approaching Inner Appenzell, you'll find a perimeter of pastoral landscape, but the country differs from the Emmental, and the one could never be mistaken for the other. The Appenzell hills have a sharper profile, crisper edges, and they are more open, with smaller patches of woods. Farmhouses, which are more widely separated in the Emmental, are in close proximity here, often several on one slope and of an architectural style different not only from the Emmental ones but from all other Swiss farmhouses as well. The distinctive facade of the Appenzell farmhouse is characterized by long rows of windows rather than by the Emmentaler tiers of balconies. (These contiguous windows fill the rooms inside with light, a boon to the women who worked on the celebrated Appenzell embroidery; when necessary, shutters could be raised or lowered vertically.) The barn, moreover, although at right angles to the house, is joined to it, so that the house roof faces one way, the barn roof another.

At the center of Inner Appenzell the landscape changes. Three long,

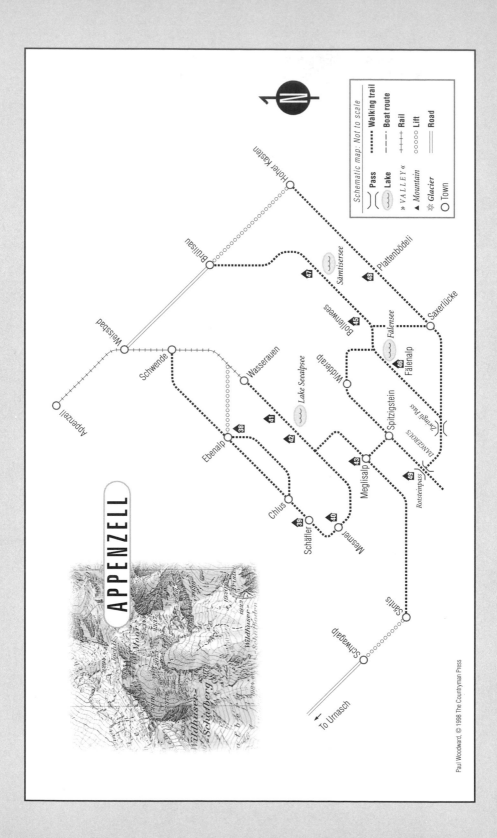

APPENZELL

Schematic map: Not to scale

Pass	)(	Walking trail	••••
Lake	⬭	Boat route	■■■
» VALLEY «		Rail	+++
Mountain	▲	Lift	ooooo
Glacier	❄	Road	===
Town	◯		

Hoher Kasten

Brülisau

Plattenbödeli

Sämtisersee

Säxerlücke

Bollenwees

Fälensee

Fälenalp

Weissbad

Widderalp

Zwinglipass

DANGEROUS

Schwende

Wasserauen

Lake Seealpsee

Spitzigstein

Appenzell

Ebenalp

38

41

42

Meglisalp

43

49

Roitsteinpass

Chlus

39

40

Schäfler

Mesmer

Säntis

Schwägalp

To Urnäsch

Chapel on the Kronberg Hill, Appenzell

craggy walls of rock, roughly parallel, suddenly erupt from the meadows. These three walls, the northern, middle, and southern chain, are together called the Alpstein. Enfolded within the walls of the Alpstein are high, narrow valleys sprinkled with alps. Most hikers are attracted to this part of Appenzell, and here are found its greatest concentration of mountain inns.

The network of trails spreads across the Alpstein, and also across the gentle meadowland around it, make it easy to design your own walking tour by consulting a map. The trails are well signposted and marked. The outline of a goblet on a trail sign means there's an inn at that place. This symbol is not customary on trail signs in other parts of Switzerland, and it is almost never seen anywhere else.

The highest peak of the Alpstein is the Säntis (2501 meters), reachable by cable car from Schwägalp or by quite delicate trails along the northern chain or the rocky wall that connects the Säntis to the Rotsteinpass. A less difficult trail exists from Meglisalp via Wagenlücke. There is a Berghotel on the Säntis and another restaurant besides, but Appenzell's most famous peak will not be described in this book because it is covered with buildings and also swarming with tourists, most of whom ride up on the lift.

The capital of Inner Appenzell is a quiet, charming small town that is itself called Appenzell. From its central square, where the canton's citizens annually cast their vote, you can see the green hills rising around the town. And from Appenzell town you can take trains to start many of these walks. As distances are small, rides are short: often only 10–15 minutes to reach the place where you start a walk. The inns mentioned here will be grouped according to whether they are on or near the northern, middle, or southern chains, but you can cross from one chain to another instead of proceeding in a linear fashion. Many of the inns up on the Alpstein have no natural source of water and must collect rainwater or pump water up.

A note about Appenzeller drinks: Apple cider, both sweet and hard, is very popular here. You may find Saft; the word means juice, as in Apfelsaft or Orangensaft, but here it can mean unpasteurized, hard apple cider. Apples are allowed to ferment until they become a little sour. Süssmost is sweet cider, Most is hard. And Ghürote, which means "married," is sweet and hard cider mixed together.

38 • BERGGASTHAUS AESCHER (ALSO ÄSCHER) • 1450 M

This must be both the tiniest Berghaus in Switzerland and the most dramatically located. It's tiny because it's perched like an eagle's nest on a bit of ledge partway up a great, sheer cliff—indeed, the rock face of the cliff is the inn's back wall, and there wasn't room to build anything larger. Just enough space was left for a little terrace, which can be quite crowded on a sunny afternoon with people admiring the exceptional view. The house, 150 years old, is very plain, made of wood (except for its back wall) and covered with weathered brown shingles. It was slightly enlarged in 1985. The menu is standard and dinner is à la carte. The inn is kept by the friendly Knechtle-Wyss family, who rent it from the canton.

There are 40 Matratzenlager places and no private rooms, a cold-water sink but no shower. It's open from May to November. Tel. 071/799 11 42; 9057 Wasserauen AI.

Getting there: Despite its location, you don't have to be a rock climber to reach the Berghaus Aescher, or even much of a walker. From the town of Appenzell, it takes 11 minutes by train to reach the village of Wasserauen, where you can take the Ebenalp cable car for a boost onto the crest of the northern chain at 1644 meters. (You can also walk up to Ebenalp from Schwende, north of Wasserauen, which would take about 2 hours.) From

Berggasthaus Aescher

the upper Ebenalp station you can see the large **Berggasthaus Ebenalp** just above, a new-looking building with a large terrace (pleasant private rooms, Matratzenlager, moderate rates; Tel. 071/799 11 94).

From the upper cable car station, instead of walking up the slope to the Ebenalp Inn, walk downward. In a few minutes you'll reach the Wild-kirchli, a large cave open at both ends, illuminated by dim electric lights. Walk through this and emerge on the other side of the ridge, where you'll find a minuscule wood cabin that houses a small collection of cave bear teeth and other relics found in the cave, and a chapel. The cabin was a hermit's shelter—it's said that for 200 years there was always a resident hermit and that Berggasthaus Aescher was built for the tourists who came to see the cave. The walk from Ebenalp to Aescher is 85 meters down and takes 20 minutes. As the trail emerges from the cave it is wide and solid, with a guardrail along the exposed side of the cliff, and in a few minutes you'll reach Aescher. No one with vertigo needs to fear this section of trail.

39 • GASTHAUS SCHÄFLER • 1924 M

Perched atop a narrow, grassy slope on the crest of the northern chain, Schäfler offers a sweeping view across the valley to the middle chain. The inn, covered with pale gray shingles and green shutters, was built in 1914–1915 and renovated in 1970. The dining room is small and simple, with a little bar. There are seven double rooms with old-fashioned bed-steads, pitchers and basins to wash in, and small towels, and 100 Matratzen-lager divided among several rooms, large and small. Schäfler depends on rainwater. There is no shower (cold-water sink only) and no drinking water except for what you buy from the inn. Meals are à la carte.

Run by the Doble family, the inn is open from June to the end of Octo-ber. Tel. 071/799 11 44; 9057 Weissbad.

Getting there: There are two ways to proceed from Aescher to Schäfler. You can proceed on the narrow trail along the cliff face, then turn and walk upward to the alp at Chlus and then on to Schäfler. Alternatively, return to the Ebenalp lift station, from which a signpost marked SCHÄFLER points to a broad trail set on grassy slopes above the cliff; this also leads to Chlus, where you can see the Schäfler inn on the slope above. From the Ebenalp lift station: 3 kilometers; 315 meters up; 1 hour, 10 minutes.

40 • BERGGASTHAUS MESMER (ALSO MESSMER) • 1613 M

Mesmer is another unpretentious little inn. The terrace was quite full at lunchtime when we arrived on a sunny day. A few goats, which live behind the inn, were wandering about among the diners. The Hehli family, who bought this inn in 1993, farm here, keeping three cows as well as the herd of goats. In the winter Herr Hehli is a housebuilder, but in summer everyone pitches in to run the inn. Peering into the small and simple kitchen, I saw the whole family working like demons: grandma at the sink, washing dishes; father at the range, frying Rösti; mother flying to and fro with trays of dishes; uncle stacking plates.

There are 50 Matratzenlager places, with down quilts instead of the more customary woolen blankets, and one double room under the eaves, which the family makes available only for people who really want to be private. The family must generate their own electricity and pump up their water (which is drinkable) from below. There's a cold-water sink outside the house and an Abort (an old word meaning "toilet").

The principal cook and his daughter at Berggasthaus Mesmer

Mesmer is open from June to the end of October. Tel. 071/799 12 55; 9057 Weissbad.

Getting there: Walking from Schäfler, the trail beyond continues along the crest of the northern chain as a Höhenweg, a high trail. It's narrow and exposed and snakes along the ridge or sometimes just below the crest. Along a few sections there's a fixed metal cable to hold onto, just to steady yourself. A few ledges of polished rock, which would be slippery in rain or snow, protrude up through the gravel path. This Höhenweg continues to the Säntis, the Alpstein's highest peak, but becomes more delicate. Instead, after about 40 minutes, you can leave the Höhenweg by turning left at a signposted junction. Descend steeply to the valley below, following sign-

Going to pasture

posts to Mesmer. From Schäfler by this route: 4 kilometers; 311 meters down; 2 hours.

From here, continue to a lovely lake, the Seealpsee. Note that if you don't want to hike from Ebenalp along the crest of the northern chain and then descend to Mesmer, as described here, the easier way to reach Mesmer is by taking the signposted trail up from Seealpsee (see below), which crosses the meadows, then switchbacks up beside a cascade and reaches Mesmer in about 2 hours. To descend to Seealpsee takes 1 hour, 10 minutes.

SEEALPSEE

This serenely beautiful lake between the north and middle chains, far from the sight or sound of traffic, is nevertheless easy to reach and also can be the starting point for hikes deeper into the Alpstein. Two Berghotels are sited on the lake's northern shore with a view across the Seealpsee to the edge of the meadows, where a rugged mountain barrier abruptly rises, perfectly reflected in the clear water. The sight line has not been spoiled, as the two hotels are partly concealed by a grove of trees, and neither hotel can be seen from the other. Every year on the morning of Assumption Day, August 15, at a chapel in the woods beside the Seealpsee, a choir in traditional Appenzell dress yodels the Mass. Many people are drawn to this event; the men sing outdoors and the audience sits on wooden benches in the grove or on the grass.

If you spend an evening at the lake, it's worth wandering through the meadows across the lake, where there are several little alps. There, on a mild summer evening, we came upon a lone farmer practicing his alpenhorn and were invited into a barn to watch a milking.

Getting there: From Wasserauen, an 11-minute train ride from the town of Appenzell , walk on an easy gravel jeep road to reach the lake in an hour.

41 • BERGGASTHAUS FORELLE • 1141 M

This very handsome Berghotel faces the lake: Its extensive terrace and also its indoor dining room offer splendid views across the water. Although the house dated only from 1935, much of it had to be rebuilt after an avalanche. The new additions retain a traditional air and blend well with the older section.

The à la carte menu offers trout, as might be expected of a lakeside hotel, served with white wine sauce and rice. Chicken is also available as well as Geschnetzeltes Kalbfleisch (veal Zurich-style: strips of veal in a sauce) with Rösti, and the more conventional fare: soup, salads, Schnitzel. Many guests order dinner on the terrace. Breakfast, however, is in the dining room, a large, new, wood-paneled room, bright because of its many windows.

The farmer's evening alpenhorn recital, Seealpsee

The private rooms have pretty bedsteads, head and footboards painted in folk-art style, warm-water sinks and towels, and thick down quilts. The Matratzenlager, with 45 places, have also been made attractive and have warm-water sinks. A shower, available for all guests, costs 1 Sfr. The hotel is open from mid-April to the beginning of November, and it is owned by the Fritsche family. Tel. 071/799 11 88; Fax: 799 15 96; 9057 Weissbad.

42 • BERGGASTHAUS SEEALP • 1141 M

A pleasant country hotel, simpler and plainer than the newly refurbished Forelle, the Seealp also has a terrace with a full, fine view of the lake and a pleasant dining room with windows onto the lake. And here too you can enjoy a dish of trout, cordon bleu, Älpler Macaroni, or other standard fare.

There are six private rooms, pine-paneled, quite fresh and light, with warm-water sinks. The Matratzenlager in the house has 70 places and a washroom with warm-water sink. Showers cost 2 Sfr for 4 minutes. Thirty more dorm places are in a separate house, where there is only cold water and toilet but no shower. Run by the Dorig family, the hotel is open from April or May until the beginning of November. Tel. 071/799 11 40; Fax: 799 18 20; 9057 Weissbad.

43 • BERGGASTHAUS MEGLISALP • 1517 M

Unlike other inns, which are isolated, the one at Meglisalp sits amid a small cluster of farms so that you are aware of the rhythm of farm life. In the early evening (and early morning), you'll hear the farmers calling for their cows and cowbells ringing as the animals troop back to the barns for milking. And as darkness falls you may also hear the Alp Segen, an old alpine tradition still practiced in this most traditional of cantons: Through a wooden megaphone, a farmer calls a prayer over the fields for the protection of beasts and people.

Berggasthaus Meglisalp is run by Sepp and Gaby Manser, who are the fifth generation of their family at the inn. It was built in 1897–1898, when all the wood and building material were carried up on men's backs. Sepp's great-grandfather promised that if everything went well he would build a chapel: It did, and he did, in 1903–1904. The inn's first guests came for a Kur (cure) and drank fresh buttermilk and goat milk. The restaurant was renovated in 1994.

Sepp Manser does a good job in the kitchen. Grilled chicken breast was moist and tender, served with an attractive array of salads. Dinner is à la carte: the menu includes Kalbgeschnetzeltes with noodles, Älpler Macaroni with applesauce, barley soup, Schnitzels, sausages, and Rösti.

If the restaurant looks new, the rooms upstairs are old and charming. Down quilts are amusingly arranged on the high, old-fashioned beds in pointed puffs; pine walls, coffered ceiling, and parquet floor are scrubbed

Saturday night dinner at Meglisalp

spotless; and there's a traditional marble washstand with a pair of pitchers and basins. It's not a new room playing at being antique but the real thing, yet smelling fresh and sweet.

There are nine double rooms and 150 Matratzenlager places. Toilet, warm–water sinks, and showers (these cost 2 Sfr) are in the hall or basement. Some of the Matratzenlager rooms have down quilts (also arranged in pointed puffs), but others have only blankets. The inn is open from mid–May to the end of October. Tel. and Fax: 071/799 11 28; 9057 Weissbad.

Getting there: From Seealpsee: 2.5 kilometers; 380 meters up; 1 hour, 40 minutes. Walk around the Seealpsee to its southern shore and take the trail that switchbacks fairly steeply up. The signposts point to Meglisalp. On a few sections there's a cable to hold, but the trail is good.

ROTSTEINPASS

This notch in the rocky wall that connects the northern and middle chains is a sort of back door to the Alpstein. Its front door is in the northeast, from which the Alpstein's valleys can be approached quite easily by gentle ascent from Wasserauen and Brülisau; coming from the southwest and Outer Appenzell, however, one must surmount this wall via the Rotsteinpass. The pass is most easily reached from Meglisalp within the Alpstein.

Maps of the Alpstein show a route connecting the Fälen Valley to the Rotsteinpass via the Zwinglipass and Rotsteinsattel. It will be noted below that this is a very difficult route with possible dangers.

44 • BERGGASTHAUS ROTSTEIN • 2124 M

The inn fits snugly between two towers of rock, as if into a slot. The pass is quite safely and most easily reached from Meglisalp. It can also be reached from the Säntis to the north, from a route along the ridge, and from the Zwinglipass to the south. Despite the difficulties of the route from the Säntis and from the Zwinglipass, neither of which is recommended in this book, many hikers reach it by those two routes, and the inn is a popular place for lunch. The house looks neither old nor new. It depends on rainwater for its water supply and on mule power for its provisions. The rest of its power comes from a windmill, solar panels, and a diesel generator. There's a good-sized terrace and large dining room to accommodate ravenous hikers. The specialty of the house is Wildpfeffer (hare) served with Spätzli and Rotkraut (red cabbage). The hare is marinated in wine, vinegar, and herbs for 10–12 days, turned in flour, sautéed, and roasted with more marinade. All meals are à la carte.

The inn has 90 Matratzenlager, and cold-water sinks. It is open from mid-June or the end of June to October 20 or thereabouts. It has been run since it was built, in 1934, by the Wyss family. Tel. 071/799 11 41; 9057 Weissbad.

Getting there: From Meglisalp, take the trail that first climbs south to Spitzigstein, then southwest to the pass: 4 kilometers; 600 meters up; 1 hour, 40 minutes.

THE FÄLENSEE

The valley of the Fälensee lies between the middle and southern chains. Whereas the Seealpsee is bordered by gentle meadows, the Fälensee is in a narrower, wilder valley with rocky walls that rise almost from the edge of the lake. A large Berghotel, Bollenwees, is at the eastern end of the lake; at its western end is a farm, Fälenalp, which also takes in overnight guests.

Getting there: The valley of the Fälensee can be reached from several directions. The most gradual approach is from the mouth of the valley, between the middle and southern chains. From the town of Appenzell take the train to Weissbad (a 6-minute ride), then a bus or shuttle van to Brülisau (a 7-minute ride). From Brülisau walk south at first, then southwest into the valley. Either the trail or the road will bring you first to a lower lake, the Sämtisersee, and the Gasthaus Plattenbödeli, then up to Bollenwees and the Fälensee.

You can also approach the Fälensee from the valley to the west, from the Seealpsee, Meglisalp, or the Rotsteinpass. If you start from Rotstein, descend to Meglisalp; from there, take the trail south to Spitzigstein, then

Berggasthaus Rotstein

east over the ridge of the Widderalpstock to the little farm at Widderalp (1644 meters). From there, follow the signposted trail down to Bollenwees.

To approach the Fälensee from Seealpsee, you can either walk up to Meglisalp and follow the route from there, or hike northeast to Hütten, then climb steeply southward to the notch at Bogartenfirst, and from there descend very steeply to the valley below, then down a gentler gradient to Bollenwees.

If you take the Geologischer Wanderweg (see p. 192), the trail will descend to Saxerlücke, just above Bollenwees.

45 • BERGGASTHAUS BOLLENWEES • 1471 M

Bol is an old family name in these parts, and *wees* means "meadow" in local dialect. The big inn at the eastern end of the Fälensee looks as if it had cloned itself; two identical buildings, joined in the center, overlook the lake. They are, however, of different dates: The new building was added in 1986 to the old one, which was constructed in 1938. The place evolved slowly to accommodate hikers. In 1880, guests could stay in the simple hut of an alp here and get milk, coffee, or tea. The alp was bought by a corporation of three men in 1903 to keep the land within the canton; the terms required the alpkeeper to continue to serve milk and coffee at "reasonable" prices and to provide Heulager (hayloft) accommodations for 50 centimes. As more guests came, attracted by the beauty of the spot, a small guesthouse was built. This burned in 1937 and was rebuilt a year later. It is still owned by an association, but has been run for many years by Röbi Manser-Dorig and his family. There is an annual Älplerfest here on the last Sunday in July, or if August 1 is a Sunday, then the week before.

Bollenwees is large, new, and impersonal; one gets no sense of the owner's (or manager's) personality as at smaller inns. The people are not cold, but a certain warmth is not there. The private rooms are comfortable, with warm-water sinks and towels. A few rooms have showers.

The dining room is large, and all meals are à la carte. The specialty of the kitchen is Kalbgeschnetzeltes with Rösti or noodles; other dishes are standard. There are 12 new private rooms with shower and toilet, a few rooms with four beds and warm-water sinks, 3 single rooms with warm-water sinks, and 130 Matratzenlager places. Downstairs are a washroom and showers (2 Sfr for 3 minutes) and a drying room for wet clothes.

Bollenwees is open from mid-May to the end of October. Tel. 071/799 11 70; Fax: 799 15 33; 9058 Brülisau.

Berggasthaus Bollenwees

46 • FÄLENALP • 1457 M

From Bollenwees, a trail follows the north shore of the Fälensee to a little farm, Fälenalp, in a spectacular location at the west end of the lake. The walk takes 25–30 minutes, and it's worth going there as the view is more dramatic at the Fälenalp end of the lake. There the narrow green valley is enfolded by mighty walls of sheer rock, 600 meters high, with a view of the lake just below. You can also stay overnight at Fälenalp. Conditions are considerably rougher than at Bollenwees; on the other hand, you can view all the operations of a working alp, run by the warm and friendly Koller family. During an hour's visit, we watched the goats being brought in and milked, saw milk cooked in a giant cauldron to make alp cheese, enjoyed the raucous spectacle of feeding time for the pigs (they dined on whey and flakes of grain), and were invited into the kitchen by Frau Koller to watch her knead butter in a wooden bowl, after which she offered us a lump to taste.

The farmhouse is small and very simple, fieldstone below and wood above. Guests at Fälenalp eat a hearty dinner in the little family dining room at a simple wooden trestle table or, in nice weather, at a weathered old table outdoors. Every evening Farmer Koller calls the Alp Segen, the

Alp blessing, beseeching protection for the little community of animals and people.

The Kollers care for 100 heifers and cows (they have 18 to milk), 300 sheep, 56 goats—animals sent up here by their owners for the summer grazing—and a few chickens and pigs. Alps like Fälenalp are not the homes of gentlemen farmers, designed to have a "country look." Don't expect antique chairs and colorful rugs. At Fälenalp the old ceramic stove that heats the downstairs is probably antique—Frau Koller splits the wood for it on a block in the kitchen. There are milk cans everywhere, a straw broom, a farm dog. Alp cheese and butter are kept cool in the cellar, which is cut right into the rock.

Guests sleep in Matratzenlager. There are 37 places in a loft above the cow barn; the cows, however, stay outside to graze during the night, and there are another 13 places in a room beside the pig barn. As one would expect, the latrine is outside.

Note that maps show a route connecting Fälenalp with the Rotsteinpass by means of a trail from Fälenalp up to the Zwinglipass, from which you turn northward to cross over the Rotsteinsattel and then descend to the

Dinnertime at Fälenalp

Rotsteinpass. The trail up to the Zwinglipass is good, and the view worth seeing. Beyond that the way becomes difficult, and the descent from the Rotsteinsattel to the Rotsteinpass is extremely difficult, involving long descents on steep rock slabs where one needs both hands free to hold onto the cables on either side. Although many Swiss do this route, we cannot recommend it. A better and quite reasonable choice would be to turn southeast at the Zwinglipass and head for Mutschen and Roslenalp, a trail that bring you down to Saxerlücke (see below and p. 195) and is said to be good. There are no inns on this section of trail.

The Koller family stays at the Fälenalp farm and accepts guests from mid-June to the first week of September. There is no telephone; just turn up.

47 • BERGGASTHAUS PLATTENBÖDELI • 1284 M

As you walk along the valley between Brülisau and the Fälensee, you pass this inn just beside the jeep road and opposite the Sämtisersee. Its name means flat (Platten) little floor (bödeli). Plattenbödeli is about an hour's walk down from Bollenwees and takes about 1½ hours up from Brülisau.

A house dating from 1911 was converted into this inn in 1931. Alois and Rita Inauen raise their children here in summer and keep the inn. Specialties of the kitchen include homemade barley soup and Chäshornli—their recipe for the well-known Älpler Macaroni, served with applesauce—and Schnitzel with mushroom-cream sauce. There are 10 pleasant double rooms, some with old bedsteads and wooden floor, walls, and ceiling; others, also attractive, have more modern beds. All the rooms have washstands with pitchers and basins. The washroom sink has warm water, and a shower is available for 2 Sfr. There are two rooms for families, containing two beds and two Matratzenlager-like sleeping spaces for kids. Thirty Matratzenlager places are in the main house, and another 50 in a separate little house that has its own toilet and cold-water sink.

The inn is open from May 1 to November 1. Tel. 071/799 11 52, Fax: 799 16 99; 9058 Brülisau.

THE GEOLOGISCHER WANDERWEG

Along the southern chain of the Alpstein is a high, narrow ridge with a trail along its crest known as the Geologischer Wanderweg, the Geologic Path. The southern chain seems to begin abruptly with the Hoher Kasten (1795 meters), a rock tower (the name means High Cupboard) that suddenly heaves up from the meadows near Brülisau. The Geologischer Wanderweg begins (or ends) atop it. At the other end is Saxerlücke, a notch in the

The operator of the farmers' lift to Alp Sigel

Berggasthaus Staubern

southern chain. Along this path are tables of orientation and information concerning the geology of the region and explaining the geological phenomena—in German. The trail is a good one but there is considerable exposure. About 15 minutes west of Staubern one must descend a few rocky steps—about 30 meters—with cables to hold onto (the most tricky section of the whole path). Hikers must go slowly and be careful and should not walk any part of the Geologische Wanderweg in bad conditions—on a misty or rainy day or if there's snow on the path. Below the ridge on one side is the valley of the Sämtisersee and Fälensee, and on the other side is the Rhine River with Liechtenstein across it.

Getting there: From Brülisau (see p. 188), you can take a little bus to the lift station, then take the cable car to the top of the Hoher Kasten. At the top are a large restaurant and hotel and an alpine garden, with labeled specimens of alpine flowers. The Geologische Wanderweg starts at the Hoher Kasten and follows the undulations of the ridge.

48 • BERGGASTHAUS STAUBERN (ALSO STAUBEREN) • 1790 M

This attractive little inn seems balanced atop the ridge of the southern chain, with a bird's-eye view into the valleys on both sides. It can be reached only by the Geologische Wanderweg or, surprisingly, by a small, four-person lift from the town of Frümsen on the Rhine. When we stopped there, we saw a few men in business shirts and ties among the hikers—they had come up on the lift for lunch. (As the lift costs 60 Sfr round-trip, or 50 just to descend, it's worth having a group of four to share the cost.)

Hikers enjoy lunch on the little terrace, overlooking the Rhine, or in the wood-paneled dining room. Dinner is à la carte. There are 60 or more Matratzenlager places, reached through a trapdoor on the top floor. There is no natural water supply and, as you would expect, no shower, and the washroom water is not potable. The house, built in 1929–1930, has been run by the Lüchinger family for three generations.

It's open from May to November. Tel. 071/799 11 77; 9058 Brülisau.

Getting there: Start the Geologischer Wanderweg from Hoher Kasten. After 2.75 km and 2–2½ hours, reach Staubern, which apart from the hotel on the Hoher Kasten is the only inn along the southern chain. From Staubern, another 3.5 km and 2 hours, 40 minutes or 3 hours will bring you down to Saxerlücke, from which you can reach Bollenwees in about 20 minutes.

CHAPTER 8

CENTRAL SWITZERLAND

The cantons in the center of the country are, historically, the heart of Switzerland. At Rütli meadow, in central Switzerland, was sworn the Eidgenossenschafr, or "Oath of Everlasting Alliance," by which three communities, Uri, Schwyz, and Unterwalden, pledged mutual defense against the tyranny of the Austrian Hapsburgs. There the nation of Switzerland was born, and August 1 is the national holiday, to commemorate the signing of that oath on that date in 1291. By tradition, the legendary Swiss hero William Tell came from this region.

Central Switzerland is the country's crossroads: To the north is Zurich and to the south is the important St. Gotthard Pass, a major route to Italy. The mountains of this region form the watershed from which the Rhône flows westward and the Rhine eastward. One of the country's loveliest cities, Lucerne, is sited at the head of Lake Lucerne, more properly called the Vierwaldstattersee, or Lake of the Four Forest Cantons. A high promontory overlooking this lake as well as Lake Zub, Mount Rigi was one of the earliest tourist attractions in Switzerland. But few travelers venture into the region's high country, beyond Lucerne, the Rigi, or another nearby popular viewpoint, Pilatus.

Although Central Switzerland has mountains and glaciers, there are no famous peaks (the highest in this region is the Titlis, 3929 meters) or internationally known summer or ski resorts. Therefore, this is another part of Switzerland not only off the tourist track but also off the "track" or trail even for most hikers from other countries; you'll find few visitors, and they are nearly all Swiss.

RIGI KULM

The Rigi is a long ridge rising from the lake region of central Switzerland and culminating at the Kulm (which means mountaintop), its highest point. The Rigi Kulm was one of the earliest famous panoramic viewpoints in the

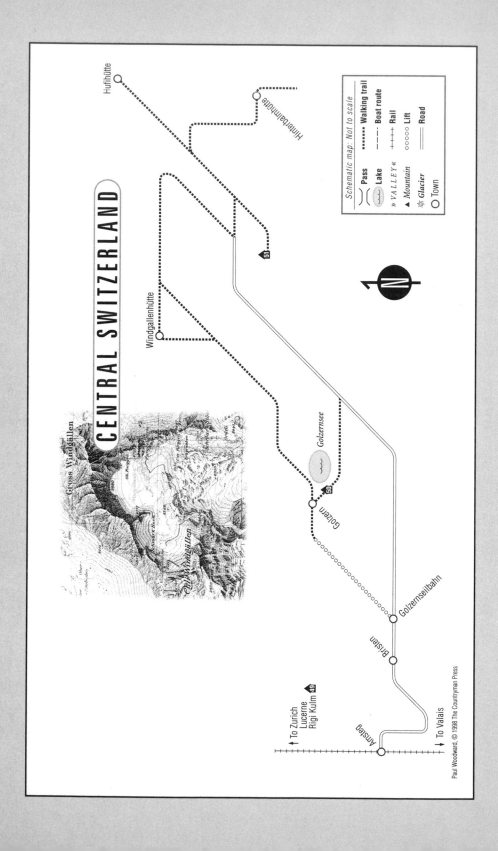

CENTRAL SWITZERLAND

Hüfihütte

Hinterbalmhütte

Windgallenhütte

51

Golzernsee

50

Golzern

Golzernseilbahn

Bristen

Cross Windgällen

Chli Windgällen

Amsteg

← To Zurich
Lucerne
Rigi Kulm 49

To Valais →

Paul Woodward, © 1998 The Countryman Press

Schematic map: Not to scale

Pass	•••••• Walking trail
Lake	– – – Boat route
» *VALLEY* «	+++++ Rail
▲ *Mountain*	ooooo Lift
❄ *Glacier*	Road
○ Town	

Alps. At 1800 meters, this summit is not comparatively high, but it stands alone and gives a sweeping, 360-degree view: To the south a snowy wall, the Bernese Oberland, forms the horizon; to the north the land seems spread out like a great quilt, a vast green expanse checkered with blue lakes. At several points along the Rigi are clusters of farms and scattered inns. And atop this promontory is one of the most famous of all Swiss mountain hotels.

49 • HOTEL RIGI KULM • 1750 M

The original inn of the Rigi Kulm was the first Swiss Gasthaus to be built on a Kulm. In 1804, a Swiss artist, Heinrich Keller, began painting the view from the Rigi Kulm. But as there was nowhere to stay at the Kulm, he had to stay below at Rigi Klösterli and hike up every day—and sometimes twice a day—to paint the scene. At last he asked his innkeeper to build an inn at the Kulm so he wouldn't have to climb up and down, and the first Gasthaus was built there in 1816, with six beds.

The Rigi Kulm became the place to go; writers, artists, and musicians making a tour of the Alps had to stop there. In the 19th century, when viewing the sunrise from a mountaintop became a cult, watching the dawn from the Rigi Kulm became de rigueur. "This is the popular mountain in Switzerland. Every body ascends it, young and old, grave and gay, men, women, and children; some walk, some ride, some are carried up in chairs with poles under them, like Guy Fawkes." (Jones 1866, p. 28) Did the famous writers who made the pilgrimage know that one day their penned words would be compared with those of the others? James Fenimore Cooper wrote in 1828 that the spectator seems literally to hang over the lake below and that behind rose "mountains in a crowd and confusion that render description hopeless . . . a congress of earthly giants." Victor Hugo, in 1839, wrote that at the Rigi one found everything necessary: an inn, an observation point, and a cross; the stomach, the eye, and the soul have a triple need, and at the Rigi Kulm, that need is satisfied. Alexandre Dumas praised the view but noted that upon entering the inn, it seemed the Tower of Babel, as 27 travelers of 11 different nations had come to see the sunrise. Other notable guests included Goethe, Wordsworth, Alphonse Daudet, Carl Maria von Weber, and Felix Mendelssohn. Escoffier served in its kitchen, César Ritz worked as a chef. But the guest who immortalized the place was Mark Twain, in the wryly humorous sketches he wrote for *A Tramp Abroad*.

Besides these notables, more ordinary visitors found the experience an ecstatic one. Most stayed up for sunset, then rose for sunrise as well. An American, Samuel Irenaeus Prime, described the ritual of a visit to the Rigi in 1860: He stood one evening among the little crowd that watched the sunset wrapped in their cloaks to protect them from the cold, then hastened down, ravenous, to the hotel, "where a table for a hundred guests was spread, with a hot supper sufficient for half the number; and before ten o'clock we were sound asleep. Those who could not find beds spent the night in the dining hall, entertaining themselves and disturbing the rest, but

The Bernese Oberland from the Rigi Kulm

we were so far above them that we heard nothing till the blast of a wooden horn rung through the halls, informing us that the sun would be up before us if we did not hasten to meet him. We hurried on our clothes, wrapped up warmly, and in a few moments stood with our faces to the East, intently watching, like worshippers of the Sun, the first signs of his coming." (The horn, he reports, was blown again as the sun emerged.) Prime found it, indeed, incomparable: ". . . the most splendid of all the prospects we had ever seen, or expect to see on earth." (Prime 1860, pp. 48–49)

The Reverend Harry Jones, writing, like Prime, in 1860, responded more wryly to the sunrise ceremony: "There was a notice in each of our rooms, desiring gentlemen not to dress themselves in the blankets when they went out to see the sun rise, under pain of a fine of one or two francs." When Jones arose to leave the hotel, very early, he saw only two or three others behind him. "Presently however I heard the row begin. I was, say, two hundred yards from the hotel, and yet I could hear the hideous noise travelling about its inside, like a mad bull in a paddock, quite distinctly. No wonder people woke; in about five minutes they began to pour out at the door like bees from a hive you have tapped. They seemed to have made a point of not dressing. It is the correct thing to hurry out, unshaved, unwashed, with wraps huddled on; some had bed-feathers in their hair, at least fluff of some kind, and noses blue with cold; they all streamed out to see the sun rise; it was very ridiculous, and very sublime." (Jones 1866, pp. 33–34)

Throughout the 19th century the little inn was enlarged and made ever grander. The cog railway up the Rigi was begun in 1871, and by 1875, when it reached the top, the hotel was like a palace. But fashions change; when Ernst Käppeli bought it in 1949 it was in utter disrepair, rain falling into the upper floor. The Käppeli family began its restoration, reopening the hotel in 1954 while continuing the work. The present owners are the next generation of Käppelis, Beat and Renate, who also run the hotel personally and oversee every detail. It is now a fine hotel, a blend of the modern and the antique. They saved as much as they could and rebuilt and refurnished the rest. The old style lives on in the formal dining room, with its coffered ceiling, parquet floor, chandeliers, and gilt mirrors. A sideboard and cabinets display fine silver and porcelain from the hotel's golden age; the tables are set with white linen and silver. There is a menu to match, with such dishes as fillet of trout with apple cider sauce and creole rice, and fillet of lamb in a crust. There's also a fixed menu with less expensive dishes that are still at the high end of the moderate-price range. Croissants are served for breakfast in the same dining room. But just outside this gracious room is a large cafeteria in a handsome, contemporary style, open during the daytime only for the crowds of sightseers.

The hotel still displays a chart with the times of sunrise and will awaken guests for sunrise viewing.

Upstairs are a small, comfortable salon and a billiards room. There are 22 private rooms with private bath and shower, 10 others without showers (there are showers in the hall), and 18 Matratzenlager places in a separate building. Rates depend on whether a room has a private tub and shower, or just a shower, or only a warm-water sink. Half-pension is available. The hotel is open all year; in winter there is both downhill and cross-country skiing here, and sledding. The only unattractive feature is the hotel's exterior. A big gray concrete structure, it resembles a huge barracks, and the steel deck also has an institutional look. But step inside, and everything is bright and attractive. From the hotel to the top of the Rigi Kulm is a walk of about 10 minutes by either of two paths, one a little more direct and steeper. Tel. 041/855 03 03; Fax. 855 00 55; 6410 Rigi Kulm.

Getting there: You can hike up to the Rigi Kulm, as Mark Twain did, or ride up on one of two cog railways, one starting from Arth-Goldau (on the Zugersee) and the other from Vitznau (on the Vierwaldstattersee). You can also ride up as far as Rigi Kaltbad by cable car from Weggis (which is also on the Vierwaldstattersee), then take the cog railway the rest of the way. All these are easily reached from nearby Lucerne. Three times during summer a special sunrise train comes up from Goldau; periodically there are also old-fashioned trains pulled by steam engine and manned by a crew in 19th-century dress.

Walks: There are trails all along the Rigi, some that simply climb to the top, others that meander around the slopes. Although the summit is a "mere" 1800 meters (there are many villages at that altitude in Switzerland), it's a climb of about 1375 meters from the lakeshore. You can take the cog railway partway up—it makes about six stops—then walk the rest of the way. Brochures outlining several hiking routes are available free of charge at the cog railway stations.

MADERANERTAL

This valley (in Canton Uri) once attracted an international clientele because of its mountain hotel. Before the development of all the modern methods that make places famous—the media, the tourist industry, and advertising—most well-to-do travelers could only get to places that were accessible (by horse and carriage) and would only go to places where they would find comfortable accommodations, conditions infrequently met before the 20th century. An old hotel in the Maderanertal met those conditions then; today it is no longer the only choice available for hikers in that valley.

From the Reuss River, which flows northward through central Switzer-

Scuol, Lower Engadine

land, the Maderanertal rises eastward. The Golzernsee is a little lake on a shelf on the Maderanertal's northern slope, near some of its best hikes.

50 • RESTAURANT (GASTHAUS) GOLZERNSEE • 1409 M

Small and simple, tucked away in a valley that few people visit, this is one of those obscure little mountain inns that can accommodate only a few guests but somehow get known anyway. The little wooden chalet is near the lake. Beside its terrace is an alp Stübli, a rustic wooden cabin where guests can have their meals. The inn itself has two rooms on the main floor: the kitchen and a small, cozy dining room. It's hard not to pile up diminutives when describing Restaurant Golzernsee, but this is not an inn in miniature, just a small and modest place. Nothing here is either remarkably handsome or the opposite; indeed, some guests find its very ordinariness (as well as its obscurity) deeply appealing. Perhaps its very simplicity and unself-consciousness—the absence of special touches that say, "Am I not charming?"—satisfy some yearning. Here we met a couple who resort to the Restaurant Golzernsee often as their weekend retreat. The house was built in 1934 by the Jauch family, who have run it ever since: Elderly Mother Jauch still helps in the kitchen and gets up early to start breakfast, while the main work is done by Walter and Hanni Jauch, brother and sister.

Half-pension guests may take the evening's menu or order à la carte. One evening menu consisted of chopped meat and pureed potatoes with vegetables, another of risotto with mushrooms, meat, and salad. The à la carte fare is standard: soup, salad, platters of dried or smoked meat, sausages, cutlets and Schnitzel, Älpler Macaroni, and, of course, Rösti. The only drawback is a small jukebox, although some of its few tunes are Swiss and most guests don't play it at all. In fine weather you can always eat outside or in the cabin on the terrace—the Stübli.

Private rooms are simple and comfortable. There are toilets and warm-water sinks in the hall. There are five double rooms and 30 Matratzenlager places divided between two rooms. The Matratzenlager and a few more single rooms are in a separate building behind the hotel, where there is also a shower—the only one available for all guests—for a charge of 3 Sfr. Towels are available.

The inn is open from May 1 to mid-November. Tel. 041/883 11 56 or 883 16 23; 6475 Bristen.

Getting there: From the rail station at Amsteg take a PTT bus to Bristen; the bus continues a little past the Bristen post office to a lift station, the Golzernseilbahn, from which most guests take a small cable car 600 meters up to Golzern. From the upper station, walk eastward on the trail up the valley (you'll pass another inn along the way, Gasthaus Edelweiss) and reach Restaurant Golzernsee in about 20–30 minutes.

Walks:

WALK 1 • A favorite destination here is the Windgallenhütte, owned not by the Swiss Alpine Club but by the Alpine Academic Club of the University of Zurich: 3 kilometers; 623 meters up; 2½ hours.

The signposted trail starts just outside Restaurant Golzernsee and climbs northeastward, mostly over meadows and then up a rocky slope; bear left at a junction and reach the hut. Recently renovated and enlarged, it's set below a long, craggy rock wall topped with snow. You can retrace your steps, but this hike can also be extended toward the scenic end of the valley.

Golzernzee

If you decide to continue from the Windgallen hut, follow the trail eastward toward Tritt, site of an old alp. In about 40 minutes turn right at an old wooden sign pointing right for Hotel SAC and Bristen (the trail to the right is blazed; the way to the left is unblazed and unmarked). Descend past many waterfalls and a fine view of the glacier. At the next signposted junction, turn right for Hotel SAC and Bristen. To return to Golzernsee you can either go back up toward the Windgallen hut, then cut off to the left (southwest) near Alp Stafel; or you can continue down to the Hotel SAC, which is the old name for the Hotel Maderanertal. If you continue to the hotel, you must then walk down the valley to the Golzernseilbahn, almost as far as Bristen, and take the lift back up, or else climb back up on the Glaspelenweg. For the latter, continue 35 minutes past the hotel to the second of two bridges on your right. A sign points to Golzern and the Windgallen hut. The trail climbs very steeply, with many wooden steps; it will take at least 1 hour to ascend; at the top, Restaurant Golzernsee is to your left, a few minutes away. (If you walk this entire route, count on 7 hours.) From the Windgallen hut via the Hotel Maderanertal to Bristen is 9.25 kilometers.

51 • HOTEL MADERANERTAL • 1394 M

This is the old hotel referred to in the opening paragraph of this section. It opened in 1865 under the name Schweizer Alpenclub but has gone by other names in its long history, some still seen on trail signposts—Hotel SAC, Hotel Alpenclub, and Kurhaus auf Balmenegg. Its first visitors were Swiss, English, German, and French; Friedrich Nietzsche was one of the notables who stayed there. The first hotel burned in 1880 and was rebuilt. It was a veritable summer resort, a compound with its own post and telegraph office, chapel, doctor, hairdresser, library, reading room (with German and English newspapers), salon for dancing, ladies' salon, bowling alley, laundry, bakery, slaughterhouse and butcher—and a camera obscura. The price list included a rate for servants. But the years rolled on and it was renovated for the last time in the 1930s. Until recently its survival was in doubt, but in 1996 Anna Fedier and her son Tobias bought the place and now run it themselves.

This hotel is undoubtedly a historic curiosity, and it's also a convenience for hikers: It's on the direct route for the Hufihütte SAC. A pleasant little lawn in front is an appealing spot for lunch; otherwise, meals and snacks are served in a large room, recently renovated, instead of in the elegant old dining room with its parquet floor. But the hotel is severely run-down, even more so now than when we were last here, in about 1980. A few other inns are as old, but none is this shabby. Guests, however, still come to stay overnight.

Dinner is à la carte and the fare is conventional, with salads, Schnitzel, platters of dried meat, sausage, Rösti. Tobias Fedier makes a very good vegetable soup. At breakfast orange juice is served, and slices of cheese.

The rooms are more problematic. The old wallpaper has been painted or papered over a dreary yellow, and here and there one spots a hole in the plaster. The floor planks are neither light pine nor warm, rich brown, but dark and grayish, and the foot rugs beside the beds look worn. There is a shower, warm-water sink, and toilet in the hall. Frau Fedier and her son are trying hard to make the hotel a welcoming place and to run a good kitchen, but the expense of full renovation is surely beyond them.

There are 19 private rooms, of which 3 are singles, in the main house and more private rooms in another building, which also holds the Matratzenlager, 21 places divided among two rooms. The hotel opens between the middle and end of May and closes at the end of October. Tel. 041/883 11 22 or 883 02 94; 6475 Bristen (Uri).

Getting there: The walk from Bristen: 7 kilometers; 624 meters up; 2½ hours. You can also go by taxi-van: telephone Rover, 041/883 14 80.

Walks:

WALK 1 • From the Maderanertal you can walk up to the Windgallen-hütte (see above), a climb of 638 meters. Either follow the signposted trail to the northeast and then west from Tritt (the reverse of Walk 1 just above), or take the shorter, steeper trail directly up (heading northwest).

WALK 2 • Hufihütte SAC: 5 kilometers; 940 meters up; 3½ hours.

Another signposted trail leads northeastward to the Hufihütte SAC at the edge of the Hufifirn Glacier. Start as to Tritt but then turn off to the right and cross the stream; the ascent steepens, with switchbacks up to the hut.

CHAPTER 9

CANTON GRAUBUNDEN

The Graubunden is in the southeast of the country. It offers a variety not only of cultures but also of landscape, from great peaks and glaciers that attract skilled climbers to rugged country through which hikers may ramble, and gentler terrain suitable for a casual stroll

Switzerland's largest canton is, paradoxically, the home of its truly minority language, Romansch—fewer people speak it than any of the other three national languages. The canton goes by three names: Graubunden in German, Grisons in French, and Grischun in Romansch. Romansch is descended from Rhaetic, a language derived from Latin. There is a Romansch culture, visible in a distinctive architectural style, and a regional cuisine. This is a living language, with several dialects and a literature, and if you visit, you can hear it spoken (except in the big international resorts, like St. Moritz). Although all speakers of Romansch also speak at least German if not other languages as well, they are determined that their own beloved language will survive. As the canton also has valleys settled by many German-speaking people, it's often called by its German name.

Romansch speakers are to be found in a number of Graubunden valleys. The regions around the sources of the Rhine, the Vorderrhein and Hinterrhein, are part of this canton. In these areas, some valleys speak Romansch, others speak German.

THE VORDERRHEIN

The Rhine originates in the southeastern Swiss Alps, its headwaters arising in two different places in Canton Graubunden. The two rivers, the Vorderrhein and the Hinterrhein, join together near Chur to become the famous Rhine, which then flows northward into Germany and the Netherlands. Very, very few non-Swiss come to these regions, near the sources of the Rhine—they are, to coin a phrase, deeply off the beaten track. There are no celebrated mountains here, or famous resorts, no well-known name to

Chapel of San Guisep

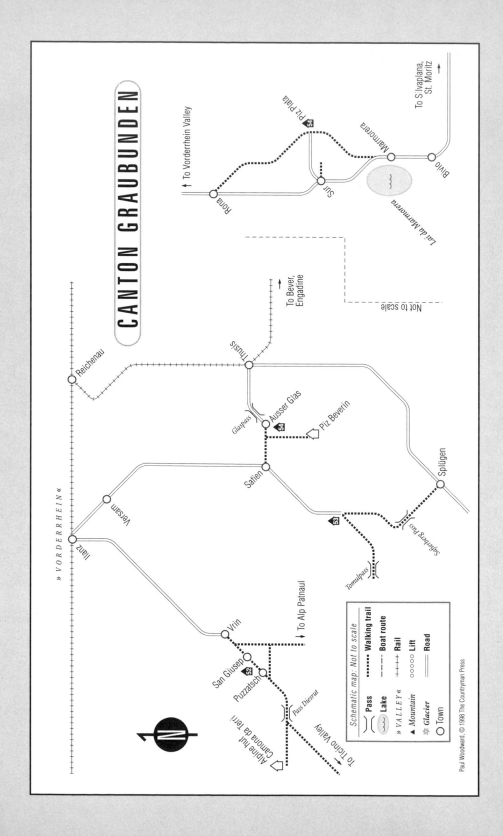

CANTON GRAUBUNDEN

To Vorderrhein Valley →

Piz Plata

54

Roma

Sur

Marmorera

To Silvaplana, St. Moritz ↑

Bivio

Lai da Marmorera

Not to scale

To Bever, Engadine ↑

Reichenau

Trusis

» VORDERRHEIN «

Ausser Glas

Glaspass

Piz Beverin

56

Splügen

Safien

Versam

55

Safierberg Pass

Ilanz

Tomulpass

Vrin

→ To Alp Patnaul

San Giusep

52

Puzzatsch

Pass Diesrut

To Ticino Valley

Alpine hut
Camona da Terri

Schematic map: Not to scale

〕〔 **Pass**	•••••• **Walking trail**
～ **Lake**	– – – **Boat route**
» VALLEY «	+++++ **Rail**
» *Mountain*	ooooo **Lift**
▲ *Mountain*	═══ **Road**
❀ *Glacier*	
○ **Town**	

N

Paul Woodward. © 1998 The Countryman Press

draw visitors. But mountains there are, and good, uncrowded hiking country, and inns, some of which are charming. As few people, and almost no international visitors, come to this region, the trails are not signposted as often or as well as in more touristed parts of the country, but for most hikes, people should be able to find their way without much difficulty.

VAL LUMNEZIA

This is one of several valleys that drain the high country around the source of the Vorderrhein. Its beautiful Romansch name reflects the language of its inhabitants. (The valley immediately to the east, the Valsertal, is German-speaking.)

Getting there: Access is from Ilanz, a town on the Vorderrhein and on the railway; from the Ilanz rail station, a PTT bus goes up the valley as far as the small village of Vrin (pronounced *Frin*), nearly an hour's ride.

52 • USTARIA TGAMANADA • 1600 M

(*Note:* In Romansch, the consonant cluster "tg" is pronounced "tch"; an Ustria, like the Italian word *Ostaria,* is an inn.)

This little guesthouse is plain, a word used to describe other inns in this book, but unlike the others its plainness is not merely a matter of simplicity (although it is simple), but of ordinariness. Here you will be very comfortable, in clean surroundings, get a good meal, and be received with a friendly greeting, but there is nothing about the inn that is particularly rustic or charming—nor is there anything disagreeable or disinviting. (Its most distinctive feature is that the menu offers a number of regional dishes.) It is kept by local people who don't appear to leave this remote valley very often, and when they renovated this old farmhouse, dating from 1779, they did not concern themselves much with appearances. They apparently just wanted to improve it a little, bring it up to date in a simple way. It's worth visiting because of some splendid hiking; it is, moreover, the only inn above Vrin. (There is another simple inn in Vrin itself, which looks cozy and pleasant: the **Ustaria dalla Posta;** Tel. 081/931 12 22; 7149 Vrin.)

The Ustaria Tgamanada is in the hamlet of San Giusep, about a 40-minute walk beyond Vrin. It is on the valley road, but the PTT bus goes no farther than Vrin. There is one small shop in Vrin and nothing beyond it, so if you need any, stock up on picnic supplies there.

The dining room at the Ustaria Tgamanada is in two sections, one near the little bar, very much frequented by local farmers, and the other used mainly by people who want a meal and not just a beer. The decoration consists of a few stuffed deer heads and some photographs of the mountains. The private rooms are comfortable, with new furnishings and warm-water sinks; good-sized towels are provided. A toilet, shower, and sink are in the hall.

Meals are à la carte. The regional specialties, each for a minimum of two people, include these: Bizochels cun truffels tsagranai (a sort of Spätzli with potatoes), Bulzani cum compot, groms e caschiel (a sort of pancake with fruit preserves), macaruns con truffels (a dish like Älpler Macaroni), and Capuns (stuffed or served with some ham and spinach). There is also standard fare: barley soup, salads, plates of dried meat, sausages, gnocchi with cheese, veal and pork Schnitzels, and cordon bleu. For children there's a plate (Kinderteller) of sautéed chicken cutlet with french fries: The kitchen will gladly prepare this as an adult portion, with Rösti—or noodles if you prefer—and vegetables. At breakfast they will ask if you would like orange juice ("Möchten sie Orangensaft?") and serve it if you wish it (just say "Ja"). I have noticed that when orange juice is served at breakfast in Swiss hotels, some Swiss people drink it after their coffee while others sip it slowly with breakfast, and perhaps the Caminada family, who own this hotel, assume that some don't really want it at all at breakfast.

There are six double rooms and 40 dormitory spaces, divided among four rooms, in another building (with indoor toilet, warm-water sink, and shower available). Anton and Genoveva Caminada speak German, Italian, and Romansch and have a waitress who speaks French. The hotel is open all year but closed on Wednesdays, except during July and August. Tel. 081/931 17 43; 7149 Vrin.

Getting there: Take the bus to Vrin, then continue walking up the road to San Giusep: 1.7 kilometers; 152 meters up; 50 minutes. If you have a car, you can drive up to the inn.

Walks:

WALK 1 • The great walk here is to the Plaun la Greina (pronounced *Gry*, to rhyme with try), a long, beautiful, uninhabited valley. This can be a shorter or longer walk, depending on how far you wish to go. Hikers not returning that evening to Vrin or San Giusep can continue to the end of the La Greina Valley, which connects with the Ticino. Some hikers walk to an alpine club hut, the Camona da Terri, which is just off the La Greina

Self-service milkbar on the way to Plaun la Greina

trail, spend the night there, and continue the next day to Campo Blenio or Olivone in the Ticino. To Pass Diesrut: 5.75 kilometers; 882 meters up; 3¼ hours.

From San Giusep, continue to Puzzatsch, the hamlet at the end of the road. There, a sign will point you left to the Pass Diesrut, Camona da Terri, and the Paso della Greina. The trail is generally distinct, but watch for blazes. At a stream (easy to cross) you'll see a sign and some objects: This is a Milch (milk) bar, set up by a local farmer. In the stream are a can of milk and another of yogurt, cooled by the water; on a wooden bar hang some

Haying near Puzzatsch

mugs, a brush, and a strainer, and there are jars of cocoa, honey, and tea-spoons. One jar is labeled KASSE—the cash box. You are asked to deposit 1.50 Sfr for a mug of milk, 2 for cocoa or yogurt, 2.50 for yogurt with honey—and please to clean out your mug with the brush when you're fin-ished. There is also a little sign in German relating the history of the pass, which has been used for millenia. Soon after this, a signposted junction will point you right for the pass. Ascend, with the brook to your right, and reach the Pass Diesrut. Even if you don't plan to go much farther, it's well worth beginning the descent, continuing for another 15 minutes or so, for a view down to the Plaun la Greina. (If you wish to go to the alpine club hut, a signpost will point the way; as you descend toward la Greina, the hut becomes visible on your right, on a promontory; it can be reached from the Pass Diesrut in about an hour. To continue to the Paso della Greina would take another 2 hours.

WALK 2 • Another route, said to be steeper and more difficult, leads to Alp Patnaul (2047 meters) and the Fuorcla Patnaul (2773 meters). From Puzzatsch, take a sharp left, descend to the river, and follow the trail along it until you reach a signpost that will point you up to those destinations.

SAFIENTAL

This is a gentler valley, more pastoral in appearance than the Val Lumnezia to the west.

Getting there: From the rail station at Ilanz, take a PTT bus to Versam, and change there for the bus that goes up the valley. The bus goes beyond Thalkirch, the last hamlet (with the valley's last shop; closed on Thursdays), to the Turrahus Inn and makes its final stop there.

53 • BERGGASTHAUS TURRAHUS (ALSO TURRAHAUS) • 1700 M

This little guesthouse is a jewel in every respect, and few inns can compare with it. It is a 300-year-old farmhouse that retains some of the original ceilings and walls. It became an inn about 1907. You enter a small central hall with a stone floor and magnificent beams on the ceiling. To one side are the two small dining rooms; the old wood of the walls and beamed ceilings is in rich, warm tones, beautifully burnished. To see either of these two little rooms makes you want to eat something in it. The private rooms are small but pretty and inviting. The corridor itself is attractive, with handsome wood floors, a colorful rag carpet, a shelf of books, dried flowers. Even the Matratzenlager is tasteful. There is a new bath facility with toilet in the hall and both separate warm–water–sink rooms and separate showers for men and women, all available for dorm guests. Towels are provided to private-room guests upon request.

All this magic has been worked by Angelika and Erwin Bandli, an energetic young couple with not only good taste but also love of innkeeping and love of the valley. Erwin was born in the Safiental and Angelika in a nearby town. Angelika, a technical artist, met Erwin, and together they became guardians of an alpine club hut, then bought the Turrahus in 1994. While they have retained nearly everything about the old inn (except for the beds), they built an impressive new kitchen (retaining its handsome ceiling beams) with a certain aim in mind: Erwin not only cooks but, with their impressive new ovens, also makes all their baked goods—all the bread, cakes, and pastries. The house is nearly always filled with the enticing smell of baking.

Guests are placed at dinner by name card, with perhaps six people at each table, and the meal is served family-style. (We were thoughtfully seated with two couples of about our age, a Swiss couple on holiday with their friends, an emigrant to Canada and his Canadian-born wife, and all four spoke English.) Vegetarians are cheerfully accommodated: Just announce your preference in advance or when you arrive. The evening's menu was an excellent green salad, polenta, cooked carrots, and meat in a sauce, and for vegetarians a tasty sort of cutlet made of wheat in an herbed tomato sauce. As a rather unusual feature, the staff came around with bowls and platters offering seconds of everything—polenta, carrots, meat, and vegetarian cutlets. Erwin's homemade bread was served with dinner and a slice of his delicious nut-cranberry cake was dessert. Another special feature of the Turrahus is that a variety of teas are available, both black and herbal (Angelika doesn't drink coffee and decided to offer a wide selection of teas); our group finished dinner by ordering a pot of Punsch-tee, a delicious blend containing apple cider, fennel, orange, and lemon, among other ingredients. And if you leave out your water bottle at night, they will fill it with tea for your next day's picnic. At breakfast there's freshly baked bread, slices of cheese and a slab of butter, and a bowl of jam. A few items are also offered for sale: blends of herb teas, honey, and fresh cheese from goats kept by the mother of one of the waitresses.

Every feature of the inn and every detail of the way it is run show thoughtful care, which Angelika can explain in her excellent English. The Bandlis' concept is to use recycled paper and buy local food as much as possible: They obtain their meat, cheese, milk, and eggs from the local farmers and use flour from wheat grown and milled in the canton. Angelika explains that she and Erwin want their inn to be a house in which guests can feel the quietness of their valley. At 11 PM they shut down. In many places local farmers use a neighborhood Berghaus for extended Saturday-night revelry, but the Bandlis do not want a place where guests come to drink all night. However, as a concession to local wishes (and because the locals asked them to do this, pleading that the Turrahus is the only Berghaus in the upper valley), they stay open until midnight on Friday and Saturday and allow a party once a month.

There are six double rooms and two with four beds, as well as 20 Matratzenlager places (half in the house and half in another building). As the Turrahus has such a small capacity, and as so much personal attention is manifestly devoted to every detail, it is clear that no one interested in merely the hotel business would take up such a life; this little inn cannot expand into a big business with more volume and larger profits.

The house is open nearly all year, closed only from about October 25 to December 15 and from April 25 to the end of May. There are more overnight guests in winter, when they come for ski mountaineering, than in summer. Angelika says that winter is her favorite time, when guests come for a week and she gets to know them—they look into the kitchen when they return from skiing and ask what's cooking. Small as it is, word gets around, and you should phone (or write) perhaps two weeks in advance for a private room and a month in advance for a Saturday night. Tel. 081/647 12 03; 7109 Thalkirch/Safiental.

Walks: Angelika Bandli enjoys hikes on tracks where you may have to find your own way a little and can suggest several such in this valley in addition to the ones listed here.

WALK 1 • Safierberg Pass: Round-trip 10 kilometers; 800 meters up; 5 hours. A good trail heads south to the Safierberg, a pass from which you could descend to Splügen on the Hinterrhein. Walk down the road, ignoring a red/yellow blaze on a gravel road to your right. Pass by a reservoir and follow the road around to its back, then continue on the road, which will eventually become a gravel jeep road. Stay on this: Don't turn off to cross a wooden bridge over a brook to the right. The trail climbs steadily but not too steeply to the pass. (According to a signpost, it's another 2¼ hours from the pass to Splügen.

WALK 2 • Another trail (cut by Polish exiles during World War II) leads southwest to the Tomulpass: 4.25 kilometers; 712 meters up; 2½ hours; thence to Vals in the Valsertal just to the west in about the same amount of time.

WALK 3 • The trail to the Glaspass can be used to hike to the Berggasthaus Beverin in the next valley; see p. 220.

THE HEINZENBERG

The Heinzenberg is a high slope along a ridge between the Vorderrhein and Hinterrhein; the Safiental is to the west, the Hinterrhein to the east. Piz Beverin (2997 meters), the highest point overlooking the Heinzenberg, dominates the region. Crystal hunters are drawn to this region because of the abundance of that mineral.

54 • BERGGASTHAUS BEVERIN • 1880 M

Near the base of Piz Beverin is a big converted farmhouse, more than 100 years old, which is now a very pleasant inn. The dining room was once the local schoolhouse, and the present postman went to school in it. Its wood paneling, perhaps deemed too dark, was painted cream color many years ago, and the room is bright and cheerful, with a handsome old country sideboard, and wildflowers on the tables. Another large room with an antique tile stove, maybe 100 years old and stoked from the kitchen, is used to serve evening coffee and drinks or special meals. Lunches and snacks are served on a terrace facing the mountain.

The character of this inn—relaxed, friendly, and warm—comes directly and precisely from the couple now running it. For many years Hans Leibacher was the skipper of a fishing boat in the Caribbean and his wife, Alice Krucker, was the cook (hence they speak English fluently). When its owner retired the boat, Hans and Alice returned to Switzerland and took up innkeeping, first managing a large hotel. But wanting a smaller, more intimate place, they found Berggasthaus Beverin, whose owners do not wish to run it but also will not sell it. Hans and Alice have a contract to run the place as they wish with only one condition: not to change any of the old-style furniture, which they don't want to do anyway. (Hans would like to strip off the dining room paint and restore the original wood paneling, but the job is too great.)

Hans and Alice believe that a hotel should be small enough so that a guest is not a number. They want it to be personal, to know all the guests by name, and to recognize former guests if they telephone. They have succeeded in making people feel at home, interacting with guests in a way that is natural and easy, not forced. A little boy was "fishing" from an upper-story window, and I saw Hans attach a chocolate bar to the hook on his fishing rod. From the easy interaction of Hans, the child, and his parents, I had thought they were visiting relatives, but they were guests like any other. An ambience is created by the personal attention and welcoming character of Hans and Alice. The best of the mountain inns make you feel that you're dining at the table of your host, not merely that of the owner. Unlike certain restaurants, where the staff are instructed to keep asking if you want another drink, at places like this they wait for you to request another. And here, as at the Turrahus and several other inns, they offer you seconds at dinner—would you like more soup, more salad, more meat and potatoes?—without ringing it up on the cash register.

Most overnight guests are on half-pension, with a fixed menu, although there is also the option of ordering à la carte. Now Hans is the cook and Alice serves, which she does in a warm and grandmotherly way. After dinner Hans comes out of the kitchen in his chef's whites and sits with the guests. At our first dinner the menu began with asparagus soup, an excellent and large mixed salad, then Schweinskotelett with fried potatoes (we asked for Rösti instead), and fresh fruit salad with ice cream. On another evening, the main dish was Älpler Macaroni with Apfelmus (applesauce). Breakfast is an excellent buffet: orange juice, Muesli, sliced cheese and meat, canisters of best-quality jam, bread, and a hot roll for each guest.

There are 10 double rooms and 2 rooms with five beds each, and no Matratzenlager. The upstairs still has the look of a farmhouse, with colorful rag rugs on the old wooden floors. Toilets, showers, and warm-water sink are in the hall, and towels are provided. Berggasthaus Beverin is open from Ascension Day in approximately mid-May to All Saints' Day, which is November 2, then again from Christmas to Easter. In winter, Hans drives guests in his van to the Heinzenberg ski area in the morning and picks them up in the afternoon; guests can also do ski mountaineering and ski cross country. The inn is closed on Tuesday except during July and August, or unless many guests come—in which case it stays open. During the summer one should phone well ahead, even two months before, for a room on Saturday or Sunday. Tel. 081/651 13 23; Fax: 651 16 88; 7428 Glas/Tschappina.

Getting there: The inn is a few steps from the Glaspass, which is also the site of the tiny hamlet of Ausser Glas. To reach it from the east, you can take a bus almost to the inn, then walk a short distance; if you have a car, you can drive to the inn. To reach it from the west you must walk. **From the east:** From the rail station at Thusis, a town on the Hinterrhein, take a PTT bus to the hamlet of Ober Tschappina, then walk, following signs for the Glaspass: 2.25 kilometers; 303 meters up; 1 hour. Both the paved road, which rises to the right, and the smaller Alter Glasweg, which drops at first, lead you there. **From the west:** Hike up to the Glaspass from Safiental (see p. 217). That trail starts from the village of Safien, at 1315 meters (if you're coming from Berggasthaus Turrahus, you can take the morning PTT bus down to Safien): 3.75 kilometers; 565 meters up; 2½ hours. A signpost in Safien between the shop and the post office points toward the Glaspass; walk down to the reservoir and there turn left, again following a sign. Turn around the edge of the reservoir and cross a bridge, after which the trail ascends steeply through trees. After 2 hours (of which 1 hour, 20 minutes is steady climbing), reach the farmhouses of Inner Glas, where the trail is less steep, and in another 30 minutes, the little community of Ausser Glas and the inn.

Why is this pass called the Glaspass? According to Hans Leibacher, there are two conflicting theories, each with its partisans. One group holds that the name means "glass," reflecting the abundance of crystals in this region; the other that the word *glasch* meant "pass" in the dialect of the Walliser (Valser) people who moved into the region centuries ago.

Walks: Many hikers climb Piz Beverin, but partway up the mountain there is a section with tremendous exposure, absolutely inadvisable for anyone with vertigo. It is also, we were told, inadvisable in wet weather, mist, and, of course, with snow on the path. But there are alternative excursions. For additional tours and information about trail conditions, ask Hans Leibacher at the inn.

WALK 1 • The Glasgrat is a long, narrow ridge extending northward from Berggasthaus Beverin and overlooking a section of heath, unusual in Switzerland. The heath's rougher, darker vegetation stands out in marked contrast to the bright green of the meadows that border it. If you climb to its highest point, you'll ascend 243 meters. A sign just behind the inn points you onto the Glasgrat, leading directly up the crest of the ridge. After coming down from the ridge, you can turn left at a fork and continue past Alp Lüsch to reach a little lake, the Bischolsee (1999 meters), in a couple of hours, or walk only as far as you like along the ridge and then retrace your steps to the inn. There are several tracks east from the Glasgrat, some across the heath, but if you wish to set off in that direction, be sure to bring your map.

WALK 2 • The Hochbüel route does not climb Piz Beverin but makes a short circuit around a promontory on its northern shoulder, just opposite the inn: 3.15 kilometers; 207 meters up; 2 hours. From the inn you can make the tour counterclockwise to the southeast.

WALK 3 • A hike into the wild, nearly empty Carnusa Valley, passing below the east face of the Piz Beverin, is lovely but long, and the route is occasionally not well marked. However, as with the Glasgrat, you can go only as far as you wish and then retrace your steps.

Walk westward on the road from the inn, not toward the Glaspass and Inner Glas but in the direction indicated by a sign near the PTT for Carnusa, Schottensee, and Wergenstein—but not to Piz Beverin. You'll soon see a little outdoor oven on your right (thought to be about 200 years old, and still used, if only to warm up pizza); across the way is a farm. Continue for about 5 minutes to the next cluster, with a house and a few barns to your left. Continue on the road; the Carnusa trail starts just beyond this cluster, heading left over a meadow and then alongside the fence, now descending. The main trail will be officially closed (GESPERRT) until the fall of 1998 for the clearance of trees. Until then, a much rougher (muddy, rocky) trail can be used. Both trails descend through woods to the stream. Cross this on a bridge, walk for about 1 minute along its left bank, then look for a dirt trail that diverges to the right: Ascend on that. The only section where the trail is indistinct is just in front of you: As you climb, at about 1935 meters, a small house (an alp) will be visible above to the right, and there is a small pond in front of you. Go left: Do not pass the pond, which should stay above you at first and to your right. (If you approach the pond, turn left just before it.) The trail switchbacks up to the clifflike rock ledges above but does not go toward the little alp. (Even if you see traces of track toward the house, do not follow them.) The true trail soon becomes clear and will lead to a second alp, above to your right. Total ascent to the second alp: 1012 meters. If you continue along this trail, you'll reach the little Lai (lake) da Scotga (Schotta-See) after ascending a rocky step at 2505 meters.

ALP FLIX

The name Alp Flix implies the usual cluster of farms, but this "alp" extends for several kilometers. It is the collective name for several little separate clusters of farms and houses, spread out across a long stretch of high, sunny meadow. Because it is relatively long and fairly level, open, and sunny, and can be reached by car, it attracts families with small children and older people who want a scenic walk that is not too strenuous. It is also completely out of the usual tourist circuit, even for hikers—so much off the tourist track that you will find no one there but Swiss. The walk along Alp Flix is pleasant: There are several pretty blue lakes, meadows with great drifts of pink and yellow wildflowers, and views of the mountains across the valley.

Those who seek something wilder can turn off to climb into higher, undeveloped country.

Roman legions once marched across the Julier and Septimer Passes, both of which connect the valley of the Upper En with the north. These two pass routes join together near the present-day town of Bivio in a valley connecting the Upper Engadine with Chur, the capital town of the Graubunden. Alp Flix is on the eastern slope overlooking this long valley, called the Oberhalbstein. (There is now a road over the Julier Pass, with PTT bus service from St. Moritz and Silvaplana to Chur; the Septimer Pass remains a hiking route only.)

55 • BERGHAUS PIZ PLATA • 1970 M

This appealing, friendly inn is near the southern end of Alp Flix. It's important to note that each of the several clusters of houses that together make up the alp has its own name; Berghaus Piz Plata is at Tigias, near Tga d'Meir, which is indicated on most maps; Tigias is not shown. (In the Romansch language, the consonant cluster "tg" is pronounced "tch.") The house was built in 1918 for Wanderung (hiking). A pleasant and attractive place, easily accessible by road, and the only restaurant anywhere on Alp Flix, the inn does a lively business at lunch, but it's quiet in the evening.

A raised terrace, overlooking the valley, attracts those who stop for lunch, and on warm evenings guests eat dinner there as well. The dining room looks cozy and intimate, an attractive space with handsome wooden beams of a warm brown hue. The private rooms are bright and cheerful, their walls, floor, and ceiling a light-colored pine. The bathroom facilities in the hall—toilet, warm-water sink, and shower—are new.

The inn is run by some older ladies of great energy. It was bought in 1989 by Helga Poetzsch and her family, and they are exerting themselves in every way to make the place inviting and attractive and to cook and serve satisfying meals. I could not finish my portion of Bundner Gerstensuppe—thick and full of barley and vegetables—the soup alone was enough for dinner. It was served in a handsome ceramic bowl, with a dollop of cream. (If you do not care for cream with your food, ask for it Ohne Rahm: The Swiss are very fond of cream, and the Poetzsch sisters aim to please.) We then had a casserole of baked noodles with slivers of turkey, mushrooms, broccoli, and other vegetables—also very filling, again a dollop of cream on top. Dinner is à la carte, and other choices include the house specialty, home-smoked ham; salad with chicken and assorted fruit; traditional Älpler

Macaroni; casserole of beef with potatoes, leeks, and other vegetables; and homemade cakes. At breakfast each guest gets a little ceramic pot of butter and a warm roll, as well as bread, jam, and sliced meat and cheese.

There are seven double rooms and 38 Matratzenlager places in three separate rooms below the dining room. The inn is closed only from early November until December 26. Tel. and Fax: 081/684 51 22; 7456 Sur.

Getting there: The nearest village on the valley floor is Sur, just north of Lai (Lake) da Marmorera (which is north of Bivio). Guests can drive up from Sur and park (for a fee) at a parking lot below the Piz Plata Inn. Sur is also a stop on the PTT bus line between Silvaplana and Chur. **To walk up from Sur:** 3.25 kilometers; 386 meters up; 1¼ hours. At Sur, start up (and remain on) the paved road. At 1785 meters, where there's a signposted junction, do *not* turn left onto an unpaved, gravel road with a little concrete bridge to your left (although the sign points left for Alp Flix, as well as for Parsettens, Tinizong, and Lais (Lakes) da Flix). This sign is on a pole with a white-red-white band. The trail it points to is confusing.

Berghaus Piz Plata

Instead, stay on the paved road, to the right. At the next junction on this paved road, a sign points you to the right for Berghaus Piz Plata (or left for the Parkplatz, or parking area). Another possibility is to walk up on a trail, instead of a road, from Marmorera, between Sur and Bivio (the bus also stops at Marmorera).

Walks:

WALK 1 • From the Berghaus Piz Plata you can walk in either direction along the Höhenweg, the balcony trail along the slope, as far as you wish. The entire route, named the Veia Surmirana, extends from Marmorera up to Alp Flix, then down again to Rona or Tinizong on the valley floor. If you walk north between Piz Plata and Plang da Crousch, where there's a big cross, you'll be essentially on the level. After Plang da Crousch, the trail descends to Rona.

WALK 2 • You can leave the Höhenweg and climb into wilder country

Descent from the Vereinapass

by turning off the main trail at the little farm at Tgalucas onto a trail that climbs northeast to a higher shelf, visible above. This is marked for Piz Colm, Tgant Pensa, Alp d'Err, and Pass d'Ela, and also for Parsettens and Tinizong. Walk as far as you wish. Before the track begins to ascend, watch for a little wooden bridge with a wooden gate across it to your left: You must cross a few rivulets to reach the bridge. It is better to cross that bridge at the outset, because although the trail on the left bank of the stream (the one you have started out on) is blazed, the blazes eventually indicate a stream crossing higher up, where there is no bridge and the crossing is more difficult. This track leads up to wild, empty slopes where you can be quite alone and enjoy an extended view.

THE VEREINATAL

Klosters, a chic ski resort, is the starting point for this valley in the northeastern Graubunden. From the Vereinatal you can hike over either of two passes and reach the Lower Engadine.

56 • BERGHAUS VEREINA • 1945 M

This exceptionally attractive inn stands nearly alone in its long, empty valley. There's a small wooden building nearby that was an old alpine club hut, which was run by the grandparents of the inn's present owner, Jakob Boner. But people kept coming and the hut was too small, he says, so his grandparents built the Berghaus Vereina in 1930–1931. (The old hut was abandoned.) The new inn is a small stone building on a sort of knoll. Everything about it is inviting. A stone terrace wraps around half the house. The dining room is wood-paneled partway and finished with white plaster for a fresh, bright look, with handsome wooden beams across its ceiling. Beside it is a cozy, smaller room, all wood-paneled, with a few more tables—a room you'd want to sit in.

The rooms are also bright and inviting, with light pine walls, carpets, pretty, matching covers on the quilts and pillows, and attractive curtains. There's a very new bath (toilet) room downstairs below the dining room, with new toilets, sinks, and showers (fluffy, good-sized towels are provided in the private rooms).

One menu is served to all overnight guests, but special requests are graciously accommodated. Dinner is served family-style at shared tables. Our meal began with soup and croutons. We were then given curried minced chicken with rice and small slices of fruit, as we had asked for something other than the evening's main dish, minced veal in a sauce with Rösti. Dessert was fruit salad. There's a standard à la carte menu for lunch. At breakfast there were jars of high-quality jam on the tables, big slices of cheese, and a slab of butter.

There are eight double rooms and two singles, 20 Matratzenlager places in the house and another 20 in a side building: The dorms are divided into rooms for four, five, and eight. Jakob Boner refuses to overbook the house because he doesn't like crowded mountain inns or alpine club huts. The rates are at the high end of the middle category.

It is open from the end of June to mid-October. Tel. 081/422 11 97, 422 12 16, or 422 25 80; 7250 Klosters.

Getting there: The easiest way to reach Berghaus Vereina is by a van that comes up from Klosters several times a day. The van leaves from Gotschna Sport, a sport shop owned by Herr Boner near the Klosters rail station; tel. 081/422 11 97. The ride takes 45 minutes and costs 12 Sfr per person; the road is private and quite narrow, so guests cannot drive their own cars. To walk the 6.5 kilometers up from Klosters (which is at 1180 meters) would take 3 hours or more.

Walks: There's a good selection of hikes from Vereina. Two of them, the trails to the Flesspass and the Vereinapass, start together but then bifurcate; both descend to the Lower En Valley.

WALK 1 • Flesspass: 11 kilometers; 513 meters up; 4 hours.

From the inn, start off toward the southeast. When the trail branches, take the path to the right, southwestward, to the Flesspass. The trail descends to Roven, which is on a road; there you can catch PTT buses back to Klosters or to Susch in the Lower Engadine, where there's a rail station.

WALK 2 • Vereinapass: 14 kilometers; 640 meters up/1170 meters down; 7½ hours.

A more strenuous, difficult route leads east from the bifurcation to climb over the Vereinapass (2585 meters). This is beautiful, wild country with views of Piz Linard (3410 meters, the highest mountain in the Lower Engadine). The upper part of the route is over snowfields. The descent to Lavin is long and the trail rough. (You can, of course, hike up to the pass, then return to Vereina; this section is less rough than the descent to Lavin.) If you decide to cross the pass to the Lower Engadine, turn left when you reach a little gravel road below; the Lavin rail station is another 30 minutes.

WALK 3 • A trail south from the inn leads to the Jori lakes: 4.5 kilometers; 544 meters up; 2 hours. This is said to be a favorite excursion from Vereina.

WALK 4 • A trail northeastward leads to the Vernelahütte and the Chessisee: 5.25 kilometers; 413 meters up; 2 hours.

LOWER ENGADINE

A very interesting and special part of Canton Graubunden is the Engadine, the region around the river En, which descends from the crown of the great glaciers around the Bernina group of mountains. Romansch culture survives best along the lower part of the river, an area called the Lower Engadine, roughly from just below the village of Bever eastward to the Italian and Austrian borders. The Lower Engadine receives far fewer international visitors than does the Upper Engadine, with its chic, cosmopolitan resorts, and for that reason the regional culture still flourishes here. In many ways, the Lower Engadine is a region of exceptional charm. A special type of house decoration has flourished here. A technique known as sgraffito was used to cut symbols, pictures, and geometric designs into the plaster walls of houses, and some houses have folk-art paintings on them as well. This style of architecture is also unique and very handsome. These houses can best be seen in the picturesque, unspoiled villages of the Lower Engadine.

Romansch is a living language, still written, and spoken everywhere throughout the Lower Engadine; one may even attend church services in this beautiful language. Regional specialties are found in restaurants in this area: Romansch cuisine is the hearty food of farm people, featuring potatoes, pancakes, and dumplings, often enlivened with fruit.

The Lower Engadine is also the site of the Swiss National Park (see p. 234), and of famous and historic spas at Scuol (recently modernized and very handsome), and nearby Tarasp and Vulpera, which still display 19th-century features and appointments and have the charm of their period.

VAL SINESTRA

At the eastern edge of the Lower Engadine is a lonely valley rather far from the region's main attractions (the spas, picture-book villages, and the Swiss National Park). Almost no one ever goes to the Val Sinestra, where are found a pair of hotels unlike any other in the Alps. These are the Kurhaus Val Sinestra and the Berghaus Val Sinestra. When we discovered them, in

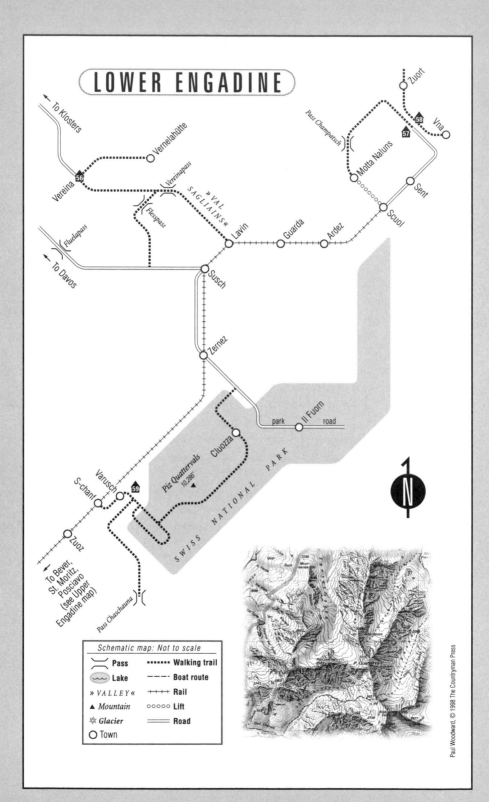

LOWER ENGADINE

To Klosters

Vernelahütte

Vereina **56**

Fluelapass

To Davos

Vereinapass

Flesspass

»VAL SAGLIAINS«

Lavin

Guarda

Ardez

Susch

Pass Champatsch

Zuort

58 Vna

57

Motta Naluns

Sent

Scuol

Zernez

park   Il Fuorn   road

SWISS   NATIONAL   PARK

Cluozza

Piz Quattervals
10.285
▲

Varusch

S-chanf   **59**

Zuoz

To Bever,
St. Moritz,
Poschiavo
(see Upper
Engadine map)

Pass Chaschauna

N

Schematic map: Not to scale

⌣ Pass	●●●● **Walking trail**
⬭ Lake	– – **Boat route**
»*VALLEY*«	++++ **Rail**
▲ *Mountain*	○○○○ **Lift**
✺ *Glacier*	══ **Road**
○ Town	

Paul Woodward, © 1998 The Countryman Press

the course of some assiduous exploration, not even the excellent tourist office in Scuol, the region's central town, knew much about them other than that the Kurhaus—"an old hotel"—exists. They had not even heard of the Berghaus.

57 • KURHAUS VAL SINESTRA • 1473 M

We traveled up the Val Sinestra by bus from Scuol and arrived midafternoon. The Kurhaus is an improbable sight: six stories high, with a turret and spire like a Schloss (castle), in a narrow, deep, and wooded valley—almost a gorge. It is isolated; there is not even a hamlet up this side of the Val Sinestra. Inside, in a huge, old-fashioned salon, we found a group of mothers drinking afternoon tea and children tumbling about in a playroom full of toys. After a search, we found a staff person to show us our room. Ordinarily, we learned, no staff is in the office in the afternoon, because nearly all the guests arrive or depart together on Saturdays. Our puzzlement increased as we passed a bulletin board on which the evening menu was posted in Dutch.

By dinnertime, the mystery had cleared up. We had stumbled inadvertently upon an unusual phenomenon: a Dutch vacation colony in a remote part of the Alps. The structure itself is in the style of an old Swiss Kurhaus, a gracious country hotel for the bourgeoisie of the 19th and early 20th centuries who came to restore body and soul with mineral waters—there is a spring near the hotel—and mountain air. A bronze plaque honors Dr. Albert Nadig, the Kur-Doktor here for 38 years, and his instruments are displayed in the entry hall.

This Kurhaus was built on the grand scale. The salon—furnished with Oriental rugs on a parquet floor, sofas and little tables, and a piano—extends almost the length of the building, with a nonsmoking parlor at one end and a library (now full of Dutch books) at the other. The stairs are equally grand, a sweeping affair with polished wood banisters. One can almost hear the rustle of the women's silk dresses as they sounded when they came down to dinner, and one can picture the men in jackets and ties. The dining room was designed for elegance: parquet floor, cream-colored walls, red drapes, and white tablecloths. But today, the atmosphere at mealtime is pure summer camp.

All guests set their own tables, fetching dishes, glasses, and silverware from the kitchen. The staff, in jeans and sweaters and indistinguishable from the guests, bring the food to the tables, but after meals guests clear the tables and wash and dry the dishes. Many families come here with children, and mealtime was noisy, lively, full of chatter (almost a din) with families and children all informal, relaxed, voluble, merry, and very much at ease. The evening's menu was potato soup, a salad of lettuce and kidney beans, spaghetti with tomato sauce and cheese, and walnut cake. A man made a speech in Dutch and everyone burst into song (a Dutch birthday song, we were later informed). A bottle of ordinary French wine was unbelievably inexpensive. Bread and cake are baked in the hotel, and salt-free bread and sugar-free desserts are available upon special request. Fresh bread is served

Berggasthaus Sinestra

for breakfast, with excellent jam, sliced cheese, and butter. Moreover, at breakfast time, lunch supplies are laid out in the kitchen—bread, cold sliced meat, cheese, and fruit—for guests to make up trail lunches.

Beyond the dining room is a cozy little Bundner Stube, Swiss-style, paneled in pine, where guests may repair for evening drinks. Others return to the salon, into which a trolley is rolled after dinner with tea and coffee.

You don't need to be Dutch or even to speak Dutch to stay there because most Dutch people speak English. The reason that all the guests are Dutch is that practically only Dutch people know about it. The Kurhaus was built in 1910 and then abandoned in the late 1950s, when mineral water cures ceased to be fashionable. A society of Swiss plumbers and roofers bought the place for their members' holidays, but they gave it up in 1972 as too expensive. In 1978 a Dutchman, Peter Kruit, bought it to make inexpensive, wholesome vacations available to Dutch families. Most of them come for a week or two, arriving and leaving on Saturdays. Ecology is important to Mr. Kruit, so to facilitate their travel and to save gas and protect the environment, a double-decker bus picks up the guests every week in Holland and brings them back again (Herr Kruit serves as one of the drivers).

As Kruit is vegetarian, the menus are also, but three times a week there is an optional meat dish. There are 67 private rooms, and dormitory space as well; if no private room is available, dorm spaces are nearly always available at the last minute. (The dorm at present is just an airy attic space that resembles a teenager's bedroom, with mattresses on the floor and with sheets and blankets provided; however, dorm renovation is planned.) All private rooms have a sink with hot water and towels, and about half have a private toilet. Showers are available, free (dorm guests must bring their own towel). During the high season, July–August, a minimum stay of one week for a private room is said to be required (although this may not be a rigid rule), and many Dutch people book for high season in January or February.

Organized programs are available, with bus trips to the National Park. Guests are dropped off at the park, can hike for 3-4 hours, and then are picked up. There's a charge for these trips.

The hotel is open from May 25 to the end of October, and again for two weeks at Christmas, and at Easter. Tel. 081/866 31 05; Fax. 866 34 52; 7554 Sent.

58 • BERGGASTHAUS SINESTRA • 1450 M

From the Kurhaus, a 5-minute walk down the road brings you to the Berggasthaus Sinestra, a much smaller inn with quite a different atmosphere. It's like a home, for several reasons. The Kurhaus, with its grand salon and huge dining room, is more noisy and bustling, but the Berggasthaus is quiet and intimate. There's a comfortable living/dining room, quite cozy, with books and plants, and a pretty glassed-in porch, airy and bright, with lots of greenery and simple, rustic furniture. After a day's hike, we came down to find afternoon tea (provided to all guests, as at the Kurhaus) and Mozart softly playing on cassette.

This inn was built in 1870 for a simple water Kur, using the nearby mineral spring. The Kurhaus was built subsequently, in 1910, for curative baths as well as drinking water. Like the Kurhaus, the inn is owned by Peter Kruit and frequented by Dutch guests. Unlike the Kurhaus, which serves meals only on a pension basis, the Berghaus is open as a restaurant to all passersby from 8 AM to 6:30 PM. It is run by a friendly Dutch couple who have two children, and the atmosphere is a bit like a home, with children's games and books strewn about. Despite the presence of the children of Liesbeth Hopman and Maarten van Wieringen and other child guests, the Berggasthaus is quiet, and the effect is more that of a cozy inn than a children's camp.

Liesbeth and Maarten cook interesting and tasty meals, far more interesting than the fare served just up the road: We had curried walnut soup, a salad of lettuce and cucumber with capers and sunflower seeds, quiche with rice and green beans, and fresh grapes. As at the Kurhaus, meals are vegetarian, with a choice of meat every other day. Breakfast was fresh bread, jam, and sliced cheese. And as at the Kurhaus, lunch supplies are laid out for guests—bread, cheese, sliced meat, and fruit—and are included in the pension price. Guests set and clear the tables and wash and dry the dishes here as well. After dinner, there's likely to be classical music playing softly.

The Berggasthaus has 14 private rooms but no dormitory. There's a toilet and sink on each floor and showers in the basement—towels are not provided. Although the Dutch clientele come for stays of a week, one can get a room, if it is available, for a minimum stay of three days for a slight surcharge. As at the Kurhaus, rooms are likely to be available in June or September, but one should reserve as early as February for July and August. The Berghaus is open from the end of May to the end of October and again from Christmas to Easter. Tel. 081/866 33 34; 7554 Sent.

Getting there: Scuol is the central town of the Lower Engadine. From its rail station, somewhat apart from the town, visitors can take a shuttle bus (Ortsbus) into the town; get off at the PTT, which is also the bus stop. Take a bus to Sent, and change there for the bus that goes up the Val Sinestra; it will stop at the Berggasthaus and the Kurhaus, which are only minutes apart.

Walks: Several walks can be taken directly from either the Kurhaus or the Berghaus; their proximity to the National Park (see page 234) and other areas of the Lower Engadine means that these two hotels can be used as a base for the entire region, especially for those who have a car, but some hikes should be possible using the PTT buses. Hikers can otherwise sign up for the bus excursions from the Kurhaus, which allow several hours of hiking.

WALK 1 • Vna: 2.75 kilometers; 130 meters up; 1 hour.

Vna (pronounced *Fna*) is a pretty hamlet with some traditional Engadine painted houses and a fine, long view across the En River Valley to the mountains of the National Park. From the Berggasthaus, walk down the road and cross the bridge over the river; at several junctions follow the signs pointing right for Vna, rather than left for Zuort. At first the trail leads through woods, then it emerges into open meadows.

WALK 2 • Zuort and Prà San Flurin: 6.25 kilometers; 558 meters up; 2½ hours.

Cross the bridge, but follow signs for Zuort. The trail follows the brook, with some washed-out sections. You'll cross another bridge, then intersect a gravel jeep road. Among Zuort's few houses is Hof Zuort, an utterly charming restaurant (no overnight accommodations). Behind the restaurant there's a signposted junction on a jeep road. Keep to the right. You'll emerge from woods onto open slopes and reach the farm at Alp Prà San Flurin. The mountains are not high and alpine, but rugged nevertheless, and despite the couple of farms in the valley, there's a sense of wildness here. (From Alp Prà San Flurin, you could strike off on a rough track for Fuorcla Champatsch.) Instead of retracing your steps through Zuort, you can bear right beyond the alp, following the loops of a gravel road, and follow signs for Sinestra. Eventually this will take you left; you can descend the last section on a steep, narrow trail through the woods or take the road.

There are more fine hikes in the Lower Engadine than can be described in this book, and for them a guidebook focused on walking should be consulted, but here are a few suggestions. One of the charms of the region is the traditional Engadine house, decorated with sgraffito or incised designs and with folk-art paintings. Ardez and Guarda, two of the prettiest villages, are connected by a pleasant trail; from Guarda you can also hike up to the Chamanna Tuoi, an alpine club hut. From Scuol, you can take a lift to Motta Naluns, then walk to Champatsch. Or you can take a PTT bus from Scuol to S-charl, from which several fine walks both in and near the National Park can be taken, including routes to Süsom Givè and to Fuorcla Sesvenna.

Across the En River, from Crusch (near Sent), a dramatic trail leads through a narrow gorge to the lovely upper meadows of the Val d'Uina.

SWISS NATIONAL PARK

Switzerland's only national park, founded in 1914, is in the Lower Engadine. It is a nature preserve, with total protection for all wildlife and everything else—organic or inorganic—that grows or is found there. The land is left completely untouched: Dead trees and branches lie where they fell, and visitors may not pick any flowers or plants or collect minerals. The landscape, with its limestone mountains, is distinctive and rugged, yet not high alpine. Hiking trails cross the park in various directions, with established rest places for stops and picnics. No camping is allowed, but accommodations are available at two places in the park. As the park is not immense, visitors can also stay in any of several nearby villages and still have a full day's hike in the park or drive through it. The Hotel Parc Naziunal at Il Fuorn, modern, handsomely decorated, and with private rooms, is on the park road and thus accessible by car and bus; the Blockhaus Cluozza is

Outdoor pool of the Scuol Kurhaus

a large, simple log house accessible only to hikers and mainly offering Matratzenlager. The third option is described below.

59 • PARKHÜTTE VARUSCH (ALSO VARUSCHHÜTTE, CHAMANNA VARUSCH) • 1770 M

These names mean the Varusch hut in German and Romansch. Despite its name, this is not an alpine club hut but a privately owned inn: a rustic wooden chalet, very small, charming, and cozy, set in a meadow at the edge of woods. A simple terrace to one side expands the inn's serving capacity, as the dining room is minute, with only four tables. It is one of only two rooms downstairs, the other being the kitchen (along with a toilet). The house was built in 1750, and except for its electric light (provided by solar panels) and a few other details, the dining room has the charm of its age. Dark wood paneling, a beamed ceiling, an old tile stove, and pretty tables made of very light, clean pine, each with a handsome iron candlestick, make a very attractive dining place.

Upstairs there are only two private rooms and a shower. Simply furnished and brightened with red-and-white-checked quilts, pillows, and curtains, the little rooms are snug and neat. (Towels are not provided.) Most of the Matratzenlager are in a separate house across the grass, but some are in the old house. In total there are 31 places distributed among four rooms.

The food is excellent and imaginative, and dinner is à la carte. Along with customary dishes, the menu offers tomato salad with fresh goat cheese, Rucola or Nüssli salads (both are bitter greens), polenta with Gorgonzola cheese or with Steinpilze (wild mushrooms), lamb marinated with herbs, and shish kebab, and Engadiner Nusstorte (nut cake), a regional specialty.

The owners, Sylvia and Gian Rico, live in Zuoz, where they keep a restaurant in an even older, historic house. When we were at Varusch, two young, friendly Portuguese people tended the kitchen and ran the inn.

Parkhütte Varusch opens at the very end of May and closes at the end of October. Tel. 081/854 31 22; Fax: 854 00 40; 7525 S-chanf.

Getting there: The Varuschhütte is reached from the village of S-chanf in the valley of the En: 4.75 kilometers; 113 meters up; 1 hour, 10 minutes. From the S-chanf rail station, walk to the left through the village, following signs for Parc Naziunal (National Park in Romansch); these lead you along a paved road that crosses below the highway by an underpass, then continues to the Parkplatz, a parking area for the National Park. From

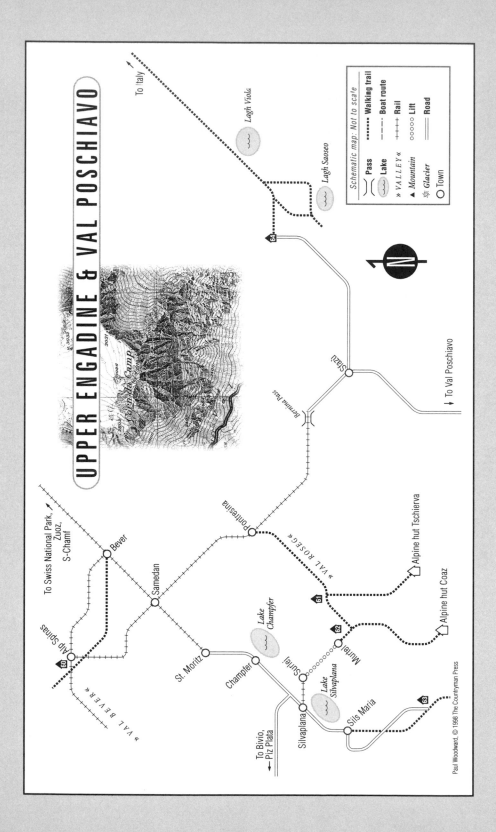

UPPER ENGADINE & VAL POSCHIAVO

Schematic map: Not to scale

Legend:
- •••• **Walking trail**
- ---- **Boat route**
- +++ **Rail**
- ooooo **Lift**
- = **Road**
- 〉〉 *VALLEY* 《
- ▲ *Mountain*
- ✳ *Glacier*
- ○ Town
-)(**Pass**
- ◯ **Lake**

N

To Italy

Lagh Viola

Lagh Saoseo

Bernina Pass

Colorda Camp

B4

Stazu

To Val Poschiavo

Pontresina

》 *VAL ROSEG* 《

Alpine hut Tschierva

Alpine hut Coaz

G1

G2

Murtel

Bever

To Swiss National Park,
Zuoz,
S-Chamf

Samedan

Alp Spinas

B0

》 *VAL BEVER* 《

St. Moritz

Champfèr

Lake Champfèr

Surlej

Lake Silvaplana

Silvaplana

To Bivio,
Piz Plata

Sils Maria

G52

Paul Woodward, © 1998 The Countryman Press

there, follow signs to Chamanna Varusch. You can either walk on the road, along the right bank of the Varusch stream, or take a footpath (the Höhenweg) through the woods above the left bank. This Höhenweg leads down to the river, which you cross on a bridge; you'll soon reach the inn. Another option is a Pferdetaxi, also known as a Pferde-Kutsche—a horse-drawn carriage—that runs on a regular schedule between the S-chanf rail station, the Parkplatz, and the Parkhütte Varusch. (You can also take a carriage from Zuoz to Varusch.) The telephone number for the Pferdetaxi is 081/854 27 31.

Walks: From the inn you can take several hikes into the National Park. All the trails are signposted.

WALK 1 • An easy walk is the one to Alp Trupchen: 4 kilometers; 270 meters up; 1¾ hours.

Two trails, on opposite banks of the river, lead to this alp. From Varusch you can follow the signs eastward to the Höhenweg and walk out to the alp on this higher forest path, above the stream's left bank, then return by the lower trail along the right bank. The alp faces a cirque of craggy Lower Engadine mountains.

WALK 2 • More strenuous hikes may also be taken. One that the inn staff recommended climbs south to Alp Chaschauna (2210 meters) and then to the Chaschauna Pass (2694 meters) on the Italian border: 5 kilometers; 440 meters up to the Alp; 1½ hours. To continue to the pass: another 1.25 kilometers; 484 meters up; and 1½ hours.

WALK 3 • We were told of a more challenging and difficult hike that leads over the Fuorcla Val Sassa (2857 meters), a steep pass below the Piz Quattervals (3154 meters), the National Park's highest mountain. There is scree at the pass. From the pass you descend, at first on scree and then down a rocky section, to the Blockhaus Cluozza (see p. 234–235).

UPPER ENGADINE

The Upper Engadine, from Bever eastward to the source of the river En, is the site of several of Switzerland's most famous resorts, especially chic, opulent St. Moritz. The region is noted also for its splendid glaciers clustered around the high peaks of the Bernina group. But there is backcountry as well, and hikers have only to leave the precincts of the great resorts to find quiet villages and good walking on scenic mountain trails.

BEVER 1708 M
On the En River in the Upper Engadine, almost at the edge of the Lower Engadine, the quiet village of Bever sees very few tourists, in striking contrast with nearby bustling, opulent St. Moritz. Bever and the country above it are out of the way; the trails from here lead into one of the least-known and least-visited parts of the Engadine. The mountains, although not the highest in the region, have a wild, rugged grandeur, and the appeal of this handsome country is heightened by its loneliness.

60 • BERGGASTHAUS (PENSION) SUVRETTA • 1815 M

This very pleasant little inn provides the only base, except for some alpine club huts higher up, for exploring the high country above Bever. The inn is actually at Alp Spinas, which is simply a small cluster of houses and a little rail stop. The house was built in 1887 as a restaurant and expanded early in the next century to become a hotel. At some time about 1916 it was used as a rest home for asthmatics and much later, in the early 1980s, as a center for the blind. The terrace in front, gaily decorated with colorful umbrellas, is a lively, cheerful place, no doubt because the few hikers who come to this valley all stop at the Suvretta. Like everything else about the inn, the rooms are pleasant and simple. There are sinks in the rooms and toilet and shower in the hall.

Meals are à la carte from a menu with several pleasant surprises. Along with the customary Berghaus fare (Bratwurst, Rösti, Schnitzel) it offers a few specialties such as spaghetti diavolo (with garlic, sage, and green pepper), gnocchi piemontese (with garlic, sage, and cheese), risotto Valtellina (with saffron and wild mushrooms), and polenta. Breakfast is also especially good, with juice; Muesli with chopped fruit; sliced cheese and meat; good-quality jam; and rolls as well as bread.

Berggasthaus Suvretta is owned by the Krättli-Kernen family. It has 15 rooms and no Matratzenlager. It's open from about the first weekend in June until about October 20, and then again from Christmas to Easter. Tel. and Fax: 081/852 54 92; 7502 Bever.

Getting there: The inn can be reached by horse-carriage, train, or by foot. **To walk:** 4.5 kilometers; 107 meters up; 1 hour. From the Bever rail station walk to the church, then turn left—a yellow hiking sign indicates Spinas and Val Bever. The trail forks but both sides lead to the inn; the way along the right bank may be more direct, the one along the left bank somewhat prettier. **By Pferde-Omnibus or horse-drawn carriage:** These leave from the Bever rail station by schedule, several times a day from July 1 to September 15; for the updated schedule phone A. Plebani, 081/852 45 90. Outside of this season, the carriages are available by special reserva-

Berggasthaus Suvretta

tion. **By rail:** Take the train heading north from Bever, which will stop at Spinas upon passengers' request—do this by pushing the green button to indicate that you want to get off there. (If you wish to leave Spinas by train, look for a little box on the platform and push the button at least 3 to 4 minutes before the train is due (do not wait until the train is in sight). After you press it, the button will flash red.

Walks: From the Suvretta Inn there are a variety of hikes. If you like the country and the inn, you could spend several days here.

WALK 1 • If you continue on the gently graded trail up the Val Bever, you'll reach little Alp Suvretta: 5.5 kilometers; 315 meters up; 2 hours. From Alp Suvretta you can continue in two different directions: You can go southwest to the end of the Val Bever and ascend to the SAC Jenatsch hut—from Alp Suvretta, an additional 5.25 kilometers; 507 meters up; 2 hours. Or you can go south to the Suvretta Pass (from which a trail descends to St. Moritz)—from Alp Suvretta, an additional 5 kilometers; 470 meters up; 1 hour, 40 minutes.

WALK 2 • Hike up to Crap ("peak" in Romansch) Alo on the Albula Pass road: 7.5 kilometers; 211 meters up; 2½ hours.

WALK 3 • Ascend a steep side valley, the Valletta Bever, to Piz Padella: 3 kilometers; 1040 meters up; 3½ hours.

VAL ROSEG

The Upper Engadine is known for its splendid glaciers, especially for the Roseg and Morteratsch, two rivers of ice that flow down from the Bernina group of mountains, the region's highest peaks. Access to the Roseg Glacier is via the Val Roseg, a valley that opens just opposite the resort of Pontresina and climbs to the foot of the glacier. The scenery is magnificent: massed glaciers within a curved line of mountains. Val Roseg is unspoiled and undeveloped, with two privately owned establishments in the valley, Hotel Roseggletscher and the Berghaus Fuorcla Surlej, as well as two alpine club huts at the edge of the glaciers. Besides those, there are no other buildings.

61 • HOTEL ROSEGGLETSCHER • 2000 M

This hotel and its few outbuildings, located partway up the Val Roseg, are the only structures on the valley floor. The view from the hotel is superb and completely unobstructed by any other building and will always remain so: The upper valley, which is owned by the community of Samedan, is a protected zone—a nature preserve—and no one is allowed to build on it. The Testa family of St. Moritz, who hold a contract for the hotel for 99 years, blocked the construction of a cable car at the end of the valley and also kept the valley closed to private cars.

Hotel Roseggletscher is substantial—no small Berghaus chalet but a large, salmon pink building with extensive space for its restaurant and terrace and a large cafeteria—because although there are few overnight guests, the hotel does a land-order business at lunch. Along with its splendid view, the hotel is very easily reached from Pontresina by horse-drawn carriage, numbers of which come up in the morning laden with people bound for the hotel. Some of them wander out a little farther with picnic lunches, but few of these day-trippers hike to the end of the valley or up its slope.

There has been a hotel here since 1865, later enlarged and renovated. The cafeteria, an extremely rare thing to find in a mountain hotel, dates from 1983.

Throughout the dining rooms there is evidence of keen interest in hunting. This region is open for hunting for three weeks every September. Under the hotel's director, Helmut Kuen, deer are fed during the fall rutting season, and there's a collection box for feeding wildlife. Everywhere there are signs of the chase: murals and pictures of hunting scenes, large numbers of antlers mounted on the walls, a variety of stuffed animals and birds, fox pelts, graphs showing the growth of antlers and teeth, and a chandelier decorated with antlers. And there are game dishes on the menu.

Some Swiss draw a distinction between a Berghotel and a Berghaus or Berggasthaus, maintaining that the name Berghotel means a place that is more "like a hotel," even though it is in the mountains, while a Berghaus is a simpler sort of inn. By that definition, and not only because of its name, Roseggletscher is a Berghotel. Although it is not formal, it is not only larger but also more elaborate than the typical Berghaus. The dining room is spacious, with a big stone fireplace, pots of flowers, and red drapes. Meals are à la carte, and along with the usual dishes are many delicacies, such as these: Nüssli Salat (a slightly bitter salad green) with smoked salmon; gnocchi alla piemontese; goat cheese with olive oil, pepper, and basil; rabbit with rosemary and polenta or risotto; polenta with porcini (wild) mushrooms; piccata; and several kinds of spaghetti (all cooked to order, al dente, in the hotel's new German-made instant spaghetti-cooking machine). Among the game dishes are a house-made pâté and deer sausage. At breakfast there are rolls as well as bread, jam, and half a wheel of Camembert cheese.

There are 17 private rooms, quite modernized and comfortable. Some have toilet and shower; for the others there's a toilet and shower in the hall. There are Matratzenlager with 120 places in a separate building (this is a popular weekend place for groups), and showers are available for the Lager guests. The hotel is open from June to the end of October and from December to the end of April. Tel. 081/842 64 45 and 842 75 65; Fax: 842 68 86; 7504 Pontresina.

Getting there: From Pontresina, the footpath to the Val Roseg begins near the bridge near the rail station and leads partly through woods, or you can walk up the center of the valley on the road used by the horse-carriages: 7 kilometers; 200 meters up; 2 hours. To ride up on a Pferde-Omnibus, also called a Pferde-Kutsch, takes an hour; these horse-drawn carriages leave near the beginning of the Val Roseg trail, between the rail station and the bridge. Places must be reserved in advance; there are several horse drivers. Tel. 081/842 83 53; 842 64 23; 842 60 57; 842 62 20.

62 • BERGHAUS FUORCLA SURLEJ • 2760 M

Perched up high on the western side of the valley, from where it commands a spectacular view, Berghaus Fuorcla Surlej cannot even be seen from Hotel Roseggletscher. Small and simple, it is a traditional kind of mountain inn. The little stone house with wooden shutters dates from 1965, when it replaced an earlier hut. A large wooden deck in front takes advantage of the magnificent view. The dining room is a small pine room with a green ceramic stove against one wall, cozy in an unaffected way.

There are dormitory accommodations only, with 60 places, but with bunk beds rather than sleeping shelves and in rooms that hold only eight people each. There's a cold-water washroom in the house but the toilet is outside. No towels are provided.

The evening half-pension meal is soup, salad, main course, and dessert. The à la carte menu offers soup, salad, sausages, platters of meat and cheese, and several kinds of spaghetti: plain, bolognese, or with pesto. The house is run by Ruth and Claudia Rähmi, a mother and daughter. The inn is open from July 1 to the end of September and offers meals during the winter ski season. Tel. 081/842 63 03; out of season, 081/852 56 74; 7504 Pontresina.

Getting there: Berghaus Fuorcla Surlej can be reached from Val Roseg by foot, or from the Upper En Valley by foot, or by lift and then by foot. **From Val Roseg:** 3.5 kilometers; 760 meters up; 2½ hours. The signposted trail starts behind Hotel Roseggletscher and climbs rather steeply to the Berghaus. At one junction, a sign points left for a trail that descends to the Coaz SAC hut; instead, continue ascending (westward). Soon the trail splits and both sections are blazed, but both lead upward to the inn. **From the Upper En Valley:** Take the Corvatsch lift from Surlej beside the Lej (Lake) of Silvaplana; get off at the intermediate station at Murtel and fol-

View from the Fuorcla Surlej

low a signposted trail to reach Fuorcla Surlej: 2 kilometers; 60 meters up; 40 minutes.

Walks: Besides the walks to the two inns, the other hikes in this valley are to its two SAC huts, set at the edge of two different glaciers, both magnificent to see.

WALK 1 • The Coaz hut sits on a bank overlooking the upper part of the Roseg Glacier: 8 kilometers; 800 meters up; 3 hours. From Hotel Roseggletscher, follow a signposted trail southward from the hotel; it rises to traverse the slope above the glacier. From Fuorcla Surlej, descend to the junction just below the inn and follow the descending, signposted trail to the hut.

WALK 2 • The Tschierva hut is tucked in beside the hanging glacier with the same name: 5.5 kilometers; 600 meters up; 2 hours. From Roseggletscher, cross the bridge and turn right (signposted junction); the trail climbs gradually above the glacier's right bank, and a final, short, steep section brings you up to the hut. From Fuorcla Surlej you must descend to Hotel Roseggletscher, then proceed as explained here.

VAL FEX

This is a tributary valley above the southern slope of the Upper En Valley, easily accessible from the pretty village of Sils (Segl in Romansch) Maria. There are two Sils villages, less than a kilometer apart: Sils Baselgia, closer to the lake, and the more elegant Sils Maria near the base of the slope. From Sils Maria, horse-drawn carriages (Pferde-Kutschen) carry people up the slope to the Fextal and then trot up and down the valley, going as far as Hotel Fex but no farther, bringing up many day visitors from the fashionable Upper En resorts: Sils Maria (site of the Waldhaus, one of the most expensive Upper En hotels), Silvaplana, and St. Moritz. There are a couple of inns near the beginning of the Fextal and a few clusters of farms, but nothing as large as a village or even a hamlet. The upper end of the valley is wild and uninhabited and culminates in a glacier. In 1900, Victor Tissot observed that "twenty years ago this long valley—one of the highest in Europe—was solitary and undreamed of. With no roads of communication, it had remained shut off from the rest of the world. And even now, to those who think of Switzerland as composed only of the Oberland and the Lake of Lucerne, it is a country absolutely new and remote from the great routes, which will give them all the joy of discovery." (Tissot 1900, p. 102)

63 • HOTEL FEX • 1970 M

The Hotel Fex and a couple of barns beside it are the last buildings in the valley (except for a single alp building at the valley's upper end). Therefore its view, facing the Fex Glacier and its cirque, is unobstructed and will remain so: The hotel owns the land in front and nothing more can be built there. (The entire Val Fex is a protected area and no new buildings are allowed, except for additions to existing farmers' houses.) Hotel Fex is comfortable, a comparatively luxurious establishment for a Berghotel—included here (although at the end of the spectrum) because it is a mountain hotel, has a certain traditional air and style, and has a striking alpine view.

Because it is accessible by Pferde-Kutsche as well as to hikers, the hotel is busy at lunchtime. A large terrace, facing the view of the glacier, has been built behind the hotel, as well as an indoor stuva for the lunch crowd. Because they are so numerous, day-trippers do not eat in the dining room reserved for overnight guests or use the parlor.

The Hotel Fex was built around 1880–90 to provide guests at a St. Moritz hotel with a change of scene and a chance to see a glacier. Guests would come up by horse-drawn carriage and stay for two weeks. Plans were afoot to turn the place into a truly grand hotel but had to be scotched because of World War II—the only good thing, says the present owner, that came out of the war. Then, when business fell off, it was rented out for school groups. It fell into bad condition and finally was closed. The mother of the present owner bought it in 1950; her son, Hans-Rudolf Zollinger, and his Malaysian wife, Mariam Mohammed, took it over in 1976 and began a careful and thoughtful renovation. Their purpose was to modernize where necessary (kitchen, bathrooms) but to keep or restore the old look of the place, at which they have been successful. This hotel is partly preserved and partly created, with a mixture of original furnishings and features (some of which the Zollingers tracked down and bought back) and others of the period. These privately owned Swiss mountain hotels and inns are free to set their own style and free to find a middle ground between luxury and simplicity, opulence and spareness. The owner is free to find a niche

Hotel Fex

between a hotel as imposing as Yosemite's Ahwahnee and the more spartan cabins and institutional cafeterias of national parks.

The one curiosity at Hotel Fex is a Jugendstil mural of the sky, with clouds and leaves, painted on the very high ceiling of the spacious entrance hall. The dining room has a country style of elegance with a fresh, clean look: handsome wooden beams on the ceiling, a fine country sideboard, old-fashioned high stove, white linen, silver, and flowers. A wall of windows faces the glacier. Beside the dining room is a wood-paneled parlor, a comfortable room with little sofas and tables. There is, deliberately, no television in the parlor or in any separate room and no radio, nor are there radios or telephones in the guests' rooms. The rooms are comfortable, neither very old-fashioned nor modern, but have had tiny bathrooms installed, some with a shower and some with only toilet and sink.

For dinner there is a set menu but with choices. We were served a traditional Gerstensuppe (barley soup), a choice of shrimp cocktail or fruit salad, and then a choice of Lammfilet (fillet of lamb) Provençal or Gemüsetorte (vegetable pie—a sort of quiche) served with gratinéed potatoes and green beans, and a sabayon pudding for dessert. The service is rather formal; the dishes are brought out under silver covers. The menu is never repeated within the same month. The excellent breakfast buffet offers juice, fruit salad, yogurt, cold cereals, cheese and sliced meat, and sliced bread, and on each table are bowls of honey and jam and a roll. For day guests there's an extensive à la carte menu.

Hans and Mariam Zollinger's idea of a small, personally run hotel like theirs is that guests should feel at home. The staff has been instructed not to approach guests and ask if they want a drink; guests should feel under no pressure, but instead request a drink if they want one. There are 13 double rooms and four singles.

Hotel Fex is open from mid-June until mid-October, and from about December 18 or 19 to the week after Easter. The hotel rates depend on the type of room. Many guests come for two weeks, but a room may be available for only a night or two, which is all that most hikers usually want. Tel. 081/ 826 53 55 or 826 57 54; 7514 Fex-Curtins.

Getting there: One remarkable feature here is that the hotel operates a daily shuttle down to Sils Maria and back (in winter it stops at the ski area), without charge; this means that guests can go down to the En Valley for the day and return for the evening. The van goes down at 9:30 AM and returns at 5:30 PM. This also serves to bring new or departing guests up or down with their luggage. Otherwise, one can reach the hotel by Pferde-Kutschen, which leave near the Sils Maria PTT on schedule—the horse-taxi telephone is 081/826 52 86. You can also walk up from Sils Maria: 3.75 kilometers; 160 meters up; 1½ hours. From Sils Maria (1809 meters), walk up on the road or take a steeper shortcut, the Schluchtweg (the gorge way). Signposts indicate three points in the Val Fex, Curtins being the last one and nearest to Hotel Fex. The Schluchtweg begins with some wooden steps and a steep but short section up through a small gorge; then it emerges from the woods and levels out. It joins the paved road at Crasta. Continue on the road or take the higher path through the woods: Both join near Hotel Fex.

Walks: There is one walk from Hotel Fex—the trail that continues up the valley toward the glacier: round-trip 4 kilometers; 200 meters up; 2 hours. You'll reach the alp building in an hour. A small track continues after that, then peters out. If you hike up in the later afternoon, when all the day hikers have gone down, you'll have this lovely place much to yourself.

VAL POSCHIAVO

Two sections of Switzerland are Italian-speaking, the Ticino (with the cities of Lugano and Locarno) and the smaller and less known Poschiavo. Centuries ago, the Swiss battled victoriously for control of all the alpine passes to the south; the Poschiavo Valley is at the southern end of the Bernina Pass, and the Ticino lies south of the St. Gotthard Pass. The main town of the Val Poschiavo is also called Poschiavo; its attractive central square is in the Italian style. The train ride over the Bernina Pass is scenic, with views of the Cambrena Glacier and Lago Bianco, a very high lake with shores at about 2200 meters. Hiking in this region gives one a taste of Italian Switzerland.

64 • RISTORANTE ALPE CAMPO • 2070 M

Amid a little alp in the high country above the Poschiavo Valley is this very small inn—a stone house with a lovely terrace overlooking the Val di Campo. The tabletops on the terrace are very handsome, some made of massive slabs of stone, some of wood. The house was built in 1961 and looks attractively simple. The interior is snugness itself: a little room with four tables and an adjoining room that would be called a Stübli in Swiss-German, with only three tables.

Alpe Campo offers Matratzenlager only: 14 places in two separate rooms, with indoor toilet and cold-water sink. There is no shower, and no towels are provided. Meals are à la carte. The menu offers traditional Swiss-German food like barley soup, Rösti, and cold sliced meat, as well as more regional dishes: pizzocheri (a sort of pasta made of dark flour, chopped and baked with vegetables, cheese, and garlic), a specialty of the Valtellina, a region of Italy culturally but not politically linked with the Poschiavo Valley—you must order this dish in advance; polenta with selvaggini (wild game); pro-

Posciavo, Swiss National Day

sciutto with melon; and bresciola carpacciata. The inn, run by its owner, Signorina Gemma Crameri, is open from mid-June to mid-October. Tel. 081/844 04 82; 7742 Sfazù (San Carlo).

Getting there: Take a PTT bus from Poschiavo through San Carlo to Sfazu, and change there to a van called an Autopostale that makes scheduled runs up to Alpe Campo. You should reserve places on the van; telephone R. Kasper SA in Poschiavo at 081/844 10 42 or the Poschiavo post office during its business hours, 844 18 70. Or you can walk up.

Walks: From Alpe Campo you can hike in several directions. Hikes are numbered on the regional trail map.

WALK 1 • Walk to nearby Lagh (Lake) Saoseo in only 20 minutes. From there, continue northwest to Lagh Viola—hike #10 on the map circles the two lakes. From Viola you can continue just across the border to an Italian alpine club hut, the Rifugio Viola, popularly known as the Polenta hut because they cook up a vat full of polenta every day and offer a lunch special that, we were told, includes polenta, meat and sausage, cheese, wine, coffee, and more, at a very moderate price. The round-trip to the hut and back should take 4–5 hours.

WALK 2 • From Alpe Campo you can also hike northeastward to Lagh da Roan: round-trip 3 kilometers; 465 meters up; 2½–3 hours.

CHAPTER 10

THE EMMENTAL

Emmental is cheese—Swiss cheese, to many—the cheese with holes in it. But the Emmental is a region of Switzerland, a countryside, a landscape, and a culture. (And the cheese made there is not the only Swiss cheese.) International tourists don't go to the Emmental: It has no ski resorts, no famous mountains— indeed, compared with the alpine terrain nearby, no real mountains at all—just hills. But this countryside has its admirers because, quite simply, it is a lovely and deeply satisfying landscape. It is far from flat: The Emmental is a great tapestry of hills, some gently rolling, others crisp in profile, covered with mixed woodland and pastures. And it is home to the handsomest farmhouses in Switzerland. Their great, superb roofs embrace and shelter both house and barn below. Across the house facades are tiers of balconies abloom with flowers, and the kitchen gardens are bright with color: roses, dahlias, and lupines growing around the cabbages, onions, and strawberries—images, it seems, from a dream of country pleasures. Walking through the Emmental yields delights quite other than those found in the high alpine country. Instead of rugged peaks and slopes of ice, here you'll find the softness of a pastoral landscape and enjoy the charm of walking through its farms.

Small Käserei (dairies where cheese is made) are scattered throughout the Emmental, and at the small village of Affoltern there is a model Käserei, where visitors can watch every step of the cheese-making process. It's open daily 8:30 to 6:30. Affoltern is east of Burgdorf, north of Sumiswald. Tel. 034/435 16 11; Fax: 435 01 51; 3416 Affoltern i.E.

A network of trails spreads over the Emmental, all well signposted, and hikers can easily devise their own itineraries by consulting a map. The region is so close to Bern that many hikes can be done as day trips from the capital, but there are also attractive inns to lure visitors to stay overnight. Nearly every village and town has one handsome inn, sometimes more, but there are also a few much more isolated inns out in the countryside. By Emmental custom, most inns and restaurants are closed one day a week; this Ruhetag varies from inn to inn and is always posted or noted in lists of

Apple storage bin in the Emmental

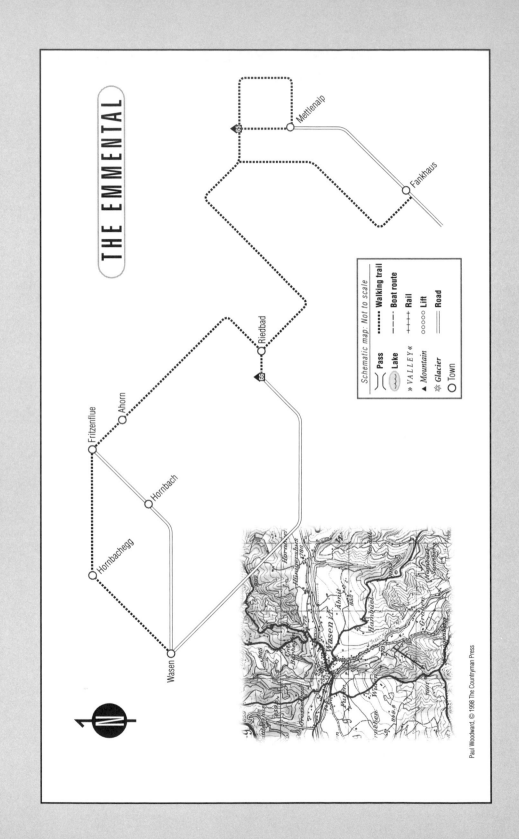

THE EMMENTAL

Schematic map: Not to scale

)(	Pass	▪▪▪▪	Walking trail
〜	Lake	– – –	Boat route
» VALLEY «		+++++	Rail
▲ Mountain		ooooo	Lift
❋ Glacier		═══	Road
○ Town			

Mettlenalp

Fankhaus

Riedbad

Ahorn

Fritzenflue

Hornbach

Hornbachegg

Wasen

inns. The trails to the country inns lead through woods, across pastures, and over hilltops. Some of the finest examples of Emmental farmhouses, however, are not on hilltops or in woods, which are somewhat remote and reachable only by footpath, but are near roads and thus more accessible for the farmers. The two guesthouses described here are in more remote parts of the Emmental and will take you past a few farmhouses, but for a tour that enables you to view a wide sample of the most beautiful farm-houses, design a walk that takes you near some of the principal villages, then strike out for one of these inns.

65 • BERGHOTEL NAPF • 1410 M

The Napf is the second highest point in the Emmental and the site of its highest hotel (the Wachthubel, 4 meters higher, has no hotel atop it). As there is nothing to block the view, the Napf offers a splendid panorama. The hotel is surrounded by a big pasture on which there are panoramic tables at the four compass points so you can identify the shapes of the dis-tant mountains, including the Eiger, Mönch, and Jungfrau. The Bernese Oberland looks like a long white wall that seems to float in the blue.

The hotel is a big, ramshackle place of no particular stylistic or archi-tectural charm; it's just a big, easy, summer-camp sort of place, bustling with people on a sunny summer afternoon, some eating and drinking at tables outdoors, some gazing at the view and munching on picnic lunches, oth-ers sprawled on the grass with children gamboling around them and maybe a few heifers grazing nearby—a scene that Brueghel might have painted. This is a real Swiss haunt; Andreas Hirschi, its owner, estimates that only about 2 percent of the guests come from other countries. Here you'll see the Swiss at ease: families, small children, and old people. Everyone has walked up—there's no other way to get to this Berghotel. They come up for an afternoon's outing, for the view, and to eat dinner, and then most walk down again. There's a dining room on one side of the hotel but nobody seems to use it; on the other side a cafeteria has been installed, and there are also tables outside, where most people eat until the sun goes down. You order your meal in the cafeteria, are given a number, then take a table and wait till your order is ready and your number is called out, then go back to get your food. The menu consists of typical Berghotel fare: soup and salads, platters of dried or smoked meat, sausages, Schnitzel, and, for vegetarians, Älpler Macaroni with Apfelmus. At breakfast you're given a warm croissant, slices of cheese, and the usual bread and jam.

The large wooden house dates from 1882 and clearly has had additions attached to it over the years. There is no source of water on this hilltop, and the hotel must pump its water up about 200 meters. You will probably see some cows or heifers grazing in the pasture because the hotel gets a fee for any cow that's sent up here to graze for 100 days. They also keep a few pigs and slaughter some of them annually on the third Sunday in October (as they have done for 40 years) for a big outdoor feast.

There are 14 private rooms and 79 Matratzenlager places, divided among several rooms, some in a different building. Our room had a warm-water sink and small towels, and a carpet on the pine floor. Toilets and big trough sinks with warm water are in the hall, and there's a shower for the private-room guests only. (Because of the water shortage, the water in the shower runs only for a minute; you must repeatedly push a blue button to start it again.)

The hotel is open all year. In the summer it's closed on Sunday (no doubt because the staff are worn out after Saturday), but from November to April its Ruhetag is Monday. The largest number of guests come in September and October. Tel. 034/495 54 08; Fax: 495 60 02; 3557 Fankhaus i.E.

Kindling wood, Emmental

Getting there: Many trails lead to Napf from various directions—so many that when you reach the top, you'll see a signpost with more than a dozen place-names. To approach from the south, take the train to the pleasant little town of Langnau, then a bus to Fankhaus at about 970 meters (the Emmental buses, although not the familiar yellow PTT buses, are public, and Swiss Passes and Cards are valid on them). From Fankhaus, the most direct way climbs up a steep, narrow ridge, much of it in the woods (pleasantly shady on a very warm day, but with greatly curtailed views). The signposts for this route list Hohstellen as an intermediate point; it will take about 2½ hours to walk up to Napf.

A less direct trail up from Fankhaus climbs by way of Hoch Sureboden and takes 4½ hours; both these trails ascend to the north, then turn east for the final approach to the hotel. From Mettlenalp, farther up the road from Fankhaus, you can take a shorter trail: either the very steep but direct one that should get you up in 45 minutes to 1 hour, or the slightly longer, more roundabout, and less steep trail through Stächelegg—1½ hours up.

For a full day's walk that brings you through a region where you'll find some handsome Emmental farmhouses, start at Langnau, walk east to Widerberg, then north through Grindlen to Schwändi and Stächengrat, and follow the trail that swings east again to Brandosch and then Fankhaus. From Fankhaus, continue on one of the two trails mentioned just above. There are other approaches as well, from points north and west of Napf. Check the map or call the Emmental Tourist Office in Langnau (it's known as Pro Emmental: Tel. 034/402 42 52).

Note that you can walk between the Hotel Napf and the Gasthof Riedbad, listed just below. The distance is 7 kilometers and should take about 2½ hours. Walking from Napf to Riedbad requires an ascent of 100 meters (because of undulations in the land) and a descent of 560 meters; from Riedbad to Napf, it's 560 meters up, 100 meters down.

66 • GASTHOF RIEDBAD • 983 M

This little inn is so deeply tucked away in an obscure side valley that for the most part probably only the very local people know about it. Although it's on a road, no bus comes up: Unless you have a car, you must walk here, by road or path. The original part of the little wooden house is 250 years old, to which a new section was added in 1981. On one side, beneath a pretty Emmental facade, is a porch. There's a sort of general idiosyncrasy about Gasthof Riedbad; it seems to exist in a nontourist dimension. For example, while we had dinner, we could see Elisabeth Widmer, the owner, ironing in her room just off the little dining room; she had left the door open and clearly did not mind that guests might see her at her ironing board. There are several signs near the inn, one asking you not to feed the dog and another requesting you to please send the dog back if you come across it on the path. When we entered the dining room, three elderly ladies, obviously locals, were finishing a card game. As they rose to leave, one pulled a little squeeze-box accordion out of her carryall and dashed off a few jolly tunes for the few of us in the room—she played the last one while holding the accordion behind her back, with a look of mischievous delight. She and her companions must have been in their late 70s.

Upper entrance of an Emmental barn

The menu is simple but along with the customary fare are a few unusual items, including Pouletflügeli (chicken wings), cordon bleu, and garlic bread. For dessert there were huge and wonderful tarts made with fresh Heubeer, which are like blueberries. The cook, Felix Willi, was off somewhere, so Frau Widmer left her ironing board to cook us up a tasty dinner.

An early-19th-century Emmental pastor, Jeremias Gotthelf, was the author of some well-loved novels about life in this region. Frau Widmer and friends had just completed the first Gotthelf festival. In the inn's more formal dining room (a simple room, nevertheless) they had built a little stage on which they acted out dramatizations of the books, in costume. Blown-up copies of pages from his novels lined the walls, and from the ceiling hung little doll-like figures representing some of the famous characters. This festival was so successful in the area that they have decided to repeat it annually.

There are five private rooms and 24 Matratzenlager in two spaces. The private rooms, quite modernized, have tiny private bathrooms and showers; there is no shower for the dorm guests, who use a cold-water sink. Dinner is à la carte. The inn is closed Thursdays and in the month of January. Tel. 034/437 15 64; 3457 Wasen i.E.

Getting there: Take a bus to the sleepy little town of Wasen (the bus stops at the train station but so few travelers go to Wasen that train service has been discontinued). You can then walk on the paved road to Gasthof Riedbad or take trails. The paved road leads directly east to Hornbach (where there is another inn, Restaurant Hornbach-Pinte), then swings southeast through Ried and climbs by a gentle grade to Riedbad.

To take the trail, you can follow the road to Hornbach and there turn left for a short ascent to Fritzenflue, where you'll turn right and pick up the trail that heads east and southeast along the crests of the hills. Alternatively, to avoid the road completely, head eastward out of Wasen, and as you near the edge of town, watch for a yellow trail signpost pointing off to the left (north). Follow signposts to Freudigenegg and then turn right (east) for Hornbachegg. If you had taken the paved road at first, then climbed up from Hornbach, you would intersect this trail along the hillcrest at Fritzenflue. Continue eastward past Ahorn, then descend to the right (south) past Badschwendi to reach Gasthof Riedbad on the road below. If you take only the trail: 9.5 kilometers; 500 meters up and 300 meters down; 4½ or 5 hours.

BIBLIOGRAPHY

Allbut, Robert. *The Tourist's Handbook to Switzerland*. London: T. Nelson & Sons, 1884.

Baedeker, K. *Switzerland, Italy, Savoy, and the Tyrol*. 15th edition. Leipsic: Karl Baedeker, 1893.

Carne, Esq., John. *The Journal of a Tour Through Switzerland and Italy*. 2nd edition. London: Henry Colburn, 1840.

Conway, Sir William M. *The Alps from End to End*. Westminster: Archibald Constable & Co., 1900.

DeBeer, G.R. *Alps and Men*. London: Edward Arnold & Company, 1932.

Jones, The Rev. Harry. *The Regular Swiss Round*. London: Alexander Strahan, 1866.

Lunn, Sir Arnold. *The Bernese Oberland*. Revised and enlarged edition, 1973. London: George Allen & Unwin, Ltd., originally published in 1958.

Murray, John. *Murray's Handbook for Travellers in Switzerland*. 1838 edition. New York: Humanities Press. Reissued by Leicester University Press, 1970.

Prime, Samuel Irenaeus. *Letters from Switzerland*. New York: Sheldon & Company, 1860.

Stephen, Leslie. *Playground of Europe*. London: Longmans, Green & Co., 1871.

Tissot, Victor. *Unknown Switzerland*. New York: James Pott & Company, 1900.

Twain, Mark. *A Tramp Abroad*. New York: Oxford University Press, 1996.

Tyndall, John. *Hours of Exercise in the Alps*. New York: D. Appleton & Company, 1898.

Aare Valley (Engstlenalp), 128
Abendberg promontory (The Kiental), 74
accommodations. *See* individual Berghaus listing
Aescher (Äscher), Berggasthaus (Appenzell), 178-80
Albrun, Pension (The Binntal), 170
Aletsch Region (Valaisian Alps), 163-70; Glacier, 163
Almagelleralp, Berghaus (Saastal), 158-59; Höhenweg, 160; walks, 159
Alp Flix (Canton Graubunden), 222-23
Alpe Campo, Ristorante (Val Poschiavo), 247-49; menu, 248; walks, 249
Alpenblumen Promenade (Valaisian Alps), 160
Älper Fest, summer festival (Reichenbachtal), 116
des Alpes, Hotel (Grindelwald), 102-3; Käseschnitte (cheese dish), 102; walks, 103
Alpfest, 15
Alpine Club, 22. *See also* Swiss Alpine Club
Alpine picnic lunch, classic, 42
alps (summer farms), 22
Alps, Swiss
    about, 20-22
    walking tips, 45
    walking to mountain inns, 35
Alpstein Mountains, 177; Säntis peak, 177
amenities (shower, toilet, etc.) Berghaus, 25-27
Anniviers, Val d' (Valaisian Alps), 143-47; lakes around, 147

Appenzell (Ausser and Inner Rhoden), 175-78
    Alpstein, 177
    Fälensee valley, 188
    The Geologischer Wanderweg, 192-95
    map of, 176
    Rotsteinpass, 187
    Seealpsee, 183
Ausser Rhoden, 175
Axalp, Bärghus and Sporthotel (Rosenlaui Valley), 124

Bachalpsee (Grindelwald), 106
backpack (pack), 39
Bagnes, Val de (Valaisian Alps), 131-37
Ballenberg (Rosenlaui Valley), 124-25
beer and wine at Berghaus, 29
Belalp, Hotel (Aletsch Region), 163-65; menu, 164; walks, 165
    Schäfersonntag at, 163
Bella Tola (Val d'Anniviers), 146
Bellevue, Hotel (Grindelwald), 100
Berggasthaus, 241. *See also* Name of Berggasthaus
Berghaus (*auberge de montagne,* Berggasthaus, Berghotel, etc.) 13, 16, 19-31, 241. *See also* Name of Berghaus; Switzerland
    address and telephone number inconsistencies, 22-23
    amenities of, 25-27
    clothes needed for, 37-39
    food offered, 27-29
    half-pension ("half-board") at, 29-30
    history of, 21-22
    necessities, 37-38

price range at (for food and lodging), 30–31
traveling to (by cable car, bus, foot, train), 33–36
vegetarian foods at, 28–29
wine and beer at, 29
Berghotels (mountain inns of Switzerland), about, 13-16, 19, 22, 24, 241. *See also* Berghaus
Bernese Oberland region, 49–129
Engstlenalp, 125–29
The Gasterntal, 55
Grindelwald and surroundings, 98–115
Iffigenalp, 49–54
Kandersteg, 54–66
The Kiental, 66–78
Kleine Scheidegg, 99–100
The Lauterbrunnental, 78–86
maps of, 50–51
Mürren, 81
Naturfreundhaus Gorneren, 73
The Oeschinensee, 63
region, 49–149
Reichenbachtal, 115–17
Rosenlaui Valley, 117–25
The Sefinental, 93–97
Selden, 59
Upper Lauterbrunnental, 86–93
Bever (Upper Engadine), 238–39; walks, 239–40
Beverin, Berggasthaus (Canton Graubunden), 218–20; walks, 220–21
bibliography, 259
Binntal (Binn) (Valaisian Alps), 170–74
Binntalhütte and Albrun Pass (Valaisian Alps), 171
Blumental (The Lauterbrunnental), 82, 85
Blümlisalphorn, cluster of mountains, 63

Bollenwees, Berggasthaus (Appenzell), 189–90
boots, importance of, 38–39
breakfast at Berghaus, 29
Brienze, lake and falls (Rosenlaui Valley), 122–23
Brig, town (Valaisian Alps), 165, 169
Bundalp, Berghaus (Berggasthof) Enzian (The Kiental), 73–74; walks, 74–78
bus routes (Iffigenalp), 54
buses, for travel, 34–35; PTT buses, 34
business hours in Switzerland, 41
Bussalp (Grindelwald), 110

Cabane de Chanrion (Valaisian Alps), 140
Cabane de Panossière (Valaisian Alps), 141
Canton Graubunden, 209–49. *See also* Graubunden
Carnusa Valley (Canton Graubunden), 221
Central Switzerland, 197–207
Maderanertal (Central Switzerland), 202–7
map of, 198
Rigi Kulm, 197–202
Chaschauna, Alp and Pass (Lower Engadine), 237
clothes need for Berghaus stay, 37–39
Corbassière Glacier (Valaisian Alps), 142
cowbells, 15
currency of Switzerland, 41

Daubensee via The Gemmipass, walk, 58
The Dom, highest mountain (Valaisian Alps), 131
drink and food in Switzerland, 30, 41–42

Dündengat, hike (The Kiental), 75

Ebenalp, Berggasthaus (Appenzell), 180

The Eiger, mountain peak, 79, 82, 98, 99. *See also* Grindelwald

electrified fencing, 44

The Emmental, 251-57
map of, 252

Engadine, The Lower (Graubunden Canton), 227-37
map of, 228
Swiss National Park, 234
Val Sinestra, 227

Engadine, The Upper (Graubunden Canton), 237-49
Bever, 238
map of, 236
Val Fex, 246
Val Poschiavo, 247
Val Roseg, 240

Engelberg (Engstlenalp), 129

Engelberg, Gstaad to, hiking route (Bernese Oberland), 115

Engelhorner (angels' peaks) (Rosenlaui Valley), 118

Engstlenalp (Bernese Oberland), 13-15, 125-29; Berghaus, 126-28; walks, 129

Fälenalp farmhouse (Appenzell), 190-92

Fälensee valley (Appenzell), 188-95

Faulhorn, Berghaus (Grindelwald), 109-10; walks, 110-12, 115

fencing, electrified, 44

Fex, Hotel (Upper Engadine), 244-47; menu, 246; walk, 247

Fex, Val (Upper Engadine), 244

Findel Glacier Overlook (Valaisian Alps), 155

Fionnay, village (Valaisian Alps), 136, 141, 143

Flesspass (Canton Graubunden), 226

Flix, Alp (Canton Graubunden), 221

Fluhalp, Hotel (Trift Valley), 153-54; walks, 155-57

food at Berghaus, 27-29. *See also* Name of Hotel; Restaurant

food and drink in Switzerland, 30-31, 41-42

Forelle, Berggasthaus (Appenzell), 183-85

Fuorcla Surlej, Berghaus (Upper Engadine), 242-43; walks, 243-44

Fuorcla Val Sassa (Lower Engadine), 237

Gastern (Selden) (Kandersteg), 59-61

Gasterntal (Bernese Oberland), 55-62; Hotel, 61-62; and Mark Twain, 55

gasthaus. *See* Name of Gasthaus

Gaststube (Stübli), 31

Geisspfadsee (Valaisian Mountains), 173

The Gemmipass route and trail, 58-59

The Geologischer Wanderweg (Appenzell), 189, 192-95

Giessbach, Grand Hotel (Rosenlaui Valley), 122; walks, 123-24; water-falls, 122

Gimmelwald (Upper Lauterbrunnen-tal), walks, 96, 97

Glasgrat (Canton Graubunden), 220, 221

The Glaspass (Canton Graubunden), 219-20

Golderli
Berggasthaus and Pension (The Kiental), 71-72, 76; menu, 72
-Griesalp-Pochtenalp cluster, 73
Naturfreundehaus Gorneren, 73

Golzernsee, Restaurant (Gasthaus) (Central Switzerland), 204; menu, 204; walks, 205
Goppenstein (The Lötschental), 160
Grand Combin (Valaisian Alps), 131, 136-37
Grand St. Bernard Hospice (Valaisian Alps), 167
Graubunden, Canton, 209-49
    Lower Engadine, 227-37. See also Engadine
    map of, 210
    Upper Engadine, 237-49. See also Engadine
    The Vorderrhein, 209-27
La Greina Valley (Canton Graubunden), 212-13
Griesalp (The Kiental), 68, 72, 74
Grindelwald and surroundings (Bernese Oberland), 98-115; Grindelwald Valley, 99, 108
The Grindjesee (Valaisian Alps), 155
Grosse Scheidegg, Berghotel (Reichenbachtal), 116-17
Grosser Aletschgletscher (Valaisian Alps), 163
Grütschalp, mountain (The Lauterbrunnental), 85-86
Gschwantenmad meadow (Rosenlaui Valley), 118
Gspaltenhornhütte hike (The Kiental), 75-76
Gstaad to Engelberg, hiking route (Bernese Oberland), 115
guesthouse. See Berghaus

half-pension ("half-board") at Berghaus, 29-30
Heimritz, Gasthaus (Berggasthaus) zur Gletscher (Kandersteg), 62; walk, 62
The Heinzenberg (Canton Graubunden), 218

hiking in Switzerland
    boots, importance of, 38-39
    clothes for, 38-39
    safety precautions, 44
The Hochbüel route (Canton Graubunden), 220
The Hochmoor (Rosenlaui Valley), 121-22
Höhbalm (Valaisian Alps), 151
Höhenweg (trail), 129. See also Name of Berghaus or Region
Hohtürli, high pass (The Kiental), 66, 74-78
hotel. See Name of Hotel
Hufihütte SAC (Central Switzerland), 206, 207

Iffigenalp (Bernese Oberland), 49-54
    Berghaus, 49-54; 53
    bus routes, 54
    Dépendance, 52
    menu, 53
    Rawilpass route, 49, 53
    walks, 53-54
Iffigensee, little blue lake (Bernese Oberland), 53
Ilanz (Canton Graubunden), 211, 215
inn, mountain. See Berghaus
Inner Rhoden, 175. See also Appenzell
Innertkirchen, village (Engstlenalp), 128

Jungfrau Express (railway), 98-99
The Jungfrau, mountain peak, 79, 80, 81-82, 98

Kaffee-Zwetschge (black coffee), 14
The Kanderfirn, glacier, 62
Kandersteg (Bernese Oberland), 54-66, 160
Käserei (cheese dairies), 251
Käseschnitte (cheese dish), 102

The Kiental (Bernese Oberland), 66-78

Kleine Scheidegg (Bernese Oberland), 99-100; walks, 79-89, 101, 103

Klosters, ski resort (Canton Graubunden), 225

Kummenalp, Berghaus (The Lötschental), 160-61

Künzi, Christian, *photo*, 60

Lac d'Armina (Val d'Anniviers), 147

Lac de Combavert (Val d'Anniviers), 147

Lac du Touno (Val d'Anniviers), 147

languages of Switzerland, 42, 131

Lauberhorn (The Lauterbrunnental), 80

Lauchernalp, Berggasthaus (The Lötschental), 161-62; walks, 162

The Lauterbrunnental (Bernese Oberland), 78-86; Upper Lauterbrunnental, 86-93

Lenk, small ski resort, 53

lodging, price of, 30. *See also* Name of Berghaus, Hotel, etc.

The Lötschental (Valaisian Alps), 160-62; Höhenweg, 162

The Lower Engadine (Graubunden Canton), 227-37. *See also* Engadine

Lumnezia, Val (Vorderrhein), 211

lunch, Alpine picnic, 42

Maderanertal (Central Switzerland), 202-7; Hotel, 206-7; walks 207

Männlichen, Berghaus (Grindelwald), 101

Map(s), 42-44
 Appenzell, 176
 Bernese Oberland, east, 51; west, 50
 Canton Graubunden, 210
 Central Switzerland, 198

The Emmental, 252

The Engadine, Lower, 228; Upper, 236

Switzerland, 8

The Valais (Valaisian Alps), 132-35

Mark Twain and the Gasterntal, 55

Martigny (Valaisian Alps), 136

Matratzenlager (*dortoirs*, Lager, Massenlager, Touristenlager) dining room and dormitories, 23, 26. *See also* Name of Berghaus

Matterhorn (mountain peak), 148, 155

Mauvoisin, 136-40; Hôtel de, 137, 138-39; walks, 139-43

Meglisalp, Berggasthaus (Appenzell), 185-87, 188

Meidpass (Val d'Anniviers), 146

Meiringen (Engstlenalp), 128-29

Melchsee-Frutt (Engstlenalp), 129

menus at Berghaus, 27-29. *See also* Name of Hotel; Restaurant

Mesmer (Messmer), Berggasthaus (Appenzell), 181

Mettelhorn (Valaisian Alps), 151

Mettlenalp (The Lauterbrunnental), 80

Mischabel Mountain Range (Saastal), 157, 159-60

The Mönch, mountain peak, 79, 80, 82, 98

mountain inns. *See also* Berghaus walking to, 35

mountains, early ideas about, 20-21

Mürren, ski resort (Bernese Oberland), 79, 96

Napf, Berghotel (The Emmental), 253-54

National Park, Swiss (Lower Engadine), 234

Naturfreundehaus Gorneren (The Kiental), 73

Nidlete (celebrating first cream), 15

Ober Bundalp (The Bernese Ober-
land), 73
The Ober Sattla (Valaisian Alps), 157
Oberland, The Bernese, 49-129; maps
of, 50-51. *See also* Bernese Oberland;
Name of Region
Oberland mountains, 49
The Oberrothorn (Valaisian Alps), 156
Obersteinberg, Hotel (Upper Lauter-
brunnental, 87, 90; walks, 92-93, 97
The Oeschinensee, mountain lake
(Bernese Oberland), 63
Oeschinensee, Berghaus (Kandersteg),
64-65
Ofenhorn, Hotel (The Binntal), 171;
walks, 171-74

pack (backpack), 39
packing for hiking trip, 38
Pferde-Omnibus (horse-drawn carriage), 239, 244
Pierre à Vire, Tour de (Valaisian Alps),
139
Piz Beverin (Canton Graubunden),
220, 221
Piz Plata, Berghaus (Canton Graubunden), 222-23; trail, 224; walks, 224-
25
Plattenbödeli, Berggasthaus (Appenzell), 188, 192
Plaun la Greina (Canton Graubunden), 212, 215
Pointes de Nava (Val d'Anniviers),
146-47
Pontresina (Upper Engadine), 242
Poschiavo, Val (Italian-speaking), 247
Post-Telephone Telegraph (PTT)
buses, 34
Prà San Flurin (Lower Engadine), 233
price range for food, drink and lodging, 30-31
Puzzatsch (Canton Graubunden), 214,
215

Raclette (cheese), 28, 56
Rawilpass Route, 53-54
Reichenbach (The Kiental), 66
Reichenbachtal (Bernese Oberland),
115-17
Restaurant-Pension. *See* Name of
Restaurant-Pension
Reuti (Engstlenalp), 129
Rhoden, Ausser, 175
Rhoden, Inner. *See* Appenzell
Riedbad, Gasthof, 255-57
Rigi Kulm (Central Switzerland), 197-
202; Hotel, 199-202; walks, 202
Roseg, Val (Upper Engadine), 240
Roseggletscher, Hotel (Upper Enga-
dine), 240, 243; menu, 241
Rosenlaui Valley (Bernese Oberland),
117-25
   Glacier, 117-18
   Hotel, 118-20; walk, 121-22
Rothornhütte (Valaisian Alps), 153
Rotstein, Berggasthaus (Appenzell),
187
Rotstockhütte (The Sefinental), 95;
walks, 96-97

Saas Valley, 157-58
Saastal (Valaisian Alps), 157-60
safety precautions, animals, 44; hiking,
44
Safiental (valley, Canton Graubunden),
215
Safierberg Pass (Canton Graubunden),
217
St. Luc (Valaisian Alps), 143-46
San Giusep (Canton Graubunden),
211, 212-14
Saoseo, Lagh (Lake) (Canton
Graubunden), 249
Schäfersonntag (Aletsch Region), 163
Schäfler, Gasthaus (Appenzell), 180;
Höhenweg, 182

Schilthorn, mountain (The Lauter-
brunnental), 84, 86
Schwarzwaldalp, Hotel-Chalet
(Reichenbachtal), 117
Schynige Platte (Grindelwald), 112;
walk, 110, 111-12
Hotel-Restaurant, 113-14; menu,
114; walks, 115
Scuol (Lower Engadine), 232
Seealp, Berggasthaus (Appenzell), 185
Seealpsee (lake) (Appenzell), 183
The Sefinenfurke, high pass (The
Kiental), 66, 74-78, 84, 96
The Sefinental (Bernese Oberland),
93-97
Selden (Gastern) (Bernese Oberland),
59-61
shopping in Switzerland, 41
shower. See amenities; Name of
Berghaus
signs and markers along trail, 35-36
Simmenfälle waterfall (Bernese Ober-
land), 53
Simplon Pass (Valaisian Alps), 166-70
Hospice du Simplon, 166-69;
walks, 169-70
Sinestra
Berggasthaus (Lower Engadine),
231-32; walks, 232-34
Val (Lower Engadine), 227-29;
Kurhaus, 229-31
Sonnenberg, Restaurant-Pension (The
Lauterbrunnental), 83-84; menu, 83;
walks, 84-86
The Sparrhorn (Valaisian Alps), 165
Spielbodenalp, Restaurant-Pension
(The Sefinental), 93, 95
Staubbach Falls (The Lauterbrunnen-
tal), 78
Staubern (Stauberen), Berggasthaus
(Appenzell), 195

Steinbock, Hotel (Kandersteg) 61
Stieregg, Bergrestaurant (Grindelwald),
103-5; menu, 105; walks, 106-7
Stockalperweg trail (Valaisian Alps),
169-70
The Sulsee, mountain (The Lauter-
brunnental), 85
summer festival, Älper Fest, (Reichen-
bachtal), 116
Sunnegga-Blauherd, lift (Valaisian
Alps), 154
Suppenalp, Pension (The Lauterbrunnental), 82-83; menu, 83
Sur, village (Canton Graubunden), 223
Suvretta, Berggastaus (Pension) (Upper
Engadine), 238; menu, 238
Swiss Alpine Club (SAC or CAS)
huts, 23
Swiss Pass card, for travel, 34
Switzerland. See also Berghaus; Central
Switzerland
Berghaus necessities, 37-38
business hours, 41
currency of, 41
food and drink in, 30-31, 41-42
hiking in, 44
languages, 42, 131
maps of, 8; about, 42-44. See also
Maps
packing for hiking trip in, 38
safety precautions, 44
shopping, 41
telephones and telephone numbers,
45
transportation system, 33-35
travel in, general information, 41-
46
walking tips, 45
weather conditions, 45-46

Tannalp (Engstlenalp), 129
telephones and telephone numbers, 45
Tgamanada, Ustaria (Canton
    Graubunden), 211-12; walks, 212-15
toilets. *See* amenities; Name of
    Berghaus
Trachsellauenen, Berghaus (Upper
    Lauterbrunnental), 87, 88
trail signs and markers, 35-36
trains, for travel, 34
Trift Valley (Valaisian Alps), 147-57
    Hôtel, 148-50; walks, 151-53
Trümmelbach Falls (The Lauterbrun-
    nental), 78, 86
Trupchen, Alp (Lower Engadine), 237
Tschingelhorn, Hotel (Upper Lauter-
    brunnental), 87, 88-90; walk, 96
The Tufternkumme (Valaisian Alps),
    156
Turrahus (Turrahaus), Berggasthaus
    (Canton Graubunden), 217
Tyndall, John, 13, 163

The Upper Engadine (Graubunden
    Canton), 237-49. *See also* Engadine
Upper Lauterbrunnental (Bernese
    Oberland), 86-93

Val (valley). *See* Name of Valley
The Valais (Valaisian Alps), 131-74. *See
    also* Name of Region
    Aletsch Region, 163-65
    The Binntal, 170-74
    The Lötschental, 160-63
    maps of, 132-35
    Saastal, 157-60
    The Simplon Pass, 166-70
    Trift Valley, 147-57
    Val d'Anniviers, 143-47
    Val de Bagnes, 131-43

Varusch, Parkhütte (Varuschhütte,
    Chamanna Varusch) (Lower Enga-
    dine), 235; walks, 237
vegetarian foods at Berghaus, 28-29
Vereina, Berghaus (Canton Graubun-
    den), 225; walks, 226-27
Vereinapass (Canton Graubunden),
    226
The Vereinatal (Canton Graubunden)
    225
Vna (Lower Engadine), 233
von Allmen, Vicki, *photo*, 91
The Vorderrhein (Canton Graubun-
    den), 209-27
Vrin (Canton Graubunden), 211, 212

Waldhaus, Hotel (Kandersteg), 56-58;
    Raclette at, 56; walks, 58-59
Waldrand, Hotel-Pension at Pochte-
    nalp (The Kiental), 68-70; menu, 69
Waldspitz Bergrestaurant (Grindel-
    wald), 107-8; menu, 107
walking to mountain inns, 35; walking
    tips, 45
weather conditions in Switzerland, 45-
    46
Weisshorn, Hotel Restaurant (St. Luc,
    Valaisian Alps), 143-45; walks, 146-47
Wengen, ski resort (The Lauterbrun-
    nental), 79; walks, 79-81
Windgallenhütte (Central Switzer-
    land), 205, 207
wine and beer at Berghaus, 29

Zermatt (Trift Valley), 147-57. *See also*
    Trift Valley
Zinalrothorn (Val d'Anniviers), 147
Zuort and Prà San Flurin (Lower
    Engadine), 233
Zwischbergen Pass (Valaisian Alps),
    159